KT-498-438

# Contents

# Bookkeeping Transactions

## Tutorial

David Cox
Michael Fard

Published by Osborne Books Limited
Tel 01905 748071
Email books@osbornebooks.co.uk
Website www.osbornebooks.co.uk

Design by Laura Ingham

Printed by CPI Group (UK) Limited, Croydon, CR0 4YY, on environmentally friendly, acid-free paper from managed forests.

MIX
Paper from
responsible sources
FSC® C019777

British Library Cataloguing in Publication Data
A catalogue record for this book is available from the British Library

ISBN 978 1909173 651

# Introduction

## Qualifications covered

This book has been written specifically to cover the Unit 'Bookkeeping Transactions' which is mandatory for the following qualifications:

AAT Foundation Certificate in Accounting – Level 2

AAT Foundation Diploma in Accounting and Business – Level 2

AAT Foundation Certificate in Bookkeeping – Level 2

AAT Foundation Certificate in Accounting at SCQF – Level 5

The book contains a clear text with worked examples and case studies, chapter summaries and key terms to help with revision. Each chapter concludes with a wide range of activities, many in the style of AAT computer based assessments.

## Osborne Study and Revision Materials

The materials featured on the previous page are tailored to the needs of students studying this unit and revising for the assessment. They include:

- **Workbooks:** paperback books with practice activities and exams
- **Wise Guides:** pocket-sized spiral bound revision cards
- **Student Zone:** access to Osborne Books online resources
- **Osborne Books App:** Osborne Books ebooks for mobiles and tablets

Visit www.osbornebooks.co.uk for details of study and revision resources and access to online material.

# 1 The accounting system

## this chapter covers...

*This chapter is a basic introduction to the accounting system of a business and gives an overview of all the topics that will be explained throughout this book.*

*You may have a general idea of how accounting and finance 'fit into' a business and the reasons why money transactions are critical to its operation, but if you are working in an accounting and finance environment it is important to appreciate fully the way accounting systems work. It is the aim of the course you are studying that you will acquire the knowledge and skills which will enable you to work effectively in an accounting and finance environment.*

*This chapter describes and explains the basic structure of an accounting system. It covers:*

- *the range of financial transactions in business, eg buying, selling, making payments*

- *the way in which financial documents such as invoices are used to record financial transactions*

- *the ways in which financial transactions are first recorded in the books of the business – using 'books of prime entry', eg a cash book*

- *the ways in which an accounting system is set up in a business, for example a double-entry system using ledger accounts*

- *the way in which the accounts are brought together in a summary known as the 'trial balance'*

- *the ways in which an accounting system can be used to provide information for the business owners and management, for example how much is owed by customers and how much profit has been made*

## FINANCIAL TRANSACTIONS

All businesses carry out a wide range of financial transactions on a daily basis. These transactions will need documenting and then recording in some form of manual or computerised accounting system. Common transactions include:

### selling goods and services

Goods and services can be sold:

- either for immediate payment – known as 'cash' sales, although confusingly this word 'cash' can involve payment by credit or debit card as well as notes and coins, or
- for payment at a later date – these are known as 'credit' sales

### making purchases and paying expenses

Examples of purchases and expenses include a wide range of large and small transactions, some more important than others:

- settling purchase invoices, eg paying by cheque or electronically for goods or services supplied during the previous month
- buying an item used in the business, eg a new delivery van, paid for by bank transfer
- buying diesel fuel for the delivery van, using the company credit card
- buying some postage stamps for the office using cash

### payments in and out of the bank account

The money received by the business and the money paid out by the business will pass through the bank account, for example:

- cash, cheques and electronic payments received from selling goods and services
- settling the company credit card by direct debit payment from the bank account
- paying the weekly wages through the bank account
- drawing cash out of the bank for use in the office

### the importance of keeping track

As you will see from the above examples, recording financial transactions will be a complex process. A business will need to keep track of:

- expenses and purchases

- wages paid
- what each customer owes, and when the money is due
- amounts owed to suppliers, and when the payment is due
- amounts paid into the bank and out of the bank

If these transactions are not recorded accurately, the owner of the business and other interested organisations such as the bank and the tax authorities will not know how much money the business is making (or losing!).

## THE FIVE STAGE ACCOUNTING SYSTEM

The accounting system, which will be set in motion by all the transactions listed on the previous page, can be broken down into five stages. These will be covered in greater detail later in this chapter. These stages (illustrated on the next page) are:

1   A **financial transaction** takes place – a sale, a purchase, a payment.

2   The transaction involves a **financial document**, for example an invoice (a sale), a credit note (returned goods), a petty cash voucher (small cash payments).

3   The document is first recorded on paper (or on computer) by the business, for example a day book (for credit transactions) recording sales of goods or goods returned, a cash book recording payments in and out of the bank, or a petty cash book which records small cash payments made (eg buying some stamps for the office).

   These books are known as the **books of prime entry**; this simply means 'the first place a transaction is recorded in the accounting records.'

4   The entries in the books of prime entry, eg the day books, will then need to be transferred to the **ledger accounts** of the business. These are a formal record of the financial transactions and normally involve **double-entry accounts.**

   The double-entry system, which involves two entries for each transaction, a debit entry and a credit entry, is explained in more detail on pages 7-9.

5   The final stage in the accounting system covered in your current studies is the **trial balance**. This is a list of the balances of the double-entry accounts. It is used as a check on the accuracy of the account entries and is also a source of information for the business owners and managers: it will enable them to monitor items such as expenses and what their customers owe, and also to calculate how much profit the business has made. The trial balance is explained in more detail on page 10.

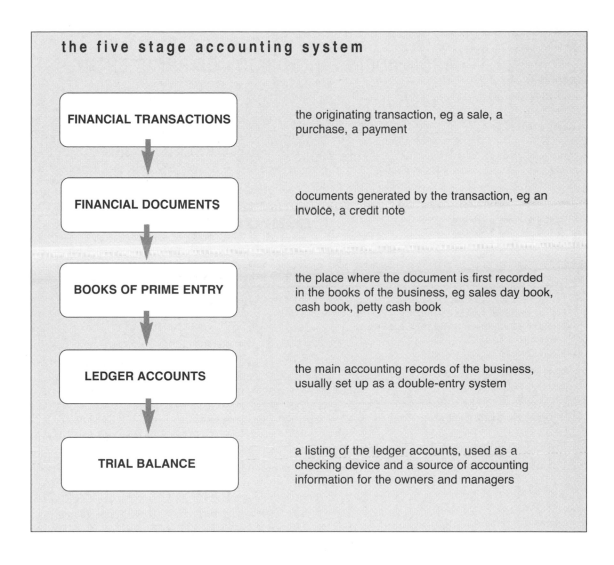

## the five stage accounting system

**FINANCIAL TRANSACTIONS** — the originating transaction, eg a sale, a purchase, a payment

**FINANCIAL DOCUMENTS** — documents generated by the transaction, eg an invoice, a credit note

**BOOKS OF PRIME ENTRY** — the place where the document is first recorded in the books of the business, eg sales day book, cash book, petty cash book

**LEDGER ACCOUNTS** — the main accounting records of the business, usually set up as a double-entry system

**TRIAL BALANCE** — a listing of the ledger accounts, used as a checking device and a source of accounting information for the owners and managers

We will now explain the last four of these five stages in more detail. The first stage, financial transactions, has already been covered on page 3.

## FROM DOCUMENTS TO BOOKS OF PRIME ENTRY

You will need to study a wide variety of financial documents as part of your course. On the next page a Case Study shows how a sales invoice – a **financial document** – is recorded in the sales day book, which is a list of sales invoices issued and a **book of prime entry**. You do not at this stage need to learn all the details of how this record is entered. This will be covered later.

# FROM DOCUMENT TO BOOK OF PRIME ENTRY

## situation

Your business, Computrade, has sold a laptop computer to R S George Limited, for £576.00 (which is list price of £480 plus £96.00 VAT at 20%). The financial document issued here is a sales invoice (see below) which requires payment in 30 days' time. The details from this invoice are recorded in a sales day book (see bottom of the page), a book of prime entry.

---

# INVOICE      COMPUTRADE

Ardent House, Mercia Way
Newtown, NT1 6TF
Tel 01722 295875  Fax 01722 295611  Email sales@computrade.com
VAT Reg GB 02756 6865 06

invoice to

R S George Limited
Unit 32 Bruges Trading Estate
Winter Road
Maidstone
ME7 2PH

| | |
|---|---|
| invoice no | 2984 |
| account | 8934 |
| your reference | CT524 |
| date/tax point | 02 04 20-3 |

| description | quantity | price | unit | total |
|---|---|---|---|---|
| Extreme 2120 Laptop | 1 | 480.00 | each | 480.00 |

terms
30 days
E & OE

| | |
|---|---|
| goods total | 480.00 |
| VAT | 96.00 |
| TOTAL | 576.00 |

---

| Sales Day Book | | | | | |
|---|---|---|---|---|---|
| Date | Customer | Invoice No. | Total | VAT | Net |
| 20-3 | | | £ | £ | £ |
| 2 April | R S George Limited | 2984 | 576.00 | 96.00 | 480.00 |
| | | | | | |
| | | | | | |
| | | | | | |

## FROM BOOKS OF PRIME ENTRY TO LEDGER ACCOUNTS

The next stage in the accounting system is the transfer of entries in the books of prime entry to the ledger accounts. Books of prime entry, as seen on the previous page, are listing devices for financial transactions. They include:

■ **day books** for
- credit sales and sales returns, ie transactions involving customers
- credit purchases and purchases returns, ie transactions with suppliers

Day books can also be used for recording certain discounts given to customers. These will be explained later in this book (Chapters 4 and 7).

■ **cash book** for recording all payments into and out of the bank account

■ **petty cash book** for recording all payments into and out of a cash float used for making small purchases and other small payments

The ledger accounts are the formal bookkeeping records of the business and are kept either in written form or, more often nowadays, on computer. They form the 'core' of the accounting system. Ledger accounts are different to the other accounting records because each transaction requires both debit and credit entries, ie entries in more than one account (normally it is in two accounts).

The flow of accounting information – transaction, book of prime entry, double-entry ledger accounts – is shown below. This gives you an overview of the accounting system. All the stages in this process are fully explained in the chapters that follow.

| TRANSACTION | BOOKS OF PRIME ENTRY | LEDGER ACCOUNTS | ACCOUNT ENTRIES |
|---|---|---|---|
| **Sales transactions** | Sales Day Book | Customer sales | debit / credit |
|  | Sales Returns Day Book | Customer returns | debit / credit |
| **Purchases transactions** | Purchases Day Book | Purchases from Suppliers | debit / credit |
|  | Purchases Returns Day Book | Returns to Suppliers | debit / credit |
| **Cash and Bank transactions** | Cash Book | Payments received / Payments made | debit / credit |
| **Small Cash transactions** | Petty Cash Book | Small cash payments made / Cash received | debit / credit |

## LEDGER ACCOUNTS

In this chapter so far we have seen that the accounting system of a business records information from financial transactions and documents (such as invoices and credit notes) into the books of prime entry and then into ledger accounts. It is useful at this point to explain what is meant by 'ledgers' and the way in which they are organised.

Most businesses use an accounting system based on the **double-entry bookkeeping system**, in which financial transactions are recorded in the accounts as **debits** and **credits**. There are two equal entries – debit and credit – of the same amount.

Bookkeeping records are kept in one of two forms: handwritten (manual) records or, increasingly often nowadays, on a computer system such as Sage.

### the ledgers

A **ledger** is traditionally a large book into which each business transaction is entered into individual **accounts**.

Because of the large number of accounts involved, there are a number of different individual ledgers, both in manual systems and also in computer systems:

- **Sales ledger** – each customer is given a personal account which contains records of sales made on credit (ie buy now, pay later), any returned goods and payments received. This account shows the business the amount owed by that particular customer. A customer buying on credit is known in accounting language as a 'trade receivable'

- **Purchases ledger** – each supplier is given a personal account which contains records of purchases made on credit (ie buy now, pay later), any returned goods and payments made to the supplier. This account shows the amount owed to that particular supplier (known as a 'trade payable')

- **General ledger** – this collection of accounts records all other transactions of the business, such as:

  - assets – these are items owned, eg premises, cars, computers and also amounts owed to a business

  - liabilities – items owed by a business, eg overdrafts and bank loans

  - the owner's capital – this includes the amount invested in the business by the owner and also the profits made by the business

  - expense items – money going out, eg wages and rent paid

  - income items – money coming in, eg sales and rent received

The **general ledger** is sometimes also known as the 'main' ledger or 'nominal' ledger (as in Sage computer accounting programs).

Also note that the term 'the ledger' is sometimes used to describe all the individual ledgers grouped together The ledger structure is shown in the diagram at the bottom of the page.

## control accounts ('total' accounts)

Many businesses use **control accounts** to provide them with information about the financial state of the organisation.

Control accounts are 'total' accounts which summarise a number of other accounts. They are set out in the same way as all other ledger accounts Examples include:

- **sales ledger control account** which contains the totals of all the trade receivable (debtor) accounts in the sales ledger – this tells the business how much is owing from all its customers, a figure that is important for business owners and managers

- **purchases ledger control account** which contains the totals of all the trade payable (creditor) accounts in the purchases ledger – this tells the business how much is owing to all its suppliers at any one time; again this is a figure that is important for anyone running a business

These control accounts are always contained in the general ledger. It is the total of these accounts that is transferred to the trial balance (see next page).

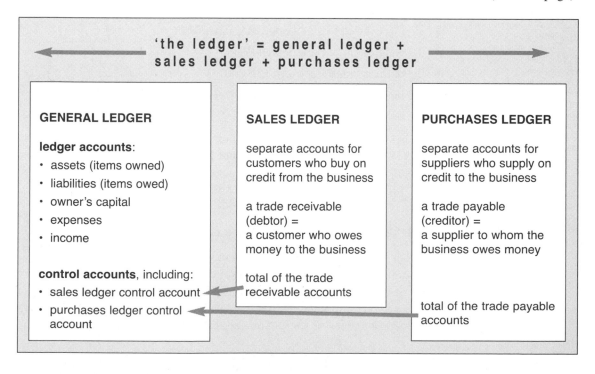

'the ledger' = general ledger + sales ledger + purchases ledger

**GENERAL LEDGER**

**ledger accounts**:
- assets (items owned)
- liabilities (items owed)
- owner's capital
- expenses
- income

**control accounts**, including:
- sales ledger control account
- purchases ledger control account

**SALES LEDGER**

separate accounts for customers who buy on credit from the business

a trade receivable (debtor) = a customer who owes money to the business

total of the trade receivable accounts

**PURCHASES LEDGER**

separate accounts for suppliers who supply on credit to the business

a trade payable (creditor) = a supplier to whom the business owes money

total of the trade payable accounts

## THE TRIAL BALANCE

### format of a trial balance

A trial balance is the important final stage in the accounting system. It brings together the balances of all the ledger accounts in the general ledger, setting them out in two columns – a debit column and a credit column – which when added up should show two equal totals.

A simplified trial balance is shown on the next page. You do not need at this stage to know how all this 'works' but just that it is an important accuracy check in the accounting system.

Note that the trial balance is headed up with:

- the **name** of the business, 'Computrade'
- the **date** on which it was drawn up – this should be done regularly, eg the end of each month, and always the end of the financial year

### what the trial balance shows

The trial balance shows the business owner and managers important and useful information. For example, the trial balance on the next page sets out the account balances of Computrade, it shows that:

- sales are £58,050
- £12,500 is owed by the customers (trade receivables)
- £9,350 is owed to suppliers (trade payables)
- the wages paid out totalled £44,100
- the delivery vans are worth £36,000
- the business has £2,000 in the bank
- the owner of the business has an investment (capital) worth £105,000

Note that the trade receivables and trade payables figures are 'total' figures and are taken from the sales ledger and purchases ledger control accounts. This makes the trial balance more manageable and meaningful – it would be rather difficult to list all the customer and supplier accounts separately!

### the trial balance – what next?

A further stage in the accounting system – which you will deal with in your later studies – is the production of **financial statements** – the **statement of profit or loss** and the **statement of financial position**. Although you will not be assessed on these statements at this level, awareness of them will help you in your current areas of study. They are briefly explained on page 12.

## the trial balance

**Name of business: Computrade**
**Trial Balance as at 30 June 20-3**

|  | Debit £ | Credit £ |
|---|---|---|
| Purchases | 35,000 |  |
| Sales |  | 58,050 |
| Trade receivables | 12,500 |  |
| Trade payables |  | 9,350 |
| Insurance | 1,400 |  |
| Rent | 6,400 |  |
| Wages | 44,100 |  |
| Bank | 2,000 |  |
| Office equipment | 35,000 |  |
| Delivery vans | 36,000 |  |
| Capital |  | 105,000 |
|  | 172,400 | 172,400 |

names of all the individual ledger accounts

totals of the two money amount columns – note that they add up to the same figure, providing an accuracy check of the accounting system

The next page gives an outline description and explanation of the financial statements of a business: the statement of profit or loss and the statement of financial position.

## FINANCIAL STATEMENTS

The financial statements of a business are the **statement of profit or loss** and the **statement of financial position**. They are compiled from the accounting records of the business, mainly from the balances of the ledger accounts which also form the basis of the trial balance.

### what the statement of profit or loss shows

| INCOME | minus | EXPENSES | equals | PROFIT |
|--------|-------|----------|--------|--------|

The **statement of profit or loss** of a business shows the day-to-day income that the business has received over a given period for goods sold or services provided. It also sets out the **expenses** incurred, including the cost of producing the products and the running expenses.

If the income of the business is greater than the expenses, the business has made a profit. If the income of the business is less than the expenses, the business has made a loss.

### what the statement of financial position shows

| ASSETS<br>what a business owns and is owed | minus | LIABILITIES<br>what a business owes to others | equals | CAPITAL<br>the owner's investment and profits |
|--------|-------|----------|--------|--------|

The statement of financial position of a business gives a 'snapshot' of the business at a particular date, eg the end of the financial year, and shows the value of the owner's investment in the business. The statement presents a simple equation, known as the **accounting equation**:

> **assets (what is owned) minus liabilities (what is owed) = capital (owner's investment)**

If a business owner invests £2,000 in the business and buys a computer, he (or she) is investing **capital** of £2,000 and also adding an **asset** in the form of a computer costing £2,000. The equation will balance because £2,000 has been added to both sides (to assets and to capital). The accounting equation is explained and expanded in full in Chapter 3, pages 57-60.

# INTERNATIONAL TERMINOLOGY USED IN ACCOUNTING

## old and new terms

In your studies of bookkeeping and accounting you will encounter some different ways of expressing common accounting terms.

You will find, at the time of writing this book, that many bookkeepers and accountants use the traditional terminology which originates in the UK.

For example, the traditional way of referring to goods held by a shop or by a manufacturer is the word 'stock'. But you will find that the American term 'inventory' is also used to mean 'stock'.

This new type of terminology is known as **'international accounting terminology'**.

Neither 'stock' nor 'inventory' is in itself right or wrong but there are situations where the international terminology is used instead of the traditional terminology. An example of this are the financial statements produced by the larger limited companies.

The table below shows both the international and traditional UK versions of terms which you are likely to come across in your accounting studies. The table also explains what the terms mean.

| international terminology | traditional UK terminology | what it means |
|---|---|---|
| inventory | stock | goods held by a business |
| trade payable | creditor | a supplier you owe money to |
| trade receivable | debtor | a customer who owes you money |
| statement of profit or loss | profit and loss account | financial statement calculating profit (or loss) made by a business |
| statement of financial position | balance sheet | financial statement showing the value of the owner's investment |

**Chapter Summary**

- The accounting system is normally made up of five stages:
  1   financial transactions
  2   financial documents
  3   books of prime entry
  4   ledger accounts
  5   trial balance

- **Financial transactions** are the starting point of the accounting system. They include sales, purchases, expenses, payments in and out of the bank account and small cash (petty cash) transactions.

- Financial transactions normally result in **financial documents**, for example an invoice (for a sale), a credit note (for returned goods), a cheque (for a payment), a petty cash voucher (for a small cash payment).

- In the next stage of the accounting system financial documents are recorded in **books of prime entry**, for example separate day books for sales and sales returns, purchases and purchases returns, the cash book and the petty cash book.

- Next the **ledger accounts** are written up from the books of prime entry. The ledger accounts are normally double-entry accounts, ie two entries are made in the accounts for each transaction – a debit entry and a credit entry.

- As there are so many ledger accounts, **the ledger** is often split into separate ledgers: sales ledger (for customer accounts), purchases ledger (for supplier accounts) and general ledger (all the other accounts, including assets, expenses, income, liabilities, and capital).

- **Control accounts** are 'total' accounts used to summarise important groups of ledger accounts, eg sales ledger control account.

- Finally, the balances of the ledger accounts are transferred to the **trial balance** which is both a checking device and also a source of accounting information for the business owners and managers.

- The **financial statements** of a business – the Statement of Profit or Loss and the Statement of Financial Position – are extracted from the accounts of a business on a regular basis.

| **Key Terms** | | |
|---|---|---|
| | **financial document** | a term given to a document which results from a financial transaction, eg an invoice |
| | **'cash' and 'credit' sales** | a 'cash' sale is a sale where payment is made straightaway, a 'credit' sale is a sale where payment is made at a later date |
| | **books of prime entry** | the place in the books of a business where a financial transaction is recorded for the first time, eg day books, cash book, petty cash book |
| | **day books** | a book of prime entry listing the details of various financial transactions, eg sales, sales returns, purchases, purchases returns and discounts |
| | **cash book** | the book of prime entry which lists payments in and out of the bank account |
| | **petty cash book** | the book of prime entry which lists small cash (notes and coins) business expense payments from an office cash fund |
| | **ledger account** | the formal accounting record (often in double-entry format) for financial transactions involving individuals (customers and suppliers) and business assets, expenses, income, liabilities and capital |
| | **double-entry accounts** | ledger accounts set up on the double-entry system (ie two entries – a debit and a credit – are made for each transaction) |
| | **the ledger** | means literally 'the book' which contains the individual accounts; it is often subdivided into different ledgers, eg sales ledger, purchases ledger, general ledger |
| | **control accounts** | 'total' accounts contained in the general ledger |
| | **trade receivable** | a customer who owes a business money |
| | **trade payable** | a supplier owed money by a business |
| | **assets** | items owned by a business, eg a delivery van |
| | **liabilities** | items owed by a business, eg a bank loan |
| | **capital** | the investment made in a business by the owner(s), ie the amount owed to the owner(s) by the business |
| | **trial balance** | a list of the balances of the ledger accounts drawn up in two columns (debit and credit) the totals of which should be the same |

# Activities

1.1 A 'cash sale' in accounting terms is:

| | |  |
|---|---|---|
| (a) | A sale involving notes and coins | |
| (b) | A sale requiring immediate payment | |
| (c) | A sale requiring payment in the future | |

Which **one** of these options is correct?

1.2 A financial document is first recorded in an accounting system in a book of prime entry.
True or false?

1.3 The following are all books of prime entry:

| | |  |
|---|---|---|
| (a) | Cash book, petty cash book, purchases ledger | |
| (b) | Sales day book, sales returns day book, sales ledger | |
| (c) | Cash book, petty cash book, sales day book | |

Which **one** of these options is correct?

1.4 Transactions recorded in the books of prime entry are then transferred to:

| | |  |
|---|---|---|
| (a) | Ledger accounts | |
| (b) | A trial balance | |
| (c) | A petty cash book | |

Which **one** of these options is correct?

1.5 A trade receivable is:

| | |  |
|---|---|---|
| (a) | A supplier owed money by the business | |
| (b) | A customer who owes money to a business | |
| (c) | A customer who settles straightaway using cash | |

Which **one** of these options is correct?

1.6 In double-entry book-keeping every transaction is recorded using:

| | |  |
|---|---|---|
| (a) | Two debits | |
| (b) | Two credits | |
| (c) | One debit and one credit | |

Which **one** of these options is correct?

**1.7**  The purchases ledger contains the ledger accounts for:

| | |
|---|---|
| (a)  Trade receivables | |
| (b)  Trade payables | |
| (c)  Expenses | |

Which **one** of these options is correct?

**1.8**  A liability of a business is:

| | |
|---|---|
| (a)  An amount owed by that business | |
| (b)  An item owned by that business | |
| (c)  A cash fund for business expenses | |

Which **one** of these options is correct?

**1.9**  An extract from the trial balance of a shop that sells tiles is shown below.

| Name of business: Style & Tile Trial Balance as at 30 June 20-3  (extract) | Debit £ | Credit £ |
|---|---|---|
| Trade receivables | 10,500 | |
| Trade payables | | 6,720 |
| Advertising | 1,400 | |
| Insurance | 780 | |
| Wages | 52,800 | |
| Bank | 3,000 | |
| Shop equipment | 22,000 | |
| Delivery vans | 28,000 | |
| Capital | | 155,000 |

On the basis of the figures shown here, answer the following questions:

**(a)**  How much do the customers of Style & Tile owe the business?

**(b)**  How much does Style & Tile owe its suppliers?

**(c)**  How much does Style & Tile have in the bank?

**(d)**  How much investment does the owner have in the business?

**(e)**  Where are the figures for trade receivables and trade payables taken from?

# 2 Financial documents for sales

## this chapter covers...

*This chapter examines the procedures involved when a business sells goods or services on credit – which means that payment is made at a later date, possibly a month later.*

*The important point here is that the business wants to get paid on time and it wants to get the right amount. It can achieve these aims through the efficient use and monitoring of financial documents.*

*This chapter covers the areas of:*

■ *the use of business documents – quotation, purchase order, invoice, delivery note, returns note, credit note, statement*

■ *the calculation of document totals and discounts*

■ *the calculation of Value Added Tax (VAT)*

■ *the coding of documents*

■ *the checking and authorisation of documents*

*Note that the documents explained in this chapter illustrate the traditional paper-based system. There is nowadays a growing trend for electronic documents, eg online orders, invoices, statements and payments. These follow the same principles as the paper-based documents.*

## FINANCIAL DOCUMENTS

When a business sells goods or services it will use a number of different documents (listed in the diagram below). A single sales transaction of course involves both seller and buyer. In this chapter we look at the situation from the point of view of the **seller** of the goods or services. The transaction from the point of view of the buyer is dealt with in Chapter 6. Documents which are used in the **selling** process include:

■ price **quotation** which the seller may be asked to provide

■ **purchase order** which the seller receives from the buyer

■ **delivery note** which goes with the goods from the seller to the buyer

■ **invoice** which lists the goods and tells the buyer what is owed

■ **returns note** which is sent with any goods that are being returned

■ **credit note** which is sent to the buyer if any refund is due

■ **statement** sent by the seller to remind the buyer what is owed

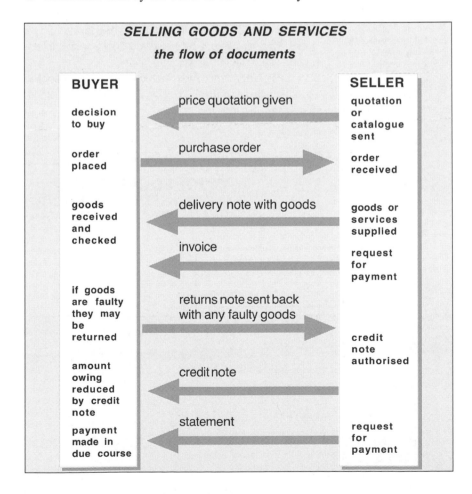

SELLING GOODS AND SERVICES
the flow of documents

### the flow of documents

Before you read the Case Study, make sure you have studied the diagram on the previous page. You will see in the columns representing the buyer and the seller that there are various activities requiring financial documents.

# COOL SOCKS – A SALES TRANSACTION

### situation

Cool Socks Limited manufactures fashion socks in a variety of colours. It supplies a number of different customers, including Trends, a fashion store in Broadfield. In this Case Study, Trends places an order for 100 pairs of socks with Cool Socks. The socks are delivered, but some are found to be faulty, so some of the socks have to be returned. The Case Study looks in detail at the documents involved.

## THE PRICE QUOTATION

Before placing the order, the buyer at Trends will need to find out the price of the socks. This can be done by consulting Cool Socks' printed catalogue or website, or by means of a written or telephoned enquiry.

Cool Socks *may* provide a written quotation for the socks if they are requested to do so, although this procedure is more common with higher value orders. A written quotation might look like this:

---

### ——— QUOTATION ———

## COOL SOCKS LIMITED

Unit 45 Elgar Estate, Broadfield, BR7 4ER
Tel 01908 765314  Fax 01908 765951 Email toni@cool.u-net.com
VAT REG GB 0745 4672 76

| Trends<br>4 Friar Street<br>Broadfield<br>BR1 3RF | date | 19 09 20-3 |
|---|---|---|

Thank you for your enquiry of 17 September 20-3. We are pleased to quote as follows:

100 pairs Toebar socks (blue)@ £2.36 a pair, excluding VAT.

*M Arnold*

Sales Department

---

## PURCHASE ORDER – THE SOCKS ARE ORDERED

The buyer at Trends, once she has accepted the quoted price will post, fax or email the authorised purchase order shown below, or she might send an online order. The order will have been processed manually, or produced on a computer accounting program.

Note the following details:

- each purchase order has a specific reference number (here it is 47609) – this is useful for filing and quoting on later documents such as invoices and statements; this reference number is an example of **coding** in accounting (see page 35)

- the catalogue number of the goods required is stated in the product code column this number is a further example of coding

- the quantity of the goods required is stated in the quantity column – socks are normally supplied in pairs!

- the description of the goods is set out in full

- the price is not essential, although some purchase orders will include a price

- the purchase order is signed and dated by the person in charge of purchasing – without this authorisation the supplier is unlikely to supply the goods (the order will probably be returned)

---

# Trends
**4 Friar Street**
**Broadfield**
**BR1 3RF**
Tel 01908 761234  Fax 01908 761987
VAT REG GB 0745 8383 56

# PURCHASE ORDER

| Cool Socks Limited, | | purchase order no | 47609 |
| Unit 45 Elgar Estate, | | date | 25 09 20-3 |
| Broadfield, | | | |
| BR7 4ER | | | |

| Product code | Quantity | Description |
|---|---|---|
| 45B | 100 pairs | Blue Toebar socks @ £2.36 per pair |

**AUTHORISED**  signature......*D Signer*.................................................date......*25/09/20-3*

## DELIVERY NOTE – THE SOCKS ARE DELIVERED

A delivery note is despatched with the goods when the order is ready. It is either processed manually in the office or printed out by a computer accounting program, often at the same time as the invoice (see next page). In this case, the delivery note travels with the socks, and a copy will be signed by Trends on receipt. Note the following details:

- the delivery note has a numerical reference (here it is 68873), useful for filing and later reference if there is a query – this is another example of coding

- the method of delivery is stated – here the delivery is by parcel carrier

- the delivery note quotes the purchase order number – 47609 – this enables the buyor to link the delivery with the original purchase order – this is another example of the use of coding

- the delivery note quotes
    - Cool Socks' catalogue reference 45B as the product code
    - the quantity supplied
    - the description of the goods, but no price – it is not needed at this stage

    these details will be checked against the goods themselves straightaway so that any discrepancies can be reported without delay

- the delivery note will be signed and dated by the person receiving the goods as proof of delivery; nowadays this process can also be carried out electronically – the person receiving the goods will be asked to sign a portable electronic device

---

## ———— DELIVERY NOTE ————
## COOL SOCKS LIMITED
Unit 45 Elgar Estate, Broadfield, BR7 4ER
Tel 01908 765314  Fax 01908 765951  Email toni@cool.u-net.com
VAT REG GB 0745 4672 76

| Trends<br>4 Friar Street<br>Broadfield<br>BR1 3RF | delivery note no | 68873 |
| | delivery method | Lynx Parcels |
| | your order | 47609 |
| | date | 02 10 20-3 |

| product code | quantity | description |
| --- | --- | --- |
| 45B | 100 pairs | Blue Toebar socks |

**Received**

signature.............*V Williams*.................name (capitals).*V WILLIAMS*...........date.*6/10/20-3*.....

## INVOICE – THE SELLER REQUESTS PAYMENT

The invoice is the trading document which is sent by the seller to the buyer stating how much is owed by the buyer of goods or services.

The invoice, like the delivery note, is prepared in the supplier's (seller's) office, and is either processed manually or produced on a computer printer using a computer accounting program.

Invoices produced by different organisations will vary to some extent in terms of detail, but their basic layout will always be the same. The invoice prepared by Cool Socks Limited – illustrated on page 25 – is typical of a modern typed or computer printed document.

An invoice will normally be printed as part of a multiple set of documents which is likely to include a delivery note and a copy invoice for the seller's own records. The copy invoice will normally be filed in numerical order (see 'coding' below). If a computer accounting program is used, the invoice can, of course, be called up on screen, referenced by its invoice number.

Note the following details, and refer to the invoice on page 25.

### addresses
The invoice shows the address:

- of the seller of the goods – Cool Socks Limited
- where the invoice should be sent – to Trends
- where the goods are to be sent – if it is different from the invoice address

### coding and references
There are a number of important coding references on the invoice:

- the numerical reference of the invoice itself – 787923
- the account number allocated to Trends by the seller – 3993 – for use in the seller's computer accounting program; note that account references can include letters as well – for example another supplier might give Trends the code TR126
- the original reference number on the purchase order sent by Trends – 47609 – which will enable the shop to link the invoice with the original order
- the product code from the seller's catalogue or product list – here it is 45B

Note that coding on a financial document can be:

- numeric – ie just numbers
- alpha-numeric – ie a mixture of letters and numbers

### date
The date on the invoice is important because the payment date (here one month) is calculated from it. It is also the transaction date used for VAT (Value Added Tax) purposes (see the next page).

## the goods

The invoice must specify accurately the goods supplied. The details – set out in columns in the body of the invoice – include:

- **product code** – this is the catalogue number which appeared on the original purchase order and on the delivery note

- **description** – the goods must be specified precisely

- **quantity** – this should agree with the quantity ordered

- **price** – this is the price of each unit shown in the next column

- **unit** is the way in which the unit is counted and charged for, eg 'boxes' of tights or single items, eg designer dresses, in which case the unit is quoted as 'each'

- **total** is the unit price multiplied by the number of units

- **discount %** is the percentage allowance (often known as 'trade' discount) given to customers who regularly deal with the supplier, ie they receive a certain percentage (eg 10%) deducted from their bill (see page 28 for further explanation of discounts)

- discounts are also given for **bulk purchases** – 'bulk discount' will also be shown in the discount column

- **net** is the amount due to the seller after deduction of trade or bulk discount, and before VAT is added on

## totals and VAT

Further calculations are made in the box at the bottom of the invoice:

- **Goods Total** is the amount due to the seller (it is the total of the net column)

- **Value Added Tax (VAT)**, here calculated as 20% of the total after deduction of any cash discount. VAT is added to produce the invoice final total

- **Total** is the VAT plus the Goods Total; it is the amount due to the seller

Note: VAT (Value Added Tax) is a 'sales tax' on the supply of goods and services. It is changed from time-to-time by the Government. In this book a standard VAT rate of 20% is used.

## terms

The terms of payment are stated on the invoice. In this case these include:

- **Net monthly** – this means that full payment of the invoice should be made within a month of the invoice date

- **Carriage paid** means that the price of the goods includes delivery

- **E & OE** stands for 'errors and omissions excepted' which means that if there is a error or something left off the invoice by mistake, resulting in an incorrect final price, the supplier has the right to rectify the mistake and demand the correct amount

Another term used (not shown here) is **Prompt Payment Discount** (also known as '**Settlement Discount**' or '**Cash Discount**') – a further percentage discount given when payment is made early. See pages 30-31 for further details.

# INVOICE

## COOL SOCKS LIMITED

Unit 45 Elgar Estate, Broadfield, BR7 4ER
Tel 01908 765314  Fax 01908 765951  Email toni@cool.u-net.com
VAT Reg GB 0745 4672 76

invoice to

| | |
|---|---|
| **Trends**<br>**1 Friar Street**<br>**Broadfield**<br>**BR1 3RF** | |

| | |
|---|---|
| invoice no | **787923** |
| account | **3993** |
| your reference | **47609** |
| date/tax point | **02 10 20-3** |

deliver to

**as above**

| Product code | Description | Quantity | Price | Unit | Total | Discount % | Net |
|---|---|---|---|---|---|---|---|
| **45B** | **Blue toebar socks** | **100** | **2.36** | **pair** | **236.00** | **0.00** | **236.00** |

**terms**
Net monthly
Carriage paid
E & OE

| | |
|---|---|
| **Goods total** | **236.00** |
| **VAT** | **47.20** |
| **TOTAL** | **283.20** |

# CREDIT NOTE – A REFUND IS DUE TO THE BUYER

A **credit note** is a 'refund' document. It reduces the amount owed by the buyer. The goods, remember, have not yet been paid for. The credit note is prepared by the seller and sent to the buyer. Examples of reasons for a refund by credit note include:

- the goods may have been damaged, lost in transit or they may be faulty
- not all the goods have been sent – this is referred to as 'shortages'
- the unit price on the invoice may be incorrect and the buyer overcharged

In this Case Study, when the staff of Trends unpack the socks in the store room they find that ten pairs are damaged. They telephone Cool Socks to report the problem and Cool Socks authorise the return of the socks for credit. These socks will then be sent back to Cool Socks with a request for credit – ie a reduction in the bill for the 10 damaged pairs – with a document known as a returns note (see page 139). Cool Socks will then issue the credit note for £28.32 shown below. Note the following details:

- the invoice number of the original consignment is quoted
- the reason for the issue of the credit note is stated at the bottom of the credit note – here 'damaged' goods
- the details are otherwise exactly the same as on an invoice

---

## —— CREDIT NOTE ——

# COOL SOCKS LIMITED

Unit 45 Elgar Estate, Broadfield, BR7 4ER
Tel 01908 765314  Fax 01908 765951  Email toni@cool.u-net.com
VAT REG GB 0745 4672 76

to

Trends
4 Friar Street
Broadfield
BR1 3RF

| credit note no | 12157 |
| account | 3993 |
| your reference | 47609 |
| our invoice | 787923 |
| date/tax point | 10 10 20–3 |

| Product code | Description | Quantity | Price | Unit | Total | Discount % | Net |
|---|---|---|---|---|---|---|---|
| 45B | Blue Toebar socks | 10 | 2.36 | pair | 23.60 | 0.00 | 23.60 |

**Reason for credit**
10 pairs of socks received – damaged

| | |
|---|---|
| GOODS TOTAL | 23.60 |
| VAT | 4.72 |
| TOTAL | 28.32 |

## STATEMENT – THE SELLER REQUESTS PAYMENT

A seller will not normally expect a buyer to pay each individual invoice as soon as it is received: this could result in the buyer having to make a number of payments during the month.  Instead, a **statement of account** is sent by the supplier to the buyer at the end of the month. This statement shows what is owed by the buyer to the seller. It contains details of:

- any balances (amounts owing) at the beginning of the month – these appear in the debit column with the wording 'balance b/f' in the details column ('b/f' stands for 'brought forward')
- any payments received from the buyer (credit column)
- invoices issued for goods supplied – the full amount due, including VAT (debit column)
- refunds made on credit notes – including VAT (credit column)
- the running balance and, in the box at the bottom, the final net total of all the items
- the bank details required for making payment by BACS or Faster Payments

The statement issued by Cool Socks to Trends for the period covering the sale and refund is shown below. Note that the balance of £150 owing at the beginning of the month has been paid off in full by a BACS payment on 2 October.

---

**STATEMENT OF ACCOUNT**

# COOL SOCKS LIMITED

Unit 45 Elgar Estate, Broadfield, BR7 4ER
Tel 01908 765314  Fax 01908 765951  Email toni@cool.u-net.com
VAT REG GB 0745 4672 76

TO

| Trends |
|---|
| 4 Friar Street |
| Broadfield |
| BR1 3RF |

account     3993

date     31 10 20-3

| Date | Details | Debit £ | Credit £ | Balance £ |
|---|---|---|---|---|
| 01 10 20-3 | Balance b/f | 150.00 | | 150.00 |
| 02 10 20-3 | BACS payment 170961 | | 150.00 | 00.00 |
| 02 10 20-3 | Invoice 787923 | 283.20 | | 283.20 |
| 10 10 20-3 | Credit note 12157 | | 28.32 | 254.88 |

Electronic payments: pay Cool Socks Ltd at Albion Bank, Account 11451226, Sort code 904717

| TOTAL | 254.88 |
|---|---|

## DISCOUNTS

The invoice in the Case Study (shown on the next page) has a column (second from the right) for a **discount** percentage. We will now explain how discounts are is calculated. The two most common discounts are bulk discount and trade discount which are simply percentage deductions from the price charged for goods and services.

### bulk discount

Discount may also be given by sellers to buyers who purchase in large quantities or over certain money amounts (eg over £10,000); this is known as **bulk discount**.

### trade discount

It is common practice for suppliers to give businesses that order from them on a regular basis an agreed discount – a percentage reduction in the invoiced amount. This is **trade discount** because it applies to businesses 'in the trade' rather than to the general public. In the example on the next page 10% trade discount has been given by Cool Socks Limited to Trends. Note how the discount percentage is shown in the discount column and the net amount is the amount after deduction of the discount.

The calculations on the Cool Socks invoice are as follows:

| | |
|---|---|
| **Step 1** | Calculate the total price before discount |
| | 100 x £2.36 = £236.00 |
| **Step 2** | Calculate the trade discount |
| | £236.00 x 10% (ie 10/100) = £23.60 |
| **Step 3** | Calculate the net price before VAT |
| | £236.00 - £23.60 = £212.40 |
| **Step 4** | Calculate the VAT |
| | £212.40 x 20% (ie 20/100) = £42.48 |
| **Step 5** | Calculate the total invoice price |
| | £212.40 + £42.48 = £254.88 |

# INVOICE

## COOL SOCKS LIMITED

Unit 45 Elgar Estate, Broadfield, BR7 4ER
Tel 01908 765314  Fax 01908 765951  Email toni@cool.u-net.com
VAT Reg GB 0745 4672 76

invoice to

| Trends<br>4 Friar Street<br>Broadfield<br>BR1 3RF |
| --- |

| | |
| --- | --- |
| invoice no | 787923 |
| account | 3993 |
| your reference | 47609 |
| date/tax point | 02 10 20-3 |

deliver to

| as above |
| --- |

| Product code | Description | Quantity | Price | Unit | Total | Discount % | Net |
| --- | --- | --- | --- | --- | --- | --- | --- |
| 45B | Blue toebar socks | 100 | 2.36 | pair | 236.00 | 10.00 | 212.40 |

**terms**
Net monthly
Carriage paid
E & OE

| | |
| --- | --- |
| Goods total | 212.40 |
| VAT | 42.48 |
| **TOTAL** | 254.88 |

*an invoice with 10% trade discount deducted*

## prompt payment discount (PPD)

**Prompt payment discount** (also known as **settlement discount** or **cash discount**) is a discount offered by the seller to the buyer to encourage the buyer to settle up straightaway or in a short space of time rather than waiting the thirty or more days specified on the invoice. For example, the seller might offer an extra 5% discount on an invoice if it is paid within 15 days.

## ways of adjusting for VAT when a PPD is deducted

It is important to remember that the VAT on an invoice will **always** be calculated on the invoice total **after** the deduction of trade or bulk discount but will **not** be adjusted for any prompt payment discount (PPD) deducted by the buyer. If PPD is taken, the goods amount and VAT actually due on the sale will therefore be **less** than the goods total and VAT shown on the invoice. These figures will need to be adjusted in the accounting records.

There are two ways in which the seller can reduce the VAT amount and goods total when a PPD (prompt payment discount) is offered. **Important note:** the first alternative listed here is the method that the AAT has set out in its Unit specifications and the second is explained here for information only.

- **Alternative 1 – the seller issues a credit note (AAT suggested method)**

    If the customer pays early, taking advantage of the lower charge, a lower amount of VAT will be due to HM Revenue & Customs (HMRC). The seller will have to issue to the customer a credit note for the amount of the prompt payment discount given. This will include the goods amount and the VAT.

- **Alternative 2 – the seller includes a PPD declaration on the invoice**

    If the seller does not want to issue a credit note, the seller's invoice must include a written declaration giving the terms of the PPD (eg discount of 5% for an invoice settled within 15 days of the invoice date) and a statement that the buyer should account to HMRC for a lower VAT amount (ie not the amount on the invoice). HMRC recommends that if this method is adopted this declaration is included on the invoice:

    *'A discount of X% of the full price applies if payment is made within Y days of the invoice date. No credit note will be issued. Following payment you must ensure you have only recovered the VAT actually paid.'*

In the Case Study on the next page a buyer is offered a prompt payment discount of 5% for settlement within 15 days and decides to take the discount **using Alternative 1** (see above) where the seller issues a credit note for the reduction in price and VAT paid.

**Case Study**

# SELAR LTD AND BIYAR LTD – DEALING WITH PPD

## situation and how the process works . . .

- Selar Ltd regularly supplies goods to Biyar Ltd and has offered Biyar Ltd a prompt payment discount of 5% for settlement within 15 days

- Selar Ltd sends an invoice for goods costing £1,000 to Biyar Ltd. An extract of this is shown below. The terms printed at the bottom of the invoice include the 5% PPD that will be offered to Biyar Ltd for payment. The invoice is sent with the goods

- Biyar Ltd decides to pay the invoice within the 15 days and calculates the 5% discount as follows:

  Goods total £1,000 x 5% = £50
  VAT payable = £200 x 5% = £10

  The total discount plus the VAT is therefore £50 + £10 = £60

- Biyar Ltd then calculates the amount due to Selar Ltd and pays the invoice:

  | | |
  |---|---:|
  | Total payable without discount (as on invoice) | £1,200 |
  | Less discount | £60 |
  | Amount payable | £1,140 |

- Selar Ltd sends Biyar Ltd a credit note for the total discount including VAT as shown below. The amounts on the £60 credit note include VAT of £10 and a goods total of £50

---

### INVOICE *(extract)*
### Selar Ltd to Biyar Ltd

| **terms** | **Goods total** | 1,000.00 |
|---|---|---:|
| 5% prompt payment discount for settlement within 15 days, otherwise net monthly | **VAT** | 200.00 |
| Carriage paid | | |
| E & OE | **TOTAL** | 1,200.00 |

---

### CREDIT NOTE *(extract)*
### Selar Ltd to Biyar Ltd

| | **Goods total** | 50.00 |
|---|---|---:|
| | **VAT** | 10.00 |
| | **TOTAL** | 60.00 |

## VALUE ADDED TAX (VAT) – A 'SALES TAX'

### what is Value Added Tax (VAT)?

**VAT is a UK sales tax on the selling price charged to buyers.**

As we have seen on some of the business documents illustrated in this chapter, VAT is added to the price of items sold after discount has been deducted. VAT is a **sales tax** paid by the consumer and administered and collected by **HM Revenue & Customs**, a Government Department.

Businesses must keep accurate records of VAT paid and collected. This means filing financial documents such as invoices and credit notes for a minimum period of six years. HM Revenue & Customs tax inspectors visit businesses from time-to-time to ensure that VAT is being charged correctly and that there are no VAT 'fiddles' taking place.

### some useful VAT calculations

In your studies you are likely to be asked to carry out a variety of calculations involving VAT. Here are some of the more common ones.

*what is the VAT to be charged?*

If you need to work out the VAT on a given amount you apply the formula:

$$amount \; x \; \frac{20 \; (ie \; the \; VAT \; rate)}{100} \; = \; VAT \; payable$$

VAT chargeable on £100 is therefore £100 $x \; \dfrac{20}{100}$ = £20.00

Note that when calculating VAT, the VAT total is usually rounded down to the nearest penny; eg VAT of £2.56<u>78</u> becomes £2.5<u>6</u> and not £2.5<u>7</u>.

*calculating the VAT when the VAT is included but not shown*

If you are given a total amount, for an example a shop till receipt which does not show the VAT amount, you may need to work out both the VAT content and also the amount before VAT is added (the 'VAT exclusive' amount). The VAT content is worked out by using the formula:

$$\frac{VAT \; percentage \; x \; amount \; which \; includes \; VAT}{100 + VAT \; percentage} \; = \; VAT \; content$$

The VAT content can also be found by using the **VAT fraction** provided by HM Revenue & Customs. For a VAT rate of 20%, the VAT fraction is $^1/6$. All you have to do to find out the VAT is to divide the amount including VAT by 6. For example, the VAT included in £12 is £12 ÷ 6 = £2.

## AUTHORISING AND CHECKING INVOICES

### credit limits

**The credit limit of a customer is the maximum amount which the seller will allow the customer to owe at any one time.**

Part of the accounting control system of a business is to set credit limits for its established customers and to establish limits for new customers. Each time that an invoice is issued, a check should be made against the credit limit of that customer.

### authorisation of invoices

Most invoices issued will be within the credit limit and processed with the authority of the person in charge of invoicing.

But what if the credit limit will be exceeded? No business will refuse to supply a good customer. It may be that payment will soon come in from the buyer, or the amount involved is relatively small. In these cases the invoice will need authorisation from a more senior person in the accounts department.

It is quite possible that a credit limit may have to be raised if a customer is buying more goods or services, and, of course, is paying invoices on time.

### the need to check invoices

Few things are more annoying to a buyer than an incorrect invoice – the wrong goods, the wrong price, the wrong discount, and so on. It wastes the buyer's time and may require an adjusting credit note to be issued. It is essential that a number of important details are checked by the accounts staff of the seller before invoices are authorised and sent out.

What will the person need to check? He or she will need to look at:

- the purchase order relating to the invoice (this is very important)
- the seller's own record of any price quoted (eg a printed or online catalogue or a product database)
- the seller's file record of the buyer (either paper-based or on the computer) which should give the credit limit and the discount allowed

### the checks to be made

- is the **correct customer** being invoiced? There are often customers with similar names; the customer coding must be carefully checked

- are the goods being sent to the **correct place**? Sometimes the delivery address can be different from the address normally held on file

- are the **correct goods** being sent? The product coding on the purchase order must be checked carefully against the description; it is possible that the buyer has quoted an incorrect code

- is the **quantity** correct?

- is the **unit** correct? Is it a box of products or an individual item being requested?

- is the **price** correct?

- is the **correct discount** percentage being allowed to the customer? Do any special terms apply? The list of discounts or customer file will need to be looked at

- are the **calculations** on the invoice correct? This is very important if the invoice has not been produced on a computer. The normal checks for a straightforward invoice with trade discount deducted are:

  *quantity  x  unit price  =  total before discount*

  *total before discount x discount %  =  discount*

  *total before discount  – discount  =  net total*

  *net total  x VAT %  =  VAT*

  *net total  + VAT = invoice total*

If the invoice is for more than one one product, all the invoice 'lines' must be carefully and individually checked and the addition also checked.

## DEALING WITH DISCREPANCIES

Discrepancies on financial documents can occur in the following situations:

- **The discrepancy is found in the internal checking process**, before the document is issued. In this case the document will have to be passed back to the person or section which made the mistake and a new corrected document will have to be issued and authorised; normally the original document reference number can be retained.

- **The buyer finds the discrepancy after the document has been issued**. In this case an apology will have to be made by the seller to the buyer and a correcting document issued; under no circumstances should the buyer alter or correct the document.

## CODING SYSTEMS

We have already seen in this chapter that **coding** is widely used in the documentation process. Coding is important for two main reasons:

- ■ it provides an instant and accurate way of referencing customers, suppliers, individual products, purchase orders
- ■ it enables documents to be filed in an efficient way so that they can be easily accessed; it is important in any business that documents can be found and referred to easily, either in paper format, or on a computer system

Filing systems are often organised using either an **alphabetic** or a **numeric** coding system:

- ■ customer files are normally filed alphabetically by name
- ■ invoices are normally filed numerically by invoice number

Sometimes coding may be **alpha-numeric**, using a mixture of letters and numbers. For example customers who have 'JON' as the first three letters of their name – 'Jones' for example – may be coded JON01, JON02, JON03, and so on. If you think about it, alpha-numeric coding is used widely in everyday life: examples include vehicle registration plates, postcodes, tax codes and National Insurance 'numbers'.

Study the invoice extract shown below and see how many accounting-related codes you can identify and what types they are. The answers are shown at the bottom of the page.

---

### invoice (extract)

Simway Ltd
4 High Street
Broadfield
BR1 2GF

| invoice no | 82346 |
| account reference | SIM003 |
| purchase order | 47609 |
| date/tax point | 07 12 20-3 |

| Product code | Description | Quantity | Price | Unit | Total | Discount % | Net |
|---|---|---|---|---|---|---|---|
| STPGR | Stapler (green) | 10 | 10.70 | each | 107.00 | 10.00 | 96.30 |

---

Alpha-numeric code: account reference SIM003

Numeric codes: invoice number 82346
purchase order number 47609

Alphabetical code: product code STPGR

# CODING AT WORK

### supplier account codes

Legno Ltd, a timber wholesaler, allocates codes to each of its suppliers. Each code is alpha-numeric, made up of the first three letters of the supplier's name followed by a two digit number to distinguish the suppliers when two or more share the same first three letters. The digits reflect the alphabetical order of the names. For example:

| Supplier | Supplier account code | Notes |
|---|---|---|
| Jonas Supplies | JON01 | *'as' comes before 'at'* |
| Jonathan UK Ltd | JON02 | *'at' comes before 'es'* |
| Jones Ltd | JON03 | |

Last week Legno Ltd opened accounts for two new suppliers: Jonty Supplies and Jonsson Ltd.

You are asked to allocate account codes to these suppliers. Apart from the three accounts listed above there are no other accounts starting with the three letters 'JON'.

What would the codes be?  The **answer** is shown below:

| Supplier | Supplier account code | Notes |
|---|---|---|
| Jonsson Ltd | JON04 | *'ss' comes after the 'es' of Jones and before the 'ty' of Jonty* |
| Jonty Supplies | JON05 | |

### sales product codes

Legno Ltd also operates a system which allocates General Ledger account codes to different types of timber sales. These are entered on the sales invoices and credit notes so that the amount can be entered in the correct account. The ledger codes are as follows:

| Product type | General Ledger Code |
|---|---|
| Pine sales | GL4000 |
| Oak sales | GL4001 |
| Beech sales | GL4002 |
| Hardwood sales | GL4003 |
| Ash sales | GL4004 |

A new trainee asks you to check that he has the right code for an invoice for the sale of oak. He asks if it is GL4002 because that is a code used very frequently on invoices. Is the trainee correct?

**Answer**: No. The code is incorrect. The code for the sale of oak is GL4001.

**Chapter Summary**

■ When a business sells goods or services on credit it will deal with a number of financial documents. The most important of these are the
- purchase order
- delivery note
- invoice
- credit note
- statement

■ The seller of the goods or services requests payment by means of an invoice and then reminds the buyer by means of a regular statement of aooount (noimally monthly).

■ Discounts – reductions in the selling price – are often given by the seller to the buyer. These include trade discount, bulk discount and prompt payment discount for early payment. Trade and bulk discounts are deducted by the seller from the invoice total. Prompt payment discount is deducted by the buyer when paying the invoice and will be adjusted by means of a credit note issued by the seller.

■ Any refund due to the buyer (eg for wrong, damaged or missing goods) will be acknowledged and documented by means of a credit note.

■ All documents are normally coded (given an alphabetic, numeric or alpha-numeric code) for reference purposes.

■ VAT (Value Added Tax), a sales tax payable on most goods and services, is included on the majority of invoices and credit notes.

■ All documents should be checked carefully by the seller to make sure that the right goods or services have been supplied, and at the right price. It is essential that items such as discounts, VAT and totals are calculated correctly.

■ Financial documents will need to be authorised before they are sent out.

■ Any discrepancies found on the documents either by the seller or the buyer should be dealt with promptly.

| | | |
|---|---|---|
| **Key Terms** | **purchase order** | a document issued by the buyer of goods and services, sent to the seller, indicating the goods or services required |
| | **delivery note** | a document sent by the seller to the buyer with the goods, detailing what has been sent |
| | **invoice** | a document issued by the seller of goods or services indicating the amount owing and the required payment date |
| | **credit note** | a document issued by the seller of the goods or services reducing the amount owed by the buyer |
| | **statement** | a document issued by the seller to the buyer summarising invoices, credit notes issued and payments received and stating the amount owed |
| | **trade discount** | a percentage reduction in the selling price given by the seller to the buyer because of the trading relationship |
| | **bulk discount** | a discount given by the seller to the buyer for bulk purchases, ie purchases over certain quantities or over certain money amounts |
| | **prompt payment discount** | a percentage reduction in the selling price given to the buyer if the buyer pays within a specified short space of time |
| | **Value Added Tax (VAT)** | a government tax on sales, normally calculated on invoices and credit notes |
| | **credit limit** | the maximum amount the seller will allow the customer to owe at any one time |
| | **coding** | document references using numeric, alphabetic or alpha-numeric identification systems |

# Activities

**2.1**   Complete the sentences below by selecting the correct words from the following list:

**invoice**      **statement of account**      **purchase order**      **delivery note**      **credit note**

**(a)**   A ⬚ Is used to order goods from the seller.

**(b)**   A ⬚ is sent with the goods by the seller to the buyer, giving details of the goods sent.

**(c)**   The document sent by the seller giving details of the terms of the transaction and stating the amount owed is an ⬚ .

**(d)**   A ⬚ is sent by the seller to remind the buyer of the amount owed to the seller.

**(e)**   The document sent to a buyer as a formal notification of a refund made is known as a ⬚ .

**2.2**   Link the three types of discount given by sellers listed on the right with the descriptions in the boxes on the left.

**(a)**   a reduction in an amount owed on an invoice where the buyer pays earlier than is normal

**bulk discount**

**(b)**   a discount given by the seller to the buyer which forms part of the terms for normal regular purchases

**prompt payment discount**

**(c)**   a discount given by the seller for purchases over certain quantities or over certain money amounts

**trade discount**

**2.3**   Tippett Brothers supplies goods priced at £159.50 to a customer at a trade discount of 30%. What would the total invoice amount be, assuming a VAT rate of 20% and no further discounts?

**2.4**   Zeta Stationery sells gel pens and has a special sales offer. A box of ten gel pens normally sells at £8.00 (excluding VAT). Zeta Stationery is offering to give a 20% bulk discount for orders of ten boxes or more. One morning it receives the following orders:

**(a)**   20 boxes ordered by Osborne Electronics Limited

**(b)**   50 boxes ordered by Helfield College

**(c)**   5 boxes ordered by Jim Masters

**(d)**   1,000 boxes ordered by Trigger Trading Limited

**You are to** calculate in each case:
   • the total cost before discount
   • the discount
   • the cost after discount
   • the VAT at the current rate
   • the total cost

**2.5**   Venables Supplies sells computer accessories. The terms it offers its regular customers are as follows:

   •   20% trade discount on all orders

   •   5% prompt payment discount for settlement of an invoice within 15 days

You are given four invoices to prepare. The goods totals before applying any discounts and applying VAT are as follows:

1   £100
2   £1,650
3   £2,500
4   £10,900

**You are to:**

**(a)**   Calculate all four invoice totals after applying trade discount and VAT @ 20%.

**(b)**   Calculate the total amounts payable after the deduction of prompt payment discount by the buyer.

**(c)**   State what document will be used by the seller in each case to deduct the prompt payment discount from the total amount shown on the invoice.

**2.6**   Examine the invoice and credit note prepared by the seller in Question 2.8 and identify five examples of coding. These examples should include:

**(a)**   Numeric coding (2 examples)

**(b)**   Alphabetic coding invoice & credit note (1 example)

**(c)**   Alpha-numeric coding (2 examples)

**2.7**   •   Check the invoice extracts shown below.

•   State what is wrong with them.

•   Calculate the correct final totals.

**Note:** VAT is rounded down to the nearest penny.

**Invoice (a)**

| Description | Quantity | Price | Total | Discount % | Net |
|---|---|---|---|---|---|
| Cotton shirts (red) | 10 | 9.50 | 95.00 | 20 | 85.50 |

| | | |
|---|---|---|
| Goods total | | 85.50 |
| VAT @ 20% | | 17.10 |
| TOTAL | | 102.60 |

**Invoice (b)**

| Description | Quantity | Price | Total | Discount % | Net |
|---|---|---|---|---|---|
| 'Crazy Surfin' T-shirts (yellow) | 50 | 5.00 | 225.00 | 10 | 202.50 |

| | | |
|---|---|---|
| Goods total | | 202.50 |
| VAT @ 20% | | 40.50 |
| TOTAL | | 243.00 |

**2.8** You work in the Accounts Department of Pool Cleaning Services Limited, a business which maintains swimming pools, spa baths and jacuzzis.

It is 31 July 20-3 and you are looking through the file for the account of Mr Henry Simpson. Your file shows that you issued an invoice on 8 July (shown below) and a credit note on 14 July for a 10% trade discount which should have been deducted from the invoice (see next page).

You also note from last month's statement that Mr Simpson still owed you £58.75 on 1 July for a call out charge he had not yet paid. You received a cheque for this amount on 4 July.

**You are to** prepare a statement for Mr H Simpson as at 31 July 20-3. It should show opening and closing balances and transactions for the month. A blank statement is shown on the next page.

---

# INVOICE

## Pool Cleaning Services Limited
Unit 5 Neptune Estate, Mereford, MR7 4EF
Tel 01908 352456  Fax 01908 352466  Email mail@poolcleaning-services.com
VAT Reg GB 0745 4872 21

invoice to

| H Simpson | |
|---|---|
| 45 Bishops Avenue | |
| Marston Hackett | |
| MR7 9JH | |

| | |
|---|---|
| invoice no | **10982** |
| account | **HS234** |
| your reference | **verbal** |
| date/tax point | **08 07 20-3** |

| Description | Total | Discount | Net |
|---|---|---|---|
| Annual swimming pool service, 27 June 20-3 (Product: ASPS) | 290.00 | 0.00 | 290.00 |

| | | |
|---|---|---|
| | **Net Total** | 290.00 |
| | **VAT** | 58.00 |
| **terms** Net monthly | **TOTAL** | 348.00 |

extract from credit note No. 2378 dated 14 July

| Description | | Total | Discount | Net |
|---|---|---|---|---|
| Annual swimming pool service (Product:ASPS) | | 29.00 | 0.00 | 29.00 |

Reason for credit
10% discount allowable on invoice

| | |
|---|---|
| NET TOTAL | 29.00 |
| VAT | 5.80 |
| TOTAL | 34.80 |

---

# STATEMENT OF ACCOUNT

## Pool Cleaning Services Limited

Unit 5 Neptune Estate, Mereford, MR7 4EF
Tel 01908 352456  Fax 01908 352466  Email mail@poolcleaning-services.com
VAT Reg GB 0745 4872 21

TO

account

date

| Date | Details | Debit £ | Credit £ | Balance £ |
|---|---|---|---|---|
| | | | | |
| | | | | |
| | | | | |
| | | | | |

Electronic payments: pay Pool Cleaning Services Ltd at Britannia Bank, Account 12397610, Sort code 83 11 20

| TOTAL | £ |
|---|---|

# 3 Double-entry and the accounting equation

## this chapter covers...

*This chapter describes and explains how double-entry accounts are set up and how they work. It covers:*

- *the need for accounts and what they are used for*

- *the way in which double-entry accounts are organised into ledgers*

- *the format of double-entry accounts*

- *the principles of debits and credits and the dual effect of each transaction*

- *the way in which the bank account fits into the double-entry system*

- *how to write up the double-entry accounts*

- *how to work out whether an entry made in a double-entry account should be a debit or a credit*

- *the way in which double-entry accounts relate to the accounting equation*

- *the operation of the accounting equation*

- *the balancing of double-entry accounts*

### important technical note

This book uses the phrase 'bank account' to mean both an account held at a bank and also a ledger account set up by a business to record bank transactions. To avoid confusion all ledger accounts in this book use capital letters for the start of the account name, but the account held at the bank is referred to using small letters. The rule is:

**B**ank **A**ccount = a ledger account in the books of the business

**b**ank **a**ccount = an account held at a bank

# AN INTRODUCTION TO DOUBLE-ENTRY ACCOUNTS

## double-entry accounts and the accounting system

As we saw in Chapter 1, double-entry accounts are written up from the books of prime entry which include day books and cash books.

Books of prime entry record financial transactions and are themselves written up from business documents, which include invoices and bank payments. The phrase 'prime entry' means 'the first place where information is entered'. Books of prime entry will be covered in detail in later chapters of this book.

The diagram below shows how the double-entry accounts fit into the earlier stages of the accounting system.

## what do double-entry accounts record?

Double-entry accounts form the 'core' of the accounting system. They are a record of financial transactions:

- what is owed on credit by individual customers as a result of sales
- what is owed on credit to individual suppliers as a result of purchases
- income items
- expense items

Double-entry accounts can be:

- accounts for types of income or expenses (sales, purchases, insurance, wages)
- accounts for assets (items owned)
- accounts for liabilities (amounts owed)

In other words, double-entry accounts cover all types of financial transaction.

### how are double-entry accounts organised?

Double-entry accounts are grouped for convenience in different **ledgers** (for credit sales, credit purchases, general accounts). These are shown in the diagram below and will be explained in more detail in later chapters.

All the ledgers grouped together are called '**the ledger**'. The word 'ledger' means 'book'.

---

**'the ledger' = sales ledger & purchases ledger & general ledger**

| **SALES LEDGER** | **PURCHASES LEDGER** | **GENERAL LEDGER** |
|---|---|---|
| accounts for customers<br>• who buy on credit from the business<br>• who owe money to the business | accounts for suppliers<br>• who supply on credit to the business, and<br>• to whom the business owes money | accounts for<br>• assets (items owned)<br>• liabilities (items owed)<br>• owner's capital<br>• expenses<br>• income |

---

## DOUBLE-ENTRY 'T' ACCOUNTS

Double-entry accounts are normally set out in the form of a 'T' with the account name at the top; they are known as 'T accounts' – see the example below:

| **Debit (dr)** | **Account name** | **Credit (cr)** |
|---|---|---|
| | | |

Each account has two sides:

■ a **debit** side (often written as 'dr') on the left

■ a **credit** side (often written as 'cr') on the right

You can remember this using the phrase '**Dr**ive on the left and **Cr**ash on the right'. If you do not normally drive on the left you could use the phrase '**D**ozy **L**ions **C**annot **R**un'.

A simple double-entry transaction makes entries in **two accounts** – a debit entry in one account and a credit entry in the other account.

In the example below a business has paid an insurance premium. The accounts record two aspects of the transaction: the insurance expense and the deduction from the bank account.

The debit entry goes to the Insurance Account and the credit entry to the Bank Account. If you are wondering why the Insurance Account entry is a debit and the Bank Account entry a credit, we will explain the rules over the next few pages.

This process is known as the **dual effect** of double-entry bookkeeping: every transaction makes a change to two accounts.

## BANK ACCOUNTS – DEBITS AND CREDITS

An organisation such as a business will need to use a bank account. Transactions passing through the account held at the bank – for example, money received, payments made – will need recording in the accounts of the business.

**Bank Account** in the accounting system of a business (see the previous page) is a separate record of the money paid into and out of the bank.

The problem for the bookkeeper is that the terms 'debit' and 'credit' are used differently by the bank and a business. In fact they are the opposite way round. This can prove confusing when dealing with a bank statement:

- banks see a **debit** as a **payment out** of a customer's account
- banks see a **credit** as a **payment into** a customer's account

Businesses, however should always think as follows:

- **money paid into the bank is always a debit** in the accounting system of the business
- **money paid out of the bank is always a credit** in the accounting system of the business

This 'left to right' flow of money in and out of the Bank Account as set up in the ledgers of a business can be seen as follows:

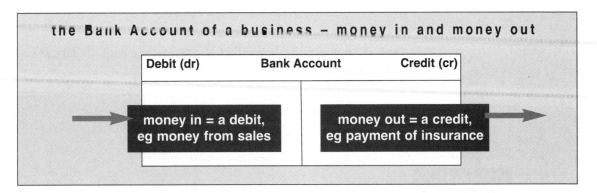

### debit or credit?

When a financial transaction is recorded as an entry in the Bank Account of a business as part of the double-entry system, it is easy to work out whether it is a credit or a debit by using the 'money in = debit and money out = credit' rule. It is then straightforward to work out whether the entry in the other account is a debit or credit. The rules are:

- **payment into the bank . . . money in = a debit . . .**

  so the other entry must be a credit

  **Example:**

  £1,000 received from sales paid into the bank. The entries are:

  **Debit: Bank Account £1,000**          **Credit: Sales Account £1,000**

- **payment out of the bank . . . money out = a credit . . .**

  so the other entry must be a debit

  **Example:**

  £500 insurance premium paid out of the bank account by electronic transfer. The entries are:

  **Debit: Insurance Account £500**          **Credit: Bank Account £500**

Note from these two entries quoted above:

- the debit and credit entries are for the same amount
- the debit entry is quoted first and the credit entry is quoted second

Not every double-entry transaction involves the Bank Account, but many do, and it is a very useful starting point for getting to grips with debits and credits. The two transactions we have just explained are illustrated below.

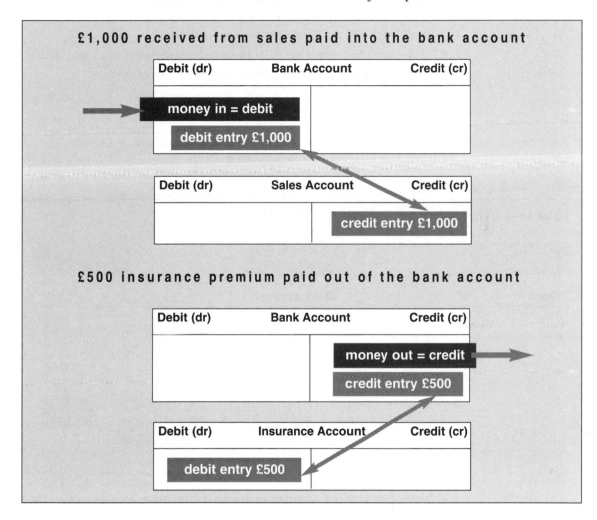

We will now go a step further and illustrate the full format of double-entry accounts and the information that needs to be recorded in the account.

## WRITING UP A DOUBLE-ENTRY ACCOUNT

In this chapter the double-entry accounts have so far been displayed as a simple 'T'. This 'T' format is a useful way of displaying the account, but a full double-entry account is more detailed and will have a number of columns. You will need to know how to enter the transaction details in these columns.

As you will see in the example below, there are two lines of detail on the account:

■ the account name and the 'debit' and 'credit' headings at the top; remember that the account name has capital letters at the beginning of each word (see the 'important technical note' on page 44)

■ on the next line down are the transaction column headings (date, details, £); these are the same on the debit and on the credit sides

Study the account format and read the notes about the transaction details that follow.

The transaction here shows how the Bank Account is written up for insurance of £500 paid out from the bank on 30 March 20-3 (remember: payment out of bank = credit entry).

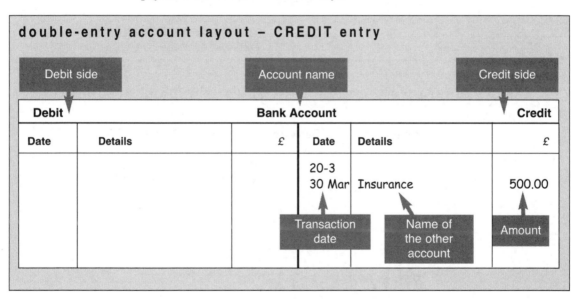

date – the year date is normally entered on the next line down of the date column and the actual date and transaction details on the following line; note that the month is often abbreviated, here it is '30 Mar' (30 March)

■ **details** – this is the other account that has been used in the double-entry transaction, here the other account is Insurance Account and the entry will be a debit because the Bank Account entry is a credit ('money out = a credit')

■ **£** – this is the **amount** column; obviously the '£' refers to the UK pound, you might also see a $ or a € sign if that is appropriate; occasionally you may also find that £ and pence (or dollars and cents) are separated into two columns

The entry to the Insurance Account for the above transaction is shown on the next page.

## double-entry account layout – DEBIT entry

| Debit | | | Insurance Account | Credit | | |
|---|---|---|---|---|---|---|
| Date | Details | £ | Date | Details | | £ |
| 20-3 30 Mar | Bank | 500.00 | | | | |

Transaction date

Name of other account

Amount

## RULES FOR DEBITS AND CREDITS

So far in this chapter we have seen that:

- money paid into the bank results in a **debit** entry to Bank Account in the accounting system of the business
- money paid out of the bank results in a **credit** entry to Bank Account in the accounting system of the business

**Bank Account**

money in = debit     money out = credit

We will now look in more detail at the 'other' accounts involved in the transactions, identifying which are normally debit or credit entries to the accounts.

### entries that are always debits

Some postings to the double-entry accounts are always debits because the other account entry is the credit side of Bank Account and the transaction involved is a payment out for something. They include:

- **purchases** – eg goods bought for selling or materials used for manufacturing items
- **expenses** – ie expenses incurred in running the business, eg rent, advertising, insurance
- **assets bought** – items bought for the business, for example computers and vehicles

### entries that are always credits

Some postings to the double-entry accounts are **always credits** because the other account entry is the **debit side of Bank Account** and the transaction involved is money coming into the business. They include:

- **sales** – money received for goods sold or services provided
- **capital** – money paid in by the owner
- **loans** – money borrowed from the bank or other sources

Examples of debits and credits are illustrated in the diagram below which uses the simple "T" account and just shows the account names in order to makes things clearer. Note that:

- money received entries: **debit** Bank Account and **credit** the account recording the amount
- money paid out entries: **credit** Bank Account and **debit** the account recording the expense
- the description entered in each account is the name of the other account in the transaction

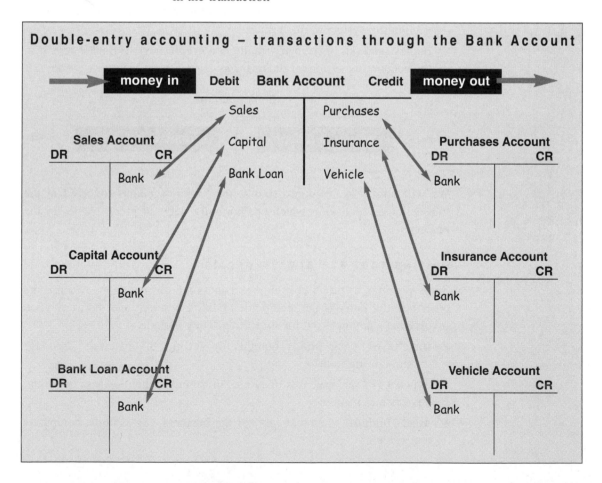

Set out below is a Case Study putting into practice all the double-entry theory covered so far in this chapter, using the full layout of the double-entry accounts.

# PRONTA PIZZA – DOUBLE-ENTRY IN PRACTICE

Riccardo has just started a new pizza home delivery business. He has put in capital of £30,000 himself and raised loans of £10,000 from the bank and £10,000 from his brother Carlo. He has paid all this money into a business account at Albion Bank so that he can then pay for all that he needs to start and run the business.

He asks his bookkeeper to enter all the transactions shown in the table below into his cash book (which contains the Bank Account). He then asks the bookkeeper to set up the ledgers and carry out all the necessary double-entry account postings.

| payments received and paid into the bank | | date of payment |
|---|---|---|
| Capital introduced by Riccardo | £30,000 | 15 January 20-3 |
| Bank loan | £10,000 | 16 January 20-3 |
| Loan from brother Carlo | £10,000 | 18 January 20-3 |
| **payments paid out of the bank** | | |
| Equipment for cooking | £10,000 | 22 January 20-3 |
| Van for pizza deliveries | £15,000 | 25 January 20-3 |
| Materials purchased | £3,000 | 28 January 20-3 |
| Insurance | £2,000 | 31 January 20-3 |

Riccardo's Bank Account in the books of Pronta Pizza after these entries have been made is shown below. The 'other' double-entry accounts follow on the next two pages.

| Debit | | | Bank Account | | | Credit |
|---|---|---|---|---|---|---|
| Date | Details | £ | Date | Details | | £ |
| 20-3 | | | 20-3 | | | |
| 15 Jan | Capital | 30,000 | 22 Jan | Equipment | | 10,000 |
| 16 Jan | Bank loan | 10,000 | 25 Jan | Van | | 15,000 |
| 18 Jan | Carlo Loan | 10,000 | 28 Jan | Purchases | | 3,000 |
| | | | 31 Jan | Insurance | | 2,000 |
| | money in = debit | | | money out = credit | | |

## The 'other entries' for payments into the Bank Account – ie credits

| Debit | | | Capital Account | | Credit |
|---|---|---|---|---|---|
| Date | Details | £ | Date | Details | £ |
| | | | 20-3<br>15 Jan | Bank | 30,000 |

| Debit | | | Bank Loan Account | | Credit |
|---|---|---|---|---|---|
| Date | Details | £ | Date | Details | £ |
| | | | 20-3<br>16 Jan | Bank | 10,000 |

| Debit | | | Carlo Loan Account | | Credit |
|---|---|---|---|---|---|
| Date | Details | £ | Date | Details | £ |
| | | | 20-3<br>18 Jan | Bank | 10,000 |

## The 'other entries' for payments out of the Bank Account – ie debits

| Debit | | | Equipment Account | | Credit |
|---|---|---|---|---|---|
| Date | Details | £ | Date | Details | £ |
| 20-3<br>22 Jan | Bank | 10,000 | | | |

| Debit | | | Van Account | | Credit |
|---|---|---|---|---|---|
| Date | Details | £ | Date | Details | £ |
| 20-3<br>25 Jan | Bank | 15,000 | | | |

| Debit | | | Purchases Account | | | Credit |
|---|---|---|---|---|---|---|
| Date | Details | £ | Date | Details | | £ |
| 20-3<br>28 Jan | Bank | 3,000 | | | | |

| Debit | | | Insurance Account | | | Credit |
|---|---|---|---|---|---|---|
| Date | Details | £ | Date | Details | | £ |
| 20-3<br>31 Jun | Bank | 2,000 | | | | |

## A NOTE ON CASH AND CREDIT TRANSACTIONS

The difference between paying for cash sales and sales made on credit terms is straightforward:

> **cash** payment = paying straightaway
>
> **credit** terms = paying at a later date

The double-entry bookkeeping described so far in this chapter relates just to **cash transactions**, ie money paid and banked straightaway.

There are also situations where goods are sold or purchased now and paid for later. These **credit transactions** will involve two double-entry transactions:

- the **first** on the date when the sale or purchase is made but no payment is made through the Bank Account – the payment due is entered in a customer or supplier account in the ledgers to record the debt

- the **second** at a later date when payment is made and passes through the Bank Account and the customer or supplier account in the ledgers

These account entries will be covered in detail in Chapter 4 'Accounting for sales, returns and discounts' and in Chapter 7 'Accounting for purchases, returns and discounts'. In conclusion, all you need to note at this stage is:

- a **cash** sale or purchase requires just **one** double-entry transaction

- a **credit** sale or purchase requires **two** double-entry transactions on different dates:

    – the first when the credit sale or credit purchase takes place

    – the second when payment is made for the transaction

## DEBITS AND CREDITS – CONCLUSION

### 'cash' transactions involving the bank account

Study the table below which gives examples of 'cash' double-entry transactions which involve payments in and out of the bank. The column 'money in/out' indicates whether the payments are into or out of the bank.

|  | money in/out | debit | credit |
|---|---|---|---|
| buying an asset | out | asset account | bank account |
| receiving a bank loan (liability) | in | bank account | loan account |
| owner contributing capital | in | bank account | capital account |
| business paying wages (expense) | out | wages account | bank account |
| business receiving rent (income) | in | bank account | rent received account |
| business purchasing materials | out | purchases account | bank account |

### balances of accounts

So far in this chapter we have concentrated on the rules for debit and credit **entries** made in the double-entry accounts. These rules also extend to the double-entry account **balances**. As we will see at the end of this chapter, double-entry accounts are regularly balanced, in other words the amount that is 'held' in each account is calculated, just as your bank calculates how much money is held in your bank account, and is your bank 'balance'.

### debits and credits – the rules

The table set out below shows which accounts normally have **debit** entries and balances and which accounts normally have **credit** entries and balances.

| DEBITS | CREDITS |
|---|---|
| **Assets** (items bought and owned by by the business) | **Liabilities** (amounts owed by the business, eg loans) |
| **Customer accounts** (money due to be paid to the business) | **Supplier accounts** (money due to be paid to suppliers by the business) |
| **Expenses** of the business | **Sales and other types of income** received by the business |
| **Purchases** | **Capital** |

# DOUBLE-ENTRY AND THE ACCOUNTING EQUATION

## the accounting equation

In Chapter 1 we outlined the final accounts of a business – the Statement of Profit or Loss and the Statement of Financial Position – which are the end result of the accounting process. The Statement of Profit or Loss shows how much profit (or loss) is made and the Statement of Financial Position shows how the assets of a business are financed. The Statement of Financial Position also reflects what is known as the accounting equation:

*assets (what a business owns and is owed)*

***minus*** *liabilities (what is owed by the business)*

***equals*** *capital (the investment of the owner and profits made)*

| ASSETS what a business owns and is owed | minus | LIABILITIES what a business owes to others | equals | CAPITAL the owner's investment and profits |
|---|---|---|---|---|

To help explain this equation we will now look at the concept of 'financial position' on a personal basis. If someone asked you what your financial position is, you might say:

'I have a total of £2,000 in the bank and in cash and I am owed £500 by a friend. I owe £100 to my brother.

My financial position is as follows: I have £2,000 plus the £500 owed to me but I have to pay £100 to my brother, so I have £2,400.'

If you then express this in accounting terms (ie assets, liabilities and capital) you can see how the accounting equation works. Study the table below and then the accounting equation on the next page.

|   | amount | personal situation | accounting term |
|---|---|---|---|
|   | £2,000 | what you own | an asset |
| + | £500 | what you are owed | an asset |
| – | £100 | what you owe | a liability |
| = | £2,400 | your financial position | capital |

| ASSETS<br>£2,000 owned +<br>£500 owed to you<br>= £2,500 | minus | LIABILITIES<br>what you owe<br>= £100 | equals | CAPITAL<br>your financial<br>position<br>= £2,400 |
|---|---|---|---|---|

## the accounting equation and double-entry

The accounting equation is a useful way of looking at the way double-entry accounting works. As we have seen, each business financial transaction is recorded in the accounting system and results in two entries being made in the ledgers – a debit and a credit

Where the accounting equation becomes relevant is that each equal debit and credit entry will always ensure that the equation will balance.

We will now illustrate this by seeing how example financial transactions . . .

■ are entered in the double-entry accounts as debits and credits

■ alter the accounting equation so that the equation still balances

**1**     **starting a business by paying money into the bank**

You pay £30,000 into the bank as capital to start your business. The account entries are:

    **Debit: Bank Account £30,000**      **Credit: Capital Account £30,000**

Here you are increasing assets by a debit entry of £30,000 and increasing capital by a credit entry £30,000.

The accounting equation (£30,000 – £0 = £30,000) balances:

| ASSETS<br>+ £30,000 in<br>Bank Account | minus | LIABILITIES<br>£0 | equals | CAPITAL<br>+ £30,000 in<br>Capital<br>Account |
|---|---|---|---|---|
| £30,000 | – | £0 | | £30,000 |

**2**     **a bank loan which is paid into the bank account**

You receive a bank loan (a liability) of £10,000 which goes straight into the business account at the bank (an asset). The account entries will be:

    **Debit: Bank Account £10,000**      **Credit: Bank Loan Account £10,000**

Here you are **increasing assets** by a debit entry of £10,000 and **increasing liabilities** by a credit entry of £10,000. The accounting equation is now £40,000 (Assets) *minus* £10,000 (Liabilities) = £30,000 (Capital). The equation still balances because the increase in assets (a 'plus') is compensated for by the increase in liabilities (a 'minus') on the same side of the equation.

| ASSETS £40,000 in Bank Account | minus | LIABILITIES £10,000 in Bank Loan Account | equals | CAPITAL £30,000 in Capital Account |
|---|---|---|---|---|
| £30,000 + £10,000 = £40,000 | – | £10,000 | = | £30,000 |

### 3 buying a computer (an asset)

You buy a computer (an asset) for £5,000 using money from the business bank account (also an asset). The account entries will be:

**Debit: Computer Account £5,000          Credit: Bank Account £5,000**

Here you are **increasing assets** by a debit entry of £5,000 to Computer Account and **decreasing assets** by a credit entry of £5,000 to Bank Account. The accounting equation is unchanged and still balances because you have just switched money from one asset (the bank account) to another asset (the computer). It now looks like this:

| ASSETS £40,000 Bank Account + Computer Account | minus | LIABILITIES £10,000 in Bank Loan Account | equals | CAPITAL + £30,000 in Capital Account |
|---|---|---|---|---|
| £40,000 – £5,000 + £5,000 = £40,000 | – | £10,000 | = | £30,000 |

### 4 paying off part of the bank loan (a liability)

You repay £1,000 of the bank loan (a liability) using money from the business bank account (an asset). The account entries will be:

**Debit: Bank Loan Account £1,000          Credit: Bank Account £1,000**

Here you are **decreasing a liability** with a debit entry of £1,000 to the Bank Loan Account and **decreasing an asset** by a credit entry of £1,000 to the Bank Account.

The equation still balances because the decrease in assets is compensated for by the decrease in liabilities on the same side of the equation. The equation now looks like this:

| ASSETS £39,000 Bank Account + Computer Account | minus | LIABILITIES £9,000 in Bank Loan Account | equals | CAPITAL £30,000 in Capital Account |
|---|---|---|---|---|
| £40,000 – £1,000 = £39,000 | – | £10,000 – £1,000 = £9,000 | | £30,000 |

### double-entry rules for changes in assets, liabilities and capital

You will see from the four examples on the last three pages that increases and decreases in assets, liabilities and capital follow a strict pattern which ensures that the accounting equation always balances:

- an **increase in an asset** is always a **debit entry**
- a **decrease in an asset** is always a **credit entry**
- an **increase in a liability** is always a **credit entry**
- a **decrease in a liability** is always a **debit entry**
- an **increase in capital** is always a **credit entry** (capital – which includes profit – increases as a business grows and makes a profit)

These rules are set out in the summaries shown below.

## asset accounts

**examples of assets:**

    property

    vehicles

    computers

    inventory

    money due from customers

    money in the bank and cash

**entries to the asset account:**

| DEBIT | CREDIT |
|---|---|
| asset increase | asset decrease |

## liability and capital accounts

**examples of liabilities:**

    bank loans

    bank overdrafts

    loans from other sources

    money due to suppliers

**entries to the liability account:**

| DEBIT | CREDIT* |
|---|---|
| liability decrease | liability increase |

*an increase in capital is also a credit entry

## BALANCING ACCOUNTS

It is normal accounting practice to balance double-entry accounts at regular intervals in order to calculate the 'total' of the account. This process provides the owner of the business with valuable information, such as:

- the amount owing to each supplier (trade payable)
- the amount owed by each customer (trade receivable)
- the amount of sales and purchases and expenses
- the amount of VAT due to, or from, HM Revenue & Customs

These accounts are set out in the purchases, sales and general ledgers:

We will now explain how to balance accounts from all three ledgers. The principles are the same for all three.

## BALANCING A PURCHASES LEDGER ACCOUNT

Set out below is an example of a supplier's account (Donato Wholesale) which has been written up in the purchases ledger of Pronta Pizza (a pizza take-away business) during the month, but has not yet been balanced. Purchases made from the supplier are entered on the credit (right-hand) side of the account and faulty goods returned to the supplier are entered on the debit (left-hand) side of the account.

| Dr | | | Donato Wholesale Account | | Cr |
|---|---|---|---|---|---|
| **20-3** | **Details** | **£** | **20-3** | **Details** | **£** |
| 14 Jul | Purchases returns | 25.00 | 13 Jul | Purchases | 320.00 |
| 22 Jul | Purchases returns | 75.00 | 20 Jul | Purchases | 80.00 |
| | | | 24 Jul | Purchases | 200.00 |

Now study the way in which this account is balanced:

| Dr | | | | Donato Wholesale Account | | Cr |
|---|---|---|---|---|---|---|
| **20-3** | **Details** | | **£** | **20-3** | **Details** | **£** |
| 14 Jul | Purchases returns | | 25.00 | 13 Jul | Purchases | 320.00 |
| 22 Jul | Purchases returns | | 75.00 | 20 Jul | Purchases | 80.00 |
| 31 Jul | Balance c/d | **1** | 500.00 | 24 Jul | Purchases | 200.00 |
| | | **2** | 600.00 | | | **2** 600.00 |
| | | | | 1 Aug | Balance b/d | **3** 500.00 |

The debit and the credit columns are separately added up and the totals noted down (eg on a piece of paper). The totals are £600 on the credit side (three purchases items) and £100 (two purchases returns items) on the debit side.

**Nothing** is entered in the account at this stage. You should then follow the following procedure:

**1**  The difference between the totals of the two sides (ie £600 – £100 = £500) is the **balance** of the account; this is entered in the account . . .

- in the money column on the side of the smaller total (here the debit side)
- on the next available line down on that side
- with the date of the balancing (here it is 31 July)
- with the words 'Balance c/d', which is an abbreviation of 'Balance carried down' in the details column

**2**  Both sides of the account are now added up and the totals (which should be identical, and the higher of the two totals calculated earlier) are entered in the money columns on both sides of the account on the same line; here the figure is £600.

A single line is drawn above the totals and a thicker single line (or a double line) underneath the totals.

**3**  As we have entered an extra £500 on the debit side in Step 1 we need to compensate for this by entering £500 on the credit side of the account, below the totals entered in Step 2. This ensures that the account shows the £500 account balance on the correct side. Note that the date here is not the month-end date (31 July) but the first day of the following month (1 August). The abbreviation 'Balance b/d' used here stands for 'Balance brought down'.

## BALANCING A SALES LEDGER ACCOUNT

On the previous page we balanced a purchases ledger account. This showed how much a supplier, Donato Wholesale, is owed by Pronta Pizza at the end of the month. The balance of this account (£500) is on the **credit** side of the account, representing an amount **owed by** a business, a liability.

It therefore follows that if you turn to the Sales Ledger which shows the opposite situation, ie amounts **owed to** Pronta Pizza by a customer, you will then find the balance of a customer account on the **debit** side of the ledger account, because an amount **owed to** a business is always a **debit**.

Study the example below of a balanced customer account – Albion Hotel – and read the notes that follow. You will see that sales are recorded on the left (debit side) and sales returns are on the right (credit side).

| Dr | | | | Albion Hotel Account | | | Cr |
|---|---|---|---|---|---|---|---|
| **20-3** | **Details** | | £ | **20-3** | **Details** | | £ |
| 6 Jul | Sales | | 200.00 | Jul 9 | Sales returns | | 20.00 |
| 8 Jul | Sales | | 50.00 | Jul 16 | Sales returns | | 30.00 |
| 22 Jul | Sales | | 150.00 | Jul 31 | Balance c/d | **1** | 350.00 |
| | | **2** | 400.00 | | | **2** | 400.00 |
| 1 Aug | Balance b/d | **3** | 350.00 | | | | |

**1**  The balance of **£350** is the difference between the total of the debit entries (**£400**, ie £200 + £50 + £150) and the total of the credit entries (**£50**, ie £20 + £30). It is entered on the credit side, ie the side with the lower total.

**2**  Both sides are added up to produce a total of £400. A single line is drawn above the totals and a thicker single line (or a double line) underneath them.

**3**  As we have entered an extra £350 on the credit side in Step 1 we need to compensate for this by entering £350 on the debit side of the account, below the totals entered in Step 2. This ensures that the account shows the £350 account balance on the correct side. Note that the date here is not the month-end date (31 July) but the first day of the following month (1 August). The abbreviation 'Balance b/d' used here stands for 'Balance brought down'.

## BALANCING GENERAL LEDGER ACCOUNTS

### general ledger balances

You can normally rely on the rule that a purchases ledger account has a balance brought down on the credit side and a sales ledger account has a balance brought down on the debit side.

The rule with General Ledger accounts is that some usually have debit balances and some usually have credit balances:

- **debit account balances** = where **money is spent by the business**, ie spent on purchases, money refunded because of returns, expenses paid
- **credit account balances** = where **money is received by the business,** ie from sales, refunds and other items of income

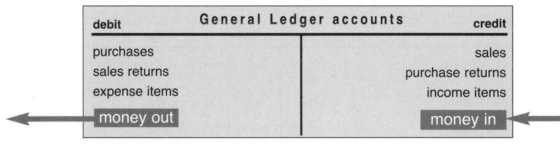

The balancing process is exactly the same as with the purchases ledger and sales ledger accounts, although it is common for the transaction entries to be on one side only.

The account below shows weekly payments for £250 recorded in the Rent Paid Account of a business. As you can see, these entries are all debits. If by any chance there was a refund of rent, it would be entered on the credit side and would reduce the final debit balance by that amount.

| Dr | | | | | | |
|---|---|---|---|---|---|---|
| **20-3** | **Details** | | **£** | **20-3** | **Details** | **£** |
| 1 Feb | Bank | | 250.00 | 28 Feb | Balance c/d | 1,000.00 |
| 8 Feb | Bank | | 250.00 | | | |
| 15 Feb | Bank | | 250.00 | | | |
| 22 Feb | Bank | | 250.00 | | | |
| | | | 1,000.00 | | | 1,000.00 |
| 1 Mar | Balance b/d | | 1,000.00 | | | |

Rent Paid Account — Cr

**Chapter Summary**

- Double-entry accounts are an integral part of the accounting system of a business and are written up from books of prime entry.

- Double-entry accounts form the core of the accounting system and record items such as income, expenses, amounts owed by customers, amounts owing to suppliers, assets, liabilities and capital.

- Double-entry accounting requires that two entries are made in the accounts for each transaction – a debit and a credit in separate accounts.

- Double-entry accounts are normally set up in the form of a 'T' with debit entries on the left and credit entries on the right.

- Double-entry accounts are organised in different ledgers (books): sales ledger (customer credit accounts), purchases ledger (supplier credit accounts) and general ledger (the rest of the accounts, including Bank Account).

- Money amounts received are recorded on the left-hand side of the Bank Account (debits) and payments made are recorded on the right-hand side (credits). This rule helps you work out your debits and credits: if the transaction is a bank payment made (credit) the other entry must be a debit; if the transaction is a bank receipt (debit) the other entry is a credit.

- The table below is a guide to which entries are debits and which entries are credits:

| Debits | Credits |
|---|---|
| Purchases | Sales |
| Expenses | Income |
| Assets | Liabilities |
| Money owed by credit customers | Money owed to credit suppliers |
| | Capital |

- The Accounting Equation relates directly to double-entry bookkeeping:

    *Assets – Liabilities = Capital*

    All double-entry transactions will change the figures in the Accounting Equation, but will ensure that it always balances. The changes in the assets, liabilities and capital in the Accounting Equation follow these rules:

| Debits | Credits |
|---|---|
| Increases in assets | Increases in liabilities |
| | Increases in capital |
| Decreases in liabilities | Decreases in assets |

- Ledger accounts are regularly balanced to provide information about the financial activity of a business. Purchases Ledger account balances are normally credit, Sales Ledger balances are normally debit and General Ledger balances can be either debit or credit.

| **Key Terms** | **books of prime entry** | the first place in the accounting records of a business where financial transactions are recorded, using details from business documents |
|---|---|---|
| | **day book** | a book of prime entry which lists the details of various financial transactions, eg Sales Day Book (a list of sales invoices) and Cash Book (compiled from bank transactions) |
| | **cash book** | the book of prime entry which lists payments in and out of an account at the bank; it can also act as the 'Bank Account' ledger account in the double-entry system |
| | **double-entry** | an accountng system which normally involves two entries for each transaction – a debit and a credit; this is known as the 'dual effect' of double-entry bookkeeping |
| | **ledger accounts** | double-entry accounts for financial transactions involving individuals (credit customers and credit suppliers), assets, purchases, expenses, income, liabilities and capital |
| | **the ledger** | means literally 'the book' which contains the individual ledger accounts; it is normally subdivided into different categories:<br>– sales ledger (customer accounts)<br>– purchases ledger (supplier accounts)<br>– general ledger (all other accounts) |
| | **statement of financial position** | one of the final accounts of a business; it shows the owner's capital in the business (investment and profits) calculated as total assets (items owned and amounts owed to the business) minus total liabilities (amounts owed by the business) |
| | **accounting equation** | total assets – total liabilities = capital<br><br>This calculates the total capital of the business (ie the owner's investment and profits made) in terms of assets and liabilities – in other words, the financial position of the business owner; it always balances if the double-entry bookkeeping is carried out correctly (see also the last bullet point in the Chapter Summary on the previous page) |
| | **account balancing** | the process of calculating the difference between the totals of the debit and credit columns of a ledger account in order to provide information to management about the financial activity of the business |

# Activities

**3.1** Which is the main source for the writing up of the double-entry accounts? Select **one** option.

| | |
|---|---|
| (a) | The ledgers | |
| (b) | Financial documents | |
| (c) | Books of prime entry | |
| (d) | The trial balance | |

**3.2** The ledger which contains the accounts of customers who buy on credit is the:

| | |
|---|---|
| (a) | General ledger | |
| (b) | Sales ledger | |
| (c) | Purchases ledger | |

Which **one** of these options is correct?

**3.3** The rule for entries in the Bank Account in the cash book is:

| | |
|---|---|
| (a) | Money in is a debit, money out is a credit | |
| (b) | Money out is a debit, money in is a credit | |
| (c) | The debit entries and credit entries always add up to the same amount | |

Which **one** of these options is correct?

**3.4** The table below lists transactions recorded in a Bank Account in the cash book of a business. Tick the appropriate column to indicate whether the entry will be a debit or a credit in the cash book.

| | **Debit** | **Credit** |
|---|---|---|
| Payment of wages | | |
| Cash received from sales | | |
| Payment of an invoice by a credit customer | | |
| Payment of an insurance premium | | |
| Loan received from a finance company | | |
| Loan repayment made | | |
| Bank charges | | |

**3.5** The table below lists transactions passed through the bank account of a business, and then recorded in the cash book of the business. Write the name of the two accounts involved in the double-entry in the correct column. The first example is completed to show what is required.  The name of the account which is not the Bank Account is shown in bold type.

|  | Debit | Credit |
|---|---|---|
| Payment of **wages** | Wages | Bank |
| Payment of **insurance** |  |  |
| Money received from **sales** |  |  |
| **Purchases** made |  |  |
| **Loan** received from the bank |  |  |
| **Loan** repayment |  |  |
| **Telephone** bill paid |  |  |
| **Rates** bill paid |  |  |
| **Rent received** from office let out |  |  |

**3.6** The Bank Account shown below has been written up by the bookkeeper, but someone still has to carry out the double-entry in the appropriate other accounts.

You have been asked to do this for her, using the blank accounts set out on the next page, completing the account name, date, details and amount for each entry. Enter the accounts in date order.

You may photocopy the blank accounts on the next page if you wish or download a copy from www.osbornebooks.co.uk.

| Debit | | | Bank Account | | | Credit |
|---|---|---|---|---|---|---|
| Date | Details | £ | Date | Details | | £ |
| 20-3 | | | 20-3 | | | |
| 1 May | Sales | 975.00 | 6 May | Telephone | | 265.00 |
| 11 May | Sales | 456.70 | 12 May | Insurance | | 678.00 |
| 14 May | Bank loan | 5,000.00 | 15 May | Purchases | | 2760.90 |

| Debit | | | ............................................Account | | Credit |
|---|---|---|---|---|---|
| Date | Detail | £ | Date | Details | £ |
| | | | | | |

| Debit | | | ............................................Account | | Credit |
|---|---|---|---|---|---|
| Date | Detail | £ | Date | Details | £ |
| | | | | | |

| Debit | | | ............................................Account | | Credit |
|---|---|---|---|---|---|
| Date | Detail | £ | Date | Details | £ |
| | | | | | |

| Debit | | | ............................................Account | | Credit |
|---|---|---|---|---|---|
| Date | Details | £ | Date | Detail | £ |
| | | | | | |

| Debit | | | ............................................Account | | Credit |
|---|---|---|---|---|---|
| Date | Details | £ | Date | Details | £ |
| | | | | | |

**3.7**    Some account **balances** are debit balances and some account balances are credit balances. Complete the table below by entering the following words in bold type in the correct column.

**Purchases   Capital   Expenses   Liabilities   Supplier Accounts** (ie money owed to suppliers)

**Customer Accounts** (ie money owed by customers)    **Assets, Sales, Income**

| Debit balances | Credit balances |
|---|---|
|  |  |

**3.8**    Some account **entries** are normally debits and some are normally credits.

Tick the appropriate column in the table below, indicating whether the type of account listed in the left-hand column normally requires a debit entry or a credit entry.

|  | Debit | Credit |
|---|---|---|
| Asset bought by the business |  |  |
| Liability (eg bank loan taken out) |  |  |
| Capital introduced by the owner |  |  |
| Sales made by the business |  |  |
| Purchases made by the business |  |  |
| Expenses of the business |  |  |
| Customer who owes the business money |  |  |
| Supplier who is owed money by the business |  |  |

**3.9**    Which is the correct formula for the accounting equation? Select **one** option.

| | |
|---|---|
| (a)    Liabilities – Assets = Capital | |
| (b)    Assets – Liabilities = Capital | |
| (c)    Assets + Liabilities = Capital | |
| (d)    Assets + Capital = Liabilities | |

**3.10**    Insert the correct figures in the blank boxes in the accounting equation table below.

| Assets | Liabilities | Capital |
|---|---|---|
| £ | £ | £ |
| 120,000 | 45,000 | |
| | 61,000 | 95,000 |
| 265,500 | 86,500 | |
| 88,000 | | 50,000 |
| | 37,500 | 90,000 |
| 345,700 | | 209,000 |

**3.11**    An increase or a decrease in an asset or liability or capital will result in either a debit or a credit to the asset, liability or capital accounts.

Indicate with a tick in the table what type of entry – debit or credit – will be brought about by the increase or decrease described in the column on the left.

| Transaction | Debit | Credit |
|---|---|---|
| Increase in capital account | | |
| Increase in liability account | | |
| Decrease in asset account | | |
| Decrease in liability account | | |
| Increase in asset account | | |

**3.12** Enter the transactions set out below in double-entry accounts.

All the transactions pass through the Bank Account, so you will have to write the entries in the Bank Account and also work out what the 'other' accounts will be. No credit sales or purchases are involved.

You can draw up your own accounts, photocopy the accounts on page 69, or download blank accounts from the Osborne Books website (www.osbornebooks.co.uk).

| Date 20-4 | Transaction |
|---|---|
| 3 Feb | Paid in capital of £10,000 |
| 4 Feb | Received bank loan of £25,000 |
| 6 Feb | Sales of £1,340 |
| 10 Feb | Purchases of £750 |
| 14 Feb | Paid rates of £450 |
| 15 Feb | Purchases of £2,760 |
| 18 Feb | Sales of £860 |
| 21 Feb | Paid for advertising costing £138 |
| 25 Feb | Sales of £2,640 |
| 28 Feb | Paid wages of £3,560 |

**3.13** You are working as a bookkeeper for Sphere Sports which acts a distributor for footballs and tennis balls. You have been handed the ledgers and asked to balance the four accounts shown on the next two pages. The date is 31 March 20-3.

(a)

| Dr | | | | Solo Supplies Account (Purchases Ledger) | | Cr |
|---|---|---|---|---|---|---|
| **20-3** | **Details** | **£** | **20-3** | **Details** | | **£** |
| | | | 23 Mar | Purchases | | 248.00 |
| | | | 25 Mar | Purchases | | 78.75 |
| | | | 30 Mar | Purchases | | 180.00 |

(b)

| Dr | Atletico Supplies Account (Purchases Ledger) | | | | | Cr |
|---|---|---|---|---|---|---|
| **20-3** | **Details** | **£** | **20-3** | **Details** | | **£** |
| 23 Mar | Purchases returns | 80.00 | 24 Mar | Purchases | | 120.00 |
| 26 Mar | Purchases returns | 70.00 | 27 Mar | Purchases | | 360.00 |
| | | | 30 Mar | Purchases | | 170.00 |

(c)

| Dr | Trajan Sports Account (Sales Ledger) | | | | | Cr |
|---|---|---|---|---|---|---|
| **20-3** | **Details** | **£** | **20-3** | **Details** | | **£** |
| 23 Mar | Sales | 450.00 | 24 Mar | Sales returns | | 80.00 |
| 26 Mar | Sales | 70.00 | 30 Mar | Sales returns | | 70.00 |
| 27 Mar | Sales | 180.00 | | | | |

(d)

| Dr | Office Expenses Account (General Ledger) | | | | | Cr |
|---|---|---|---|---|---|---|
| **20-3** | **Details** | **£** | **20-3** | **Details** | | **£** |
| 4 Mar | Bank | 75.20 | | | | |
| 6 Mar | Bank | 191.00 | | | | |
| 8 Mar | Bank | 34.65 | | | | |
| 15 Mar | Bank | 63.46 | | | | |

# 4 Accounting for sales, returns, and discounts

## this chapter covers...

*This chapter focuses on using the accounting system to record the details of sales, sales returns, and discounts allowed (using the credit note system – see pages 30-31)*

*Having looked in the previous chapter at the documents and procedures involved in selling on credit we will now take the financial documents of sales invoices, credit notes for sales returns and discounts allowed and record them in books of prime entry (day books) and in the bookkeeping system of general ledger and sales ledger.*

*We will be using three books of prime entry:*

- *sales day book*
- *sales returns day book*
- *discounts allowed day book*

*Information from these day books will then be transferred into the bookkeeping system using accounts in general ledger and sales ledger.*

*The chapter also covers the methods of coding, used to trace transactions through the accounting system*

***Notes:***

- *in this chapter we focus on the accounting for credit sales, sales returns, and discounts allowed. Cash sales will be seen when we study the cash book in Chapter 9*
- *we use the international financial reporting standards term 'trade receivable' to mean a person who owes money to a business; normally this is a customer. In your studies you may also come across the traditional term 'debtor' which means exactly the same thing*

## THE ACCOUNTING SYSTEM

We have seen earlier in Chapter 1 (page 4) that the accounting system comprises a number of stages of recording and presenting financial transactions:

■ financial documents

■ books of prime entry (eg day books)

■ double-entry bookkeeping

■ trial balance

In this chapter we look at how financial documents for credit sales, sales returns, and discounts allowed transactions are recorded in the books of prime entry, together with the entries to be made in the double-entry bookkeeping accounts. Later in the book we will see how a list of the balances of the double-entry accounts is used to form the trial balance (Chapter 11).

## ACCOUNTING FOR CREDIT SALES, SALES RETURNS, AND DISCOUNTS ALLOWED

In accounting, the term 'sales' means: **the sale of goods in which the business trades**.

This means that an office stationery shop will record as sales things such as photocopier paper, ring binders, etc – the income from the goods in which the business trades is described as **revenue income**. By contrast, if the shop sells off its old cash till when it is replaced with a new one, this is not recorded as sales but, instead, is accounted for as the sale of an asset – such income is described as **capital income**.

'Sales returns' are when goods previously sold on credit are returned to the business by its customers.

'Discounts allowed' (or **prompt payment discount**) is a discount offered by a supplier to customers in order to encourage customers to settle up straightaway or in a short time from the invoice date; it is discounts allowed in the accounting system of the seller.

The diagram on the next page shows the order in which the accounting records are prepared for credit sales, sales returns, and discounts allowed transactions. You will see that the steps are:

- start with a **financial document**, either a sales invoice (for sales) or a credit note issued (for sales returns and discounts allowed)

- enter it in the appropriate **book of prime entry** (the first accounting book in which the financial document is recorded and summarised), sales day book, sales returns day book, or discounts allowed day book

- transfer the information from the book of prime entry into the double-entry accounts in the **general ledger**

- transfer the information from the book of prime entry into the accounts of trade receivables – ie the customers – in the **sales ledger**

### accounting for credit sales and sales returns

**financial documents**

- sales invoices
- credit notes for sales returns and discounts allowed

**books of prime entry**

- sales day book
- sales returns day book
- discounts allowed day book

**general ledger**

*double-entry accounts*

- sales account
- sales returns account
- discounts allowed account
- sales ledger control account
- Value Added Tax account

**sales ledger**

*subsidiary accounts*

- accounts of trade receivables (customers)

We will now look in more detail at the mechanics of the books of prime entry and the double-entry bookkeeping system. We shall then apply the accounting system to the recording of credit sales, sales returns, and discounts allowed.

## BOOKS OF PRIME ENTRY

The books of prime entry include a number of **day books** which list money amounts and other details taken from financial documents.

The day books used for credit sales, sales returns and discounts allowed are:

■ sales day book

■ sales returns day book

■ discounts allowed day book

These are called books of prime entry because they are the first place in the accounting system where financial documents are recorded. Note that books of prime entry are not part of double-entry bookkeeping, but are used to give totals which are then entered into the accounts.

The reasons for using books of prime entry are:

■ the totals from the books of prime entry can be checked before they are entered into the ledger accounts

■ the use of books of prime entry for a large number of regular transactions, such as sales, means that there are fewer transactions to enter into the double-entry accounts

■ the work of the accounts department can be divided up – one person can enter transactions in the books of prime entry, while another can concentrate on the double-entry accounts

A sales day book is written up as shown below, with sample entries which will have been taken from individual sales invoices:

| Sales Day Book | | | | | | SDB21 |
|---|---|---|---|---|---|---|
| Date | Details | Invoice number | Account code | Total | VAT* | Net |
| 20-4 | | | | £ | £ | £ |
| 5 Jan | Doyle & Co Ltd | 901 | SL058 | 144 | 24 | 120 |
| 8 Jan | Sparkes & Sons Ltd | 902 | SL127 | 192 | 32 | 160 |
| 13 Jan | T Young | 903 | SL179 | 96 | 16 | 80 |
| 15 Jan | A-Z Supplies Ltd | 904 | SL003 | 240 | 40 | 200 |
| 21 Jan | Sparkes & Sons Ltd | 905 | SL127 | 144 | 24 | 120 |
| 31 Jan | Totals for month | | | 816 | 136 | 680 |
| | | | | GL1200 | GL2200 | GL4100 |

*VAT = 20 per cent

**Notes:**

- sales day book is prepared from financial documents – sales invoices issued to customers

- the code 'SDB21' at the top of the day book is used for cross-referencing to the bookkeeping system: here it indicates that this is page 21 of the sales day book (SDB)

- the **account code** column cross-references here to 'SL' – the Sales Ledger – followed by the account number of the trade receivable (customer)

- the **total** or **gross** column records the amount of each financial document, ie after VAT has been included

- the code 'GL' beneath the totals amounts refers to the account numbers in the General Ledger

- sales day book is totalled at appropriate intervals – daily, weekly, or monthly (as here) – and the total of the **net** column tells the business the amount of credit sales for the period

- the amounts from sales day book are recorded in the ledger accounts

## a note on day books and Value Added Tax

When a business is VAT-registered, VAT is charged on invoices and credit notes issued to customers. When writing up day books from VAT invoices and credit notes:

- enter the total amount of the invoice or credit note into the 'total' column

- enter the VAT amount in the VAT column

- enter the net amount of the invoice or credit note, before VAT is added, in the 'net' column

Later in this chapter we shall see how the VAT columns from the sales, sales returns, and discounts allowed day books are entered into the double-entry accounts.

## WRITING UP THE SALES DAY BOOK

The sales day book lists the credit sales made by a business. Following the issue of an invoice for each transaction, the sales day book is prepared from sales invoices, as seen on page 77. In order to write up the sales day book, we take the sales invoices that have been checked and authorised and enter the details:

- date of invoice

- name of customer

- sales invoice number

- cross reference to the customer's account number in the sales ledger, eg 'SL058'

- enter the total amount of the invoice into the total or gross column

- enter the VAT amount shown on the invoice

- enter the net amount of the invoice (often described as 'goods or services total'), before VAT is added

The next step in the accounting process is to make entries in the ledger accounts contained in the general ledger and in the sales ledger.

## GENERAL LEDGER AND SALES LEDGER

Within an accounting system there are often a number of ledger sections – for example general ledger, sales ledger and purchases ledger. In accounting for sales transactions we will make use of the following ledgers:

- **general ledger** (also often referred to as the main or nominal ledger) containing sales account, sales returns account, sales ledger control account, Value Added Tax account, together with other accounts kept by the business

- **sales ledger**, which is a subsidiary ledger to general ledger, and contains the accounts of the trade receivables

The diagram on the next page illustrates the way in which ledgers and accounts are used in connection with sales:

**GENERAL LEDGER**

- **sales account** – to record sales invoices issued

- **sales returns account** – to record credit notes issued for sales returns

- **discounts allowed account** – to record credit notes issued for prompt payment discount allowed

- **sales ledger control account** – to record the total amount of trade receivables

- **Value Added Tax account** – to record the VAT amounts of credit sales and sales returns

**SALES LEDGER**

ledger containing the separate subsidiary accounts for each **trade receivable**, ie customers who owe money to the business

Notes:

- **General ledger** also contains a number of other accounts, for example accounts for items such as purchases, expenses, receipts and payments, and also the assets and liabilities of the business.

- **Sales ledger** is a subsidiary ledger to general ledger because it gives a detailed breakdown of the amount of the sales ledger control account in the general ledger. It does this by showing the separate accounts for each trade receivable of the business: these accounts are called **subsidiary accounts** because they provide a record of individual amounts owed by each trade receivable. The total of these accounts should always equal the balance (total amount) of the sales ledger control account.

## ACCOUNTING SYSTEM FOR CREDIT SALES

The accounting system for credit sales fits together in the following way:

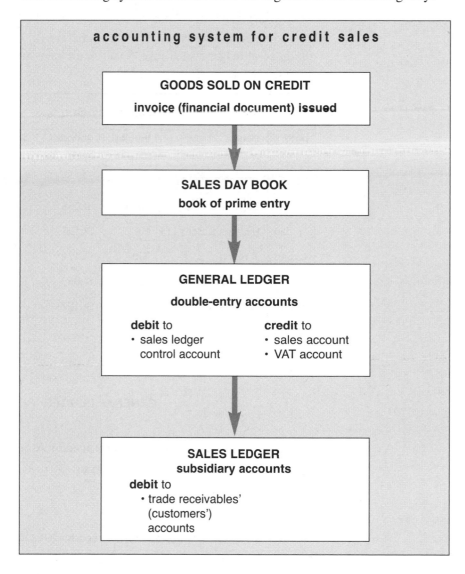

We will now look in more detail at the sales day book and the accounting system for credit sales.

In the examples which follow we will assume that the business is registered for Value Added Tax, and therefore VAT is charged on invoices issued to customers.

The VAT rate used in the examples is 20%.

## BOOKKEEPING FOR CREDIT SALES

After the sales day book has been written up and totalled, the information from it is transferred to the double-entry system in the general ledger.

The completed sales day book is shown below, followed by the accounts in the general ledger which record the credit sales transactions listed in the sales day book.

| | Sales Day Book | | | | | SDB21 |
|---|---|---|---|---|---|---|
| **Date** | **Details** | **Invoice number** | **Account code** | **Total** | **VAT** | **Net** |
| 20-4 | | | | £ | £ | £ |
| 5 Jan | Doyle & Co Ltd | 901 | SL058 | 144 | 24 | 120 |
| 8 Jan | Sparkes & Sons Ltd | 902 | SL127 | 192 | 32 | 160 |
| 13 Jan | T Young | 903 | SL179 | 96 | 16 | 80 |
| 15 Jan | A-Z Supplies Ltd | 904 | SL003 | 240 | 40 | 200 |
| 21 Jan | Sparkes & Sons Ltd | 905 | SL127 | 144 | 24 | 120 |
| 31 Jan | Totals for month | | | 816 | 136 | 680 |
| | | | | GL1200 | GL2200 | GL4100 |

### GENERAL LEDGER

| Dr | | Sales ledger control account (GL1200) | | Cr |
|---|---|---|---|---|
| 20-4 | £ | 20-4 | | £ |
| 31 Jan Sales Day Book SDB21 | 816 | | | |

| Dr | | Value added tax account (GL2200) | | Cr |
|---|---|---|---|---|
| 20-4 | £ | 20-4 | | £ |
| | | 31 Jan Sales Day Book SDB21 | | 136 |

| Dr | | Sales account (GL4100) | | Cr |
|---|---|---|---|---|
| 20-4 | £ | 20-4 | | £ |
| | | 31 Jan Sales Day Book SDB21 | | 680 |

Note that from the sales day book on the previous page:

■ the total of the total column, £816, has been debited to sales ledger control account (which records the asset of receivables)

■ the total of the VAT column, £136, has been credited to VAT account (which has given value)

■ the total of the net column, £680, has been credited to sales account (which has given value)

■ each entry in the general ledger is cross-referenced back to the page number of the sales day book; here the reference is 'SDB21'

The last step is to record the amount of sales made to each trade receivable. We do this by recording the sales invoices in sales ledger as follows:

**SALES LEDGER**

| Dr | | A-Z Supplies Ltd (SL003) | | Cr |
|---|---|---|---|---|
| 20-4 | £ | 20-4 | | £ |
| 15 Jan   Sales SDB21 | 240 | | | |

| Dr | | Doyle & Co Ltd (SL058) | | Cr |
|---|---|---|---|---|
| 20-4 | £ | 20-4 | | £ |
| 5 Jan   Sales SDB21 | 144 | | | |

| Dr | | Sparkes & Sons Ltd (SL127) | | Cr |
|---|---|---|---|---|
| 20-4 | £ | 20-4 | | £ |
| 8 Jan   Sales SDB21 | 192 | | | |
| 21 Jan   Sales SDB21 | 144 | | | |

| Dr | | T Young (SL179) | | Cr |
|---|---|---|---|---|
| 20-4 | £ | 20-4 | | £ |
| 13 Jan   Sales SDB21 | 96 | | | |

**Notes:**

■ the sales day book (see page 82) incorporates an account code column, used to cross-reference each transaction to the account of each trade receivable in the sales ledger (SL); this enables a particular transaction to be traced from financial document (invoice issued), through the book of prime entry (sales day book), to the trade receivable's account

■ each entry in the sales ledger is cross-referenced back to the page number of the sales day book; here the reference is 'SDB21'

### subsidiary accounts

The accounts in sales ledger are prepared following the principles of double-entry bookkeeping. However, they are **subsidiary accounts,** which means they are used to provide a note of how much each trade receivable owes to the business.

As such they are not part of double-entry but are represented in the general ledger by sales ledger control account. This means that, here, the £816 debit entry is split up in the sales ledger between the four trade receivables' subsidiary accounts. Note that subsidiary accounts are often referred to as **memorandum accounts**.

## ACCOUNTING SYSTEM FOR SALES RETURNS

**Sales returns** (or returns in) are when goods previously sold on credit are returned to the business by its customers. A credit note (see page 26) is the financial document issued by a business when it makes a refund to a customer who has bought goods on credit. A credit note reduces the amount owed by the trade receivable.

The accounting procedures for sales returns involve:

■ **financial documents** – credit notes issued to customers

■ **book of prime entry** – sales returns day book

■ **double-entry accounts** – general ledger (sales returns account, which records the total net amount of credit notes issued, Value Added Tax account, which records the VAT amount of sales returns, and sales ledger control account, which records the asset of trade receivables)

■ **sales ledger** – the subsidiary accounts for each individual trade receivable of the business

The accounting system for sales returns is shown in the diagram on the next page.

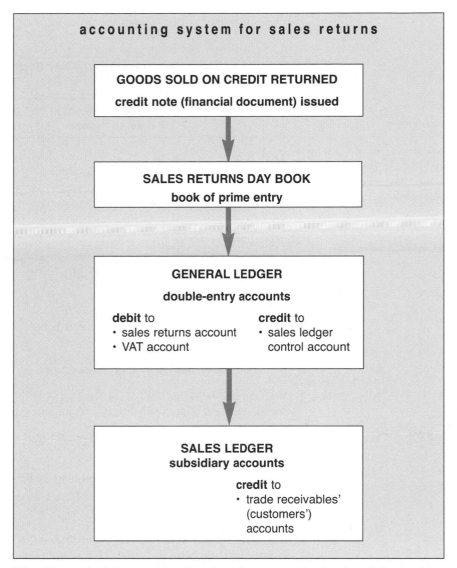

**accounting system for sales returns**

**GOODS SOLD ON CREDIT RETURNED**

**credit note (financial document) issued**

**SALES RETURNS DAY BOOK**

**book of prime entry**

**GENERAL LEDGER**

**double-entry accounts**

**debit** to
• sales returns account
• VAT account

**credit** to
• sales ledger
  control account

**SALES LEDGER**
**subsidiary accounts**

**credit** to
• trade receivables'
  (customers')
  accounts

We will now look in more detail at the sales returns day book and the double-entry accounts for sales returns. Note that the business is registered for Value Added Tax.

## SALES RETURNS DAY BOOK

The sales returns day book uses virtually the same layout as the sales day book seen on page 82 of this chapter. It operates in a similar way, storing up information about sales returns transactions until such time as a transfer is made into the double-entry accounts system. The financial documents for sales returns day book are credit notes issued to customers.

The sales returns day book is written up as follows, with sample entries:

| Sales Returns Day Book | | | | | | SRDB5 |
|---|---|---|---|---|---|---|
| **Date** | **Details** | **Credit note no** | **Account code** | **Total** | **VAT*** | **Net** |
| 20-4 | | | | £ | £ | £ |
| 15 Jan | T Young | 702 | SL179 | 48 | 8 | 40 |
| 27 Jan | A-Z Supplies Ltd | 703 | SL003 | 144 | 24 | 120 |
| 31 Jan | Totals for month | | | 192 | 32 | 160 |
| | | | | GL1200 | GL2200 | GL4110 |

* VAT = 20 per cent

**Notes:**

■ the sales returns day book is prepared from credit notes (or copies of credit notes) issued to customers

■ the day book is totalled at appropriate intervals – weekly or monthly

■ the VAT-inclusive amounts from the total column are credited to the trade receivables' individual subsidiary accounts in sales ledger

■ the total of the VAT column is transferred to the debit of the VAT account in general ledger

■ the total of the net column tells the business the amount of sales returns for the period. This amount is transferred to the debit of sales returns account in general ledger

■ the total or gross column records the amount of each credit note issued, ie after VAT has been included. This amount is transferred to the credit of sales ledger control account in general ledger

## BOOKKEEPING FOR SALES RETURNS

After the sales returns day book has been written up and totalled, the information from it is transferred into the double-entry system.

The accounts in the general ledger to record the transactions from the above sales returns day book (including any other transactions already recorded on these accounts) are as follows (see next page):

**GENERAL LEDGER**

| Dr | Sales ledger control account (GL1200) | | Cr |
|---|---|---|---|
| 20-4 | £ | 20-4 | £ |
| 31 Jan Sales Day Book SDB21 | 816 | 31 Jan Sales Returns Day Book SRDB5 | 192 |

| Dr | Value added tax account (GL2200) | | Cr |
|---|---|---|---|
| 20-4 | £ | 20-4 | £ |
| 31 Jan Sales Returns Day Book SRDB5 | 32 | 31 Jan Sales Day Book SDB21 | 136 |

| Dr | Sales returns account (GL4110) | | Cr |
|---|---|---|---|
| 20-4 | £ | 20-4 | £ |
| 31 Jan Sales Returns Day Book SRDB5 | 160 | | |

The last step is to record the amount of sales returns from each trade receivable. We do this by recording the sales returns in the subsidiary accounts for each trade receivable in the sales ledger as follows:

**SALES LEDGER**

| Dr | A-Z Supplies Ltd (SL003) | | Cr |
|---|---|---|---|
| 20-4 | £ | 20-4 | £ |
| 15 Jan Sales SDB21 | 240 | 27 Jan Sales Returns SRDB5 | 144 |

| Dr | T Young (SL179) | | Cr |
|---|---|---|---|
| 20-4 | £ | 20-4 | £ |
| 12 Jan Sales SDB21 | 96 | 15 Jan Sales Returns SRDB5 | 48 |

## ACCOUNTING SYSTEM FOR DISCOUNTS ALLOWED

As noted on page 30, HM Revenue & Customs permits two methods of accounting for Value Added Tax when a prompt payment discount (PPD) is offered by the supplier:

1 The supplier's invoice charges the normal rate of VAT (currently 20%) on the net value of the goods or services, eg net £100, VAT £20, total £120. If a 5% PPD is offered by the supplier and taken up by the customer, then the supplier issues a credit note for the amount of the PPD which, for the example above, will be net £5, VAT £1, total £6.

2 If the supplier does not wish to have a policy of issuing credit notes then the supplier's invoice must include:

 – the terms of the PPD

 – a statement that the customer can only recover as input tax (see Chapter 7) the VAT paid to the supplier which, for the example above, will be net £95, VAT £19, total £114

 HM Revenue & Customs recommends that the following statement is used on the invoice: '*A discount of X% of the full price applies if payment is made within Y days of the invoice date. No credit note will be issued. Following payment you must ensure you have only recovered the VAT actually paid.*'

**Important note:** in this section we see how the accounting for PPD in the supplier's books, ie discounts allowed, is carried out using the method where a credit note is issued by the supplier. Note that this method is used by AAT to assess PPD transactions. A sample credit note for PPD is shown on page 31.

When accounting for discounts allowed by using credit notes, a Discounts Allowed Day Book (DADB) is used to record credit notes issued by the supplier for PPD and sent to the customer. The accounting system is shown on the next page.

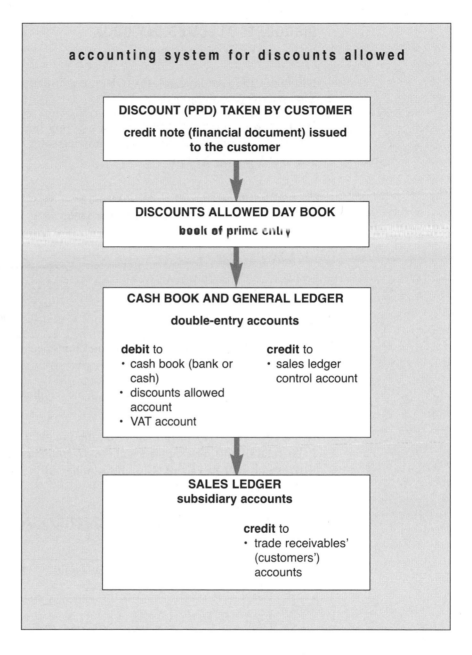

We will now look in detail at the discounts allowed day book and the double-entry accounts to record prompt payment discount in the books of the supplier. Note that the business is registered for Value Added Tax.

## DISCOUNTS ALLOWED DAY BOOK

Discounts allowed day book (DADB) uses virtually the same layout as the sales day book seen on page 82.

In order to see how the discounts allowed day book and the bookkeeping entries are recorded we will use the following sales invoice issued by James Ltd to a customer, XJ Ltd:

| | INVOICE | |
|---|---|---|
| | **Number 5480** | |
| From James Ltd | | 10 August 20-2 |
| To XJ Ltd | | |

| | £ |
|---|---|
| Goods Net | 1,000.00 |
| VAT | 200.00 |
| Total | 1,200.00 |

Terms: 5 per cent prompt payment discount for payment within ten days

**Note:** if the customer pays after ten days, the payment will be for £1,200 and no PPD entries will be required.

If the customer pays within ten days, the payment will be net £950, VAT £190, total £1,140. The supplier will issue a credit note for £60 (ie £50 + VAT £10) which will be recorded by the supplier in the discounts allowed day book as follows:

| Discounts Allowed Day Book | | | | | | DADB1 |
|---|---|---|---|---|---|---|
| **Date** | **Details** | **Credit note no** | **Account code** | **Total** | **VAT** | **Net** |
| 20-2 | | | | £ | £ | £ |
| 19 Aug | XJ Ltd | DA100 | SL243 | 60 | 10 | 50 |
| 31 Aug | Totals for month | | | 60 | 10 | 50 |
| | | | | GL1200 | GL2200 | GL3480 |

**Notes:**

■ the discounts allowed day book is prepared from credit notes (or copies of credit notes) for PPD issued to customers

■ the day book is totalled at appropriate intervals – weekly or monthly (only one transaction in the example on the previous page)

■ the VAT-inclusive amounts from the total column are credited to the trade receivables' individual subsidiary accounts in sales ledger

■ the total of the VAT column is transferred to the debit of the VAT account in the general ledger

■ the total of the net column tells the business the amount of discounts allowed for the period. This amount is transferred to the debit of discounts allowed account in the general ledger

■ the total column records the amount of each credit note issued, ie after VAT has been included. This amount is transferred to the credit of sales ledger control account in the general ledger

## BOOKKEEPING FOR DISCOUNTS ALLOWED

After the discounts allowed day book has been written up and totalled, the information from it is transferred into the double-entry system as follows:

| Cash Book* (debit side) | | | | | | | | CB015 |
|---|---|---|---|---|---|---|---|---|
| Date | Details | Account code | Cash | Bank | VAT | Cash sales | Trade receivables | Other income |
| 20-2 | | | £ | £ | £ | £ | £ | £ |
| 19 Aug | XJ Ltd | SL243 | | 1,140 | | | 1,140 | |

*the layout of the cash book is explained fully in Chapter 9.

## GENERAL LEDGER

| Dr | Discounts allowed account (GL3480) | | Cr |
|---|---|---|---|
| 20-2 | £ | 20-2 | £ |
| 19 Aug  Discounts Allowed | | | |
| Day Book DADB1 | 50 | | |

| Dr | Value added tax account (GL2200) | | Cr |
|---|---|---|---|
| 20-2 | £ | 20-2 | £ |
| 19 Aug  Discounts Allowed | | | |
| Day Book DADB1 | 10 | | |

| Dr | Sales ledger control (GL1200) | | Cr |
|---|---|---|---|
| 20-2 | £ | 20-2 | £ |
| | | 19 Aug  Bank  CB015 | 1,140 |
| | | 19 Aug  Discounts Allowed | |
| | | Day Book DADB1 | 60 |

The last step is to record the amount of discounts allowed in the subsidiary account of the trade receivable in the sales ledger as follows:

## SALES LEDGER

| Dr | XJ Ltd (SL 243) | | Cr |
|---|---|---|---|
| 20-2 | £ | 20-2 | £ |
| 10 Aug  Sales SDB | 1,200 | 19 Aug  Bank  CB015 | 1,140 |
| | | 19 Aug  Discounts Allowed | |
| | | Day Book DADB1 | 60 |

## THE USE OF ANALYSED SALES DAY BOOKS

As well as the layout of the day books we have seen so far in this chapter, a business can use analysed day books whenever it needs to analyse its sales and sales returns between:

- different types of goods sold, eg paint, wallpaper, brushes, or services supplied

- different departments, eg a store with departments for furniture, carpets and curtains, hardware

For example, a business with two different types of sales – sales type 1 and sales type 2 – will write up its sales day book as follows:

| Sales Day Book | | | | | | | | SDB48 |
|---|---|---|---|---|---|---|---|---|
| Date | Details | Invoice number | Account code | Total | VAT* | Net | Sales type 1 | Sales type 2 |
| 20-4 | | | | £ | £ | £ | £ | £ |
| 9 Aug | DIY Limited | 1478 | SL059 | 240 | 40 | 200 | 200 | – |
| 12 Aug | T Lane | 1479 | SL108 | 144 | 24 | 120 | 100 | 20 |
| 16 Aug | Comet Traders Limited | 1480 | SL038 | 336 | 56 | 280 | 100 | 180 |
| 23 Aug | Southern Ltd | 1481 | SL211 | 192 | 32 | 160 | 160 | – |
| 31 Aug | Totals for month | | | 912 | 152 | 760 | 560 | 200 |
| | | | | GL1200 | GL2200 | | GL4160 | GL4170 |

* VAT = 20 per cent

Analysed sales day books and sales returns day books can be adapted to suit the particular needs of a business. Thus, there is not a standard way in which to present the books of prime entry – the needs of the user of the information are all important. By using analysed day books, the owner of the business can see how much has been sold by types of goods and services, or by departments.

**Notes:**

- the account code column is to 'SL' (Sales Ledger) and the customer's account number

- the code 'GL' beneath the totals amounts refers to the account numbers in General Ledger

- the analysis columns – here sales type 1 and sales type 2 – show the amount of sales net of VAT (ie before VAT is added)

- the analysis columns analyse the net amount – by products sold or services supplied – from sales invoices

# METHODS OF CODING IN ACCOUNTING SYSTEMS

As a business grows, methods of coding need to be used to trace transactions through the accounting system, ie through financial documents, books of prime entry, double-entry bookkeeping and the trial balance. There are a number of different systems of coding in use:

- **alphabetical**, where letters are used, eg 'ABC'
- **numeric**, where numbers are used, eg '123'
- **alpha-numeric**, where both letters and numbers are used, eg 'ABC123'

Uses of coding in the stages of the accounting system are:

## financial documents

- each document, eg invoice, credit note, is numbered
- goods listed on invoices have reference number or letters, eg catalogue reference, which, if a computer accounting system is used, will enable the business to analyse sales by product

## books of prime entry

- each page of the day books is numbered
- the number of the document, eg invoice, credit note is recorded
- the code of the trade receivables or trade payables account is recorded, eg 'SL' for sales ledger, followed by the account number or short name (see below)

## ledger accounts

- the accounting system is divided into sections: general ledger, sales ledger, and purchases ledger
- general ledger accounts are numbered and are often arranged in a particular order, for example

| | |
|---|---|
| 0100 – 1399 | Assets |
| 2100 – 2399 | Liabilities |
| 3100 – 3399 | Capital |
| 4100 – 4399 | Sales |
| 5100 – 5399 | Purchases |
| 6100 – 6399 | Expenses |

- each account in the sales ledger is coded eg 'SL058' (or some accounting systems use an abbreviated name, or short name, eg the account of Peterhead Trading Company might be coded as 'PETER')
- alternatively, in sales ledger an alpha-numeric code – such as 'PET001' – is used; this comprises the first three letters of the customer's name followed by three numbers indicating the first (001) second (002) third (003) etc account use of the same first letter (here 'PET001' is coded as the first account to use 'P')

**Case Study**

# WYVERN TRADERS – CREDIT SALES AND RETURNS

This Case Study shows how credit sales and sales returns are recorded in the accounting system of a business. The Case Study makes use of:

*   **books of prime entry**
    *   sales day book
    *   sales returns day book
*   **general ledger accounts**
    *   sales account
    *   sales returns account
    *   Value Added Tax account
    *   sales ledger control account
*   **sales ledger accounts**
    *   trade receivables' subsidiary accounts

The Chapter Summary (pages 98-100) also includes diagrams which summarise the procedures for recording credit sales and sales returns transactions in the accounting system.

### situation

Wyvern Traders is a wholesaler of stationery and office equipment. The business is registered for VAT. The VAT rate is 20%. The following are the credit sales and sales returns transactions for April 20-4:

| 20-4 | |
|---|---|
| 2 Apr | Sold goods to P Woodhouse, £200 + VAT, invoice no 2416 |
| 9 Apr | P Woodhouse returns goods, £80 + VAT, we issue credit note no 12 |
| 14 Apr | Sold goods to Blackheath Limited, £80 + VAT, invoice no 2417 |
| 21 Apr | Blackheath Limited returns goods, £40 + VAT, we issue credit note no 13 |
| 26 Apr | Sold goods to P Woodhouse, £160 + VAT, invoice no 2418 |

The day books, general ledger and sales ledger accounts are illustrated on the next two pages: arrows indicate the transfers from the day books to the individual accounts. Note that some accounts have been repeated on both pages in order to show, on the same page, the accounts relating to a particular day book: in practice a business would keep all the transactions together in one account.

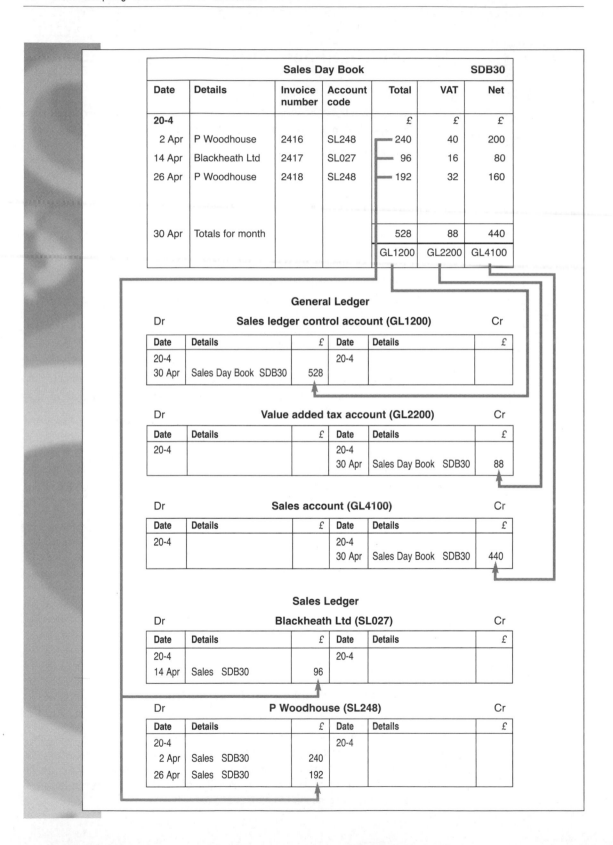

**Sales Day Book** SDB30

| Date | Details | Invoice number | Account code | Total | VAT | Net |
|---|---|---|---|---|---|---|
| **20-4** | | | | £ | £ | £ |
| 2 Apr | P Woodhouse | 2416 | SL248 | 240 | 40 | 200 |
| 14 Apr | Blackheath Ltd | 2417 | SL027 | 96 | 16 | 80 |
| 26 Apr | P Woodhouse | 2418 | SL248 | 192 | 32 | 160 |
| | | | | | | |
| 30 Apr | Totals for month | | | 528 | 88 | 440 |
| | | | | GL1200 | GL2200 | GL4100 |

**General Ledger**

Dr **Sales ledger control account (GL1200)** Cr

| Date | Details | £ | Date | Details | £ |
|---|---|---|---|---|---|
| 20-4 | | | 20-4 | | |
| 30 Apr | Sales Day Book  SDB30 | 528 | | | |

Dr **Value added tax account (GL2200)** Cr

| Date | Details | £ | Date | Details | £ |
|---|---|---|---|---|---|
| 20-4 | | | 20-4 | | |
| | | | 30 Apr | Sales Day Book  SDB30 | 88 |

Dr **Sales account (GL4100)** Cr

| Date | Details | £ | Date | Details | £ |
|---|---|---|---|---|---|
| 20-4 | | | 20-4 | | |
| | | | 30 Apr | Sales Day Book  SDB30 | 440 |

**Sales Ledger**

Dr **Blackheath Ltd (SL027)** Cr

| Date | Details | £ | Date | Details | £ |
|---|---|---|---|---|---|
| 20-4 | | | 20-4 | | |
| 14 Apr | Sales  SDB30 | 96 | | | |

Dr **P Woodhouse (SL248)** Cr

| Date | Details | £ | Date | Details | £ |
|---|---|---|---|---|---|
| 20-4 | | | 20-4 | | |
| 2 Apr | Sales  SDB30 | 240 | | | |
| 26 Apr | Sales  SDB30 | 192 | | | |

| Sales Returns Day Book | | | | | | SRDB4 |
|---|---|---|---|---|---|---|
| Date | Details | Credit note number | Reference | Total | VAT | Net |
| **20-4** | | | | £ | £ | £ |
| 9 Apr | P Woodhouse | 12 | SL248 | 96 | 16 | 80 |
| 21 Apr | Blackheath Ltd | 13 | SL027 | 48 | 8 | 40 |
| 30 Apr | Totals for month | | | 144 | 24 | 120 |
| | | | | GL1200 | GL2200 | GL4110 |

**General Ledger**

Dr  **Sales ledger control account (GL1200)**  Cr

| Date | Details | £ | Date | Details | £ |
|---|---|---|---|---|---|
| 20-4 | | | 20-4 | | |
| 30 Apr | Sales Day Book SDB30 | *528 | 30 Apr | Sales Returns Day Book SRDB4 | 144 |

Dr  **Value added tax account (GL2200)**  Cr

| Date | Details | £ | Date | Details | £ |
|---|---|---|---|---|---|
| 20-4 | | | 20-4 | | |
| 30 Apr | Sales Returns Day Book SRDB4 | 24 | 30 Apr | Sales Day Book SDB30 | *88 |

Dr  **Sales returns account (GL4110)**  Cr

| Date | Details | £ | Date | Details | £ |
|---|---|---|---|---|---|
| 20-4 | | | 20-4 | | |
| 30 Apr | Sales Returns Day Book SRDB4 | 120 | | | |

**Sales Ledger**

Dr  **Blackheath Ltd (SL027)**  Cr

| Date | Details | £ | Date | Details | £ |
|---|---|---|---|---|---|
| 20-4 | | | 20-4 | | |
| 14 Apr | Sales   SDB30 | *96 | 21 Apr | Sales Returns SRDB4 | 48 |

Dr  **P Woodhouse (SL248)**  Cr

| Date | Details | £ | Date | Details | £ |
|---|---|---|---|---|---|
| 20-4 | | | 20-4 | | |
| 2 Apr | Sales   SDB30 | *240 | 9 Apr | Sales Returns SRDB4 | 96 |
| 26 Apr | Sales   SDB30 | *192 | | | |

*transactions entered previously

**Chapter Summary**

The diagrams below and on the two next pages summarise the material we have studied so far in this chapter. They show the procedures for recording transactions in the accounting system for credit sales, sales returns and discounts allowed.

Further chapter summary points follow on page 101.

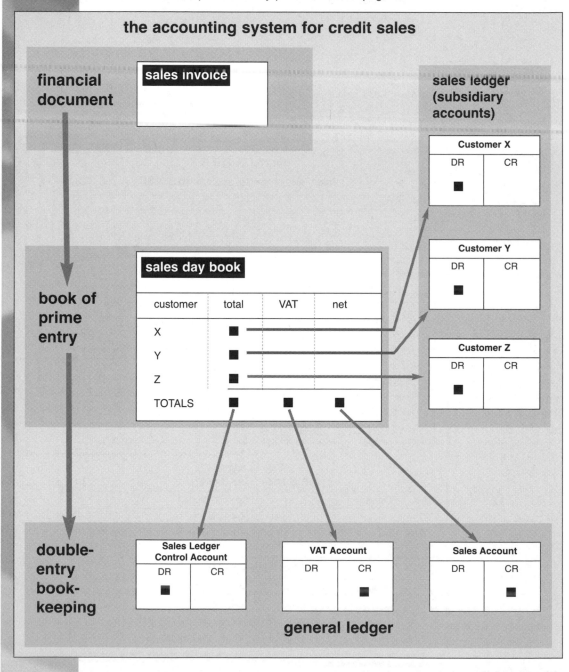

the accounting system for credit sales

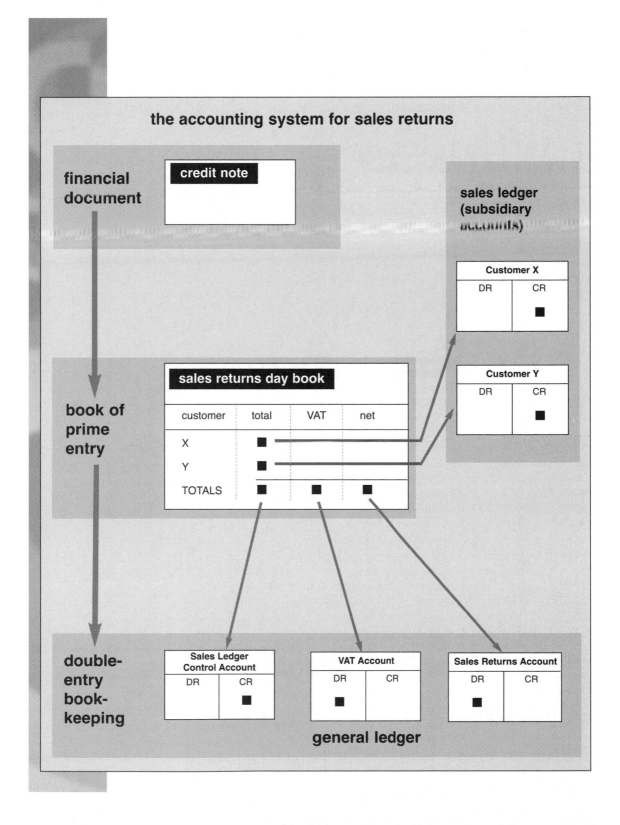

# the accounting system for discounts allowed

**financial document**

**credit note**

**sales ledger (subsidiary accounts)**

| Customer X | |
|---|---|
| DR | CR |
| | ■ |

**book of prime entry**

### discounts allowed day book

| customer | total | VAT | net |
|---|---|---|---|
| X | ■ | | |
| Y | ■ | | |
| TOTALS | ■ | ■ | ■ |

| Customer Y | |
|---|---|
| DR | CR |
| | ■ |

**double-entry book-keeping**

| Sales Ledger Control Account | |
|---|---|
| DR | CR |
| | ■ |

| VAT Account | |
|---|---|
| DR | CR |
| ■ | |

| Discounts Allowed Account | |
|---|---|
| DR | CR |
| ■ | |

**general ledger**

■ The accounting system comprises a number of specific stages of recording and presenting financial transactions:

- financial documents
- books of prime entry (eg day books)
- double-entry bookkeeping
- trial balance

■ The financial documents relating to credit sales are:

- sales invoices
- credit notes for sales returns and discounts allowed

■ Sales day book is the book of prime entry for credit sales. It is prepared from sales invoices sent to customers.

■ Sales returns day book is the book of prime entry for sales returns. It is prepared from credit notes issued to customers.

■ Discounts allowed day book is the book of prime entry for discounts allowed. It is prepared from credit notes for prompt payment discount issued to customers.

■ Analysed sales and sales returns day books are used when a business wishes to analyse its sales between different departments or different types of goods sold or services supplied.

■ Recording credit sales in the double-entry system uses:

- financial documents, sales invoices
- book of prime entry, sales day book
- double-entry accounts in the general ledger
- subsidiary accounts in the sales ledger

■ Recording sales returns in the double-entry system uses:

- financial documents, credit notes for sales returns issued to customers
- book of prime entry, sales returns day book
- double-entry accounts in the general ledger
- subsidiary accounts in the sales ledger

■ Recording discounts allowed in the double-entry system uses:

- financial documents, credit notes for prompt payment discount issued to customers
- book of prime entry, discounts allowed day book
- double-entry accounts in the general ledger
- subsidiary accounts in the sales ledger

| | | |
|---|---|---|
| **Key Terms** | **financial documents** | source documents for the accounting records |
| | **books of prime entry** | the first accounting books in which transactions are recorded |
| | **coding** | cross-referencing methods used to trace transactions through the accounting system |
| | **ledger** | section of an accounting system, eg general ledger, sales ledger, purchases ledger |
| | **sales** | the sale of goods in which the business trades |
| | **revenue income** | income from the goods in which the business trades |
| | **capital income** | income from items other than the goods in which the business trades, eg a shop selling its old cash till |
| | **sales returns** | goods previously sold on credit which are returned to the business by its customers |
| | **discounts allowed** | prompt payment discount offered by a supplier to customers in order to encourage customers to settle up straightaway or in a short time from the invoice date; it is discounts allowed in the accounting system of the seller |
| | **sales day book** | book of prime entry prepared from sales invoices |
| | **sales returns day book** | book of prime entry prepared from credit notes issued to customers |
| | **discounts allowed day book** | book of prime entry prepared from credit notes for prompt payment discount issued to customers |
| | **analysed sales day book** | day books which incorporate analysis columns, for example between <br> – different departments <br> – different types of goods sold, or services supplied |

| | |
|---|---|
| **general ledger** | ledger section which includes |
| | – sales account |
| | – sales returns account |
| | – discounts allowed account |
| | – sales ledger control account |
| | – Value Added Tax account |
| **sales ledger** | subsidiary ledger section which contains the subsidiary accounts of the trade receivables (customers) |
| **subsidiary account** | a subsidiary ledger (eg sales ledger) account which provides a record of individual amounts (eg owing by trade receivables to the business) |

# Activities

**4.1**  Which **one** of the following is a book of prime entry?

| (a) | Sales day book | |
|---|---|---|
| (b) | Sales account | |
| (c) | Sales ledger account of T Smith | |
| (d) | Value Added Tax account | |

**4.2**  Which **one** of the following is in the right order?

| (a) | Sales invoice; sales day book; sales account; sales ledger control account; customer's account | |
|---|---|---|
| (b) | Sales day book; sales ledger control account; customer's account; sales account; sales invoice | |
| (c) | Sales day book; sales invoice; customer's account; sales account; sales ledger control account | |
| (d) | Sales account; sales ledger control account; customer's account; sales invoice; sales daybook | |

**4.3** Which **one** of the following shows the correct general ledger entries to record discounts allowed?

| | |
|---|---|
| (a) | Debit sales ledger control; debit VAT; credit discounts allowed |
| (b) | Credit sales ledger control; credit discounts allowed; credit VAT |
| (c) | Debit discounts allowed; debit VAT; credit sales ledger control |
| (d) | Debit discounts allowed; credit sales ledger control; credit VAT |

**4.4** Explain in note format:

**(a)** The principles of recording a credit sales transaction in the accounting system.

**(b)** The principles of recording a sales returns transaction in the accounting system.

---

**For Activities 4.5 and 4.6:**

• work in pounds and pence, where appropriate

• the rate of Value Added Tax is to be calculated at 20% (when calculating VAT amounts, you should ignore fractions of a penny, ie round down to a whole penny)

• use a coding system incorporating the following:

| | | | |
|---|---|---|---|
| sales day book | – SDB50 | general ledger account numbers | |
| sales returns day book | – SRDB18 | sales ledger control account – GL1200 | |
| | | sales account | – GL4100 |
| sales ledger account numbers | | sales returns account | – GL4110 |
| A Cox | – SL032 | Value Added Tax account | – GL2200 |
| Dines Stores | – SL048 | | |
| E Grainger | – SL055 | | |
| M Kershaw | – SL090 | | |
| D Lloyd | – SL095 | | |
| Malvern Stores | – SL110 | | |
| Pershore Retailers | – SL145 | | |
| P Wilson | – SL172 | | |

**4.5**  Wyvern Wholesalers sells office stationery to other businesses in the area. During April 20-5 the following credit transactions took place:

20-5

  2 Apr    Sold goods to Malvern Stores £55 + VAT, invoice no 4578 issued

  5 Apr    Sold goods to Pershore Retailers £65 + VAT, invoice no 4579 issued

  7 Apr    Sold goods to E Grainger £28 + VAT, invoice no 4580 issued

  9 Apr    Sold goods to P Wilson £58 + VAT, invoice no 4581 issued

12 Apr    Sold goods to M Kershaw £76 + VAT, invoice no 4582 issued

14 Apr    Sold goods to D Lloyd £66 + VAT, invoice no 4583 issued

19 Apr    Sold goods to A Cox £33 + VAT, invoice no 4584 issued

22 Apr    Sold goods to Dines Stores £102 + VAT, invoice no 4585 issued

23 Apr    Sold goods to Malvern Stores £47 + VAT, invoice no 4586 issued

26 Apr    Sold goods to P Wilson £35 + VAT, invoice no 4587 issued

29 Apr    Sold goods to A Cox £82 + VAT, invoice no 4588 issued

**You are to:**

**(a)**    Enter the above transactions in Wyvern Wholesaler's sales day book for April 20-5, using the format shown below.

**(b)**    Record the accounting entries in Wyvern Wholesaler's general ledger and sales ledger. (You will need to retain the ledger accounts for use with Activity 4.6)

| Sales Day Book | | | | | | SDB50 |
|---|---|---|---|---|---|---|
| **Date** | **Details** | **Invoice number** | **Account code** | **Total** £ | **VAT** £ | **Net** £ |
| | | | | | | |
| | | | | | | |
| | | | | | | |
| | | | | | | |
| | | | | | | |
| | | | | | | |
| | | | | | | |
| | | | | | | |
| | | | | | | |
| | | | | | | |

**4.6**    The following details are the sales returns of Wyvern Wholesalers for April 20-5. They are to be:

**(a)**    Entered in the sales returns day book for April 20-5, using the format shown below.

**(b)**    Recorded in the general ledger and sales ledger (use the ledgers already prepared in the answer to Activity 4.5).

20-5

8 Apr       Pershore Retailers returns goods £20 + VAT, credit note no 572 issued

12 Apr      E Grainger returns goods £28 + VAT, credit note no 573 issued

16 Apr      D Lloyd returns goods £33 + VAT, credit note no 574 issued

28 Apr      Malvern Stores returns goods £20 + VAT, credit note no 575 issued

30 Apr      A Cox returns goods £40 + VAT, credit note no 576 issued

| | | | | | | |
|---|---|---|---|---|---|---|
| **Sales Returns Day Book** | | | | | | **SRDB18** |
| **Date** | **Details** | **Credit note number** | **Account code** | **Total £** | **VAT £** | **Net £** |
| | | | | | | |
| | | | | | | |
| | | | | | | |
| | | | | | | |
| | | | | | | |

**4.7** You are employed by Johnson Limited as an accounts assistant. The business has a manual accounting system. Double-entry takes place in the general ledger; individual accounts of trade receivables are kept as subsidiary accounts in the sales ledger. The VAT rate is 20%.

**Notes:**
- show your answer with a tick, words or figures, as appropriate
- coding is not required

**(a)** The following credit transactions all took place on 30 June 20-9 and have been entered into the sales day book as shown below. No entries have yet been made into the ledger system.

**Sales day book**

| Date 20-9 | Details | Invoice number | Total £ | VAT £ | Net £ |
|---|---|---|---|---|---|
| 30 June | Bowne Ltd | 610 | 960 | 160 | 800 |
| 30 June | Jamieson & Co | 611 | 4,944 | 824 | 4,120 |
| 30 June | Pottertons | 612 | 3,888 | 648 | 3,240 |
| 30 June | Wells plc | 613 | 2,928 | 488 | 2,440 |
| | Totals | | 12,720 | 2,120 | 10,600 |

What will be the entries in the general ledger?

**General ledger**

| Account name | Amount £ | Debit | Credit |
|---|---|---|---|
| | | | |
| | | | |
| | | | |

What will be the entries in the sales ledger?

**Sales ledger**

| Account name | Amount £ | Debit | Credit |
|---|---|---|---|
| | | | |
| | | | |
| | | | |
| | | | |

**(b)**    The following credit transactions all took place on 30 June 20-9 and have been entered into the sales returns day book as shown below. No entries have yet been made into the ledger system.

**Sales returns day book**

| Date 20-9 | Details | Credit note number | Total £ | VAT £ | Net £ |
|---|---|---|---|---|---|
| 30 June | Lloyd & Co | CN 47 | 576 | 96 | 480 |
| 30 June | Wyvern Stores | CN 48 | 1,248 | 208 | 1,040 |
| | Totals | | 1,824 | 304 | 1,520 |

What will be the entries in the general ledger?

**General ledger**

| Account name | Amount £ | Debit | Credit |
|---|---|---|---|
| | | | |
| | | | |
| | | | |

What will be the entries in the sales ledger?

**Sales ledger**

| Account name | Amount £ | Debit | Credit |
|---|---|---|---|
| | | | |
| | | | |

(c)   The following discounts allowed transactions all took place on 30 June 20-9 and have been entered into the discounts allowed day book as shown below. No entries have yet been made into the ledger system.

**Discounts allowed day book**

| Date 20-9 | Details | Credit note number | Total £ | VAT £ | Net £ |
|---|---|---|---|---|---|
| 30 June | Sanchos Ltd | DA 122 | 24 | 4 | 20 |
| 30 June | Belton Stores | DA 123 | 36 | 6 | 30 |
| | | Totals | 60 | 10 | 50 |

What will be the entries in the general ledger?

**General ledger**

| Account name | Amount £ | Debit | Credit |
|---|---|---|---|
| | | | |
| | | | |
| | | | |

What will be the entries in the sales ledger?

**Sales ledger**

| Account name | Amount £ | Debit | Credit |
|---|---|---|---|
| | | | |
| | | | |

**4.8**   The following is taken from the coding lists used at a business called Fashion Trading.

| Customer | Sales ledger account code |
|---|---|
| Allens Stores | ALL001 |
| Dart Enterprises | DAR001 |
| Dennis & Co | DEN002 |
| Eden Contracts | EDE001 |
| Ginger Trading | GIN001 |
| Jarvis & Co | JAR001 |
| New Wave Fashions | NEW001 |
| Number 1 Store | NUM002 |
| Riverside Trading | RIV001 |
| Toast Ltd | TOA001 |
| Ye Olde Stores | YEO001 |

You are to set up the sales ledger account codes for the new customers shown below.

| Customer | Sales ledger account code |
|---|---|
| Dymock Trading Co | |
| Hedgehog Fashions | |
| Jones & Co | |

**4.9**   Sales invoices have been prepared and partially entered in the sales day book, as shown below.

**(a)**   Complete the entries in the sales day book by inserting the appropriate figures for each invoice.

**(b)**   Total the last five columns of the sales day book.

**Sales day book**

| Date 20-9 | Details | Invoice number | Total £ | VAT £ | Net £ | Sales type 1 £ | Sales type 2 £ |
|---|---|---|---|---|---|---|---|
| 30 June | Yanez & Co | 1621 | | 240 | | | 1,200 |
| 30 June | Napier Stores | 1622 | 1,920 | | | 1,600 | |
| 30 June | Beale Ltd | 1623 | 768 | | 640 | | 640 |
| | **Totals** | | | | | | |

# 5 Process payments from customers

## this chapter covers...

*The earlier chapters of this book have explained how a business sets about selling its goods and services on credit, issuing invoices, credit notes and statements which help to ensure that the right money is received at the right time. The entry of these sales transactions into the book-keeping system has also been described.*

*This chapter will now explain the next stage in the process – the way in which a business will process a payment received from a customer who has bought goods on credit. It will continue the Case Study in Chapter 2 in which Cool Socks, a manufacturer of fashion socks, sold socks to Trends, a fashion store.*

*A payment sent by a business such as Trends in settlement of sales transactions will need to be checked and verified against documentation including:*

- *the remittance advice sent by the buyer and any payment sent by the buyer*
- *sales invoices and credit notes issued by the seller*
- *the statement of account sent by the seller*
- *the record of what is owing in the buyer's account in the sales ledger of the seller*

*In checking this documentation the seller will have to look out for any discrepancies which may be the result of an error made by the buyer, for example:*

- *an overpayment*
- *an underpayment*
- *the buyer taking prompt payment discount when the period for early payment has expired, or even when it is not offered*

## FINANCIAL DOCUMENTS – SOME REVISION

When a business makes a sale on credit terms it uses a number of financial documents which are sent to the buyer, these include:

- the **invoice**, which sets out the details of the sales transaction, including
  - the date
  - the sales price and any discount given and VAT (sales tax) added
  - the total due
  - the date when payment is required (which is often 30 days after the date of the invoice)

- the **credit note**, which is used if any refund is due and can be deducted from the amount owing to the seller – for example a deduction made for faulty goods

- the **customer statement**, which sets out all the invoices and credit notes issued and any payments received over a set period (often a month), all resulting in a final amount due to be paid

## FINANCIAL DOCUMENTS – REMITTANCE ADVICE

A further financial document which is important to the payment process is the **remittance advice**. This is an advice which can be posted, faxed or emailed, stating that a certain amount of money has been sent by a credit customer in settlement of an account. A remittance advice is used:

- to advise the sending of a payment **direct to the seller's bank account** by electronic bank transfer such as **BACS** or **Faster Payment** or . .

- **to accompany a cheque** – a practice which is becoming less common as more businesses and individuals make payments elecronically and online

These two types of remittance advice are illustrated on the next two pages. The remittance advices both relate to payments made to Cool Socks, the business introduced as a Case Study in Chapter 2. You will see that they both contain references. These are:

- the buyer's purchase order reference
- the seller's invoice number

Other details include the amount being sent and the means of payment, ie a cheque enclosed or a payment direct to the bank account of the seller through using BACS or Faster Payments electronic bank transfer systems.

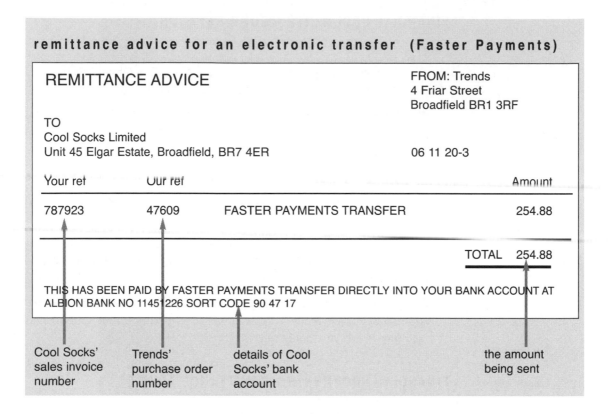

**remittance advice for an electronic transfer (Faster Payments)**

REMITTANCE ADVICE

FROM: Trends
4 Friar Street
Broadfield BR1 3RF

TO
Cool Socks Limited
Unit 45 Elgar Estate, Broadfield, BR7 4ER

06 11 20-3

| Your ref | Our ref | | Amount |
| --- | --- | --- | --- |
| 787923 | 47609 | FASTER PAYMENTS TRANSFER | 254.88 |
| | | TOTAL | 254.88 |

THIS HAS BEEN PAID BY FASTER PAYMENTS TRANSFER DIRECTLY INTO YOUR BANK ACCOUNT AT
ALBION BANK NO 11451226 SORT CODE 90 47 17

Cool Socks'
sales invoice
number

Trends'
purchase order
number

details of Cool
Socks' bank
account

the amount
being sent

## electronic payment remittance advice

■ this remittance advice relates to a Faster Payments bank transfer made by Trends in payment of their account with Cool Socks Limited. The advice has been emailed from Trends' accounts department

■ the details do not include the invoice amount or the credit note amount, but only the final payment made. An alternative to this is to list the various documents (invoices, credit notes) which make up the payment. This method is shown on the remittance advice on the next page

■ the bank account details on the advice set out Cool Socks' bank account number and sort code in full. Some remittance advices may not provide the account number in full for security reasons

■ cool Socks will need to check its bank statement in due course to see if the payment has been received

## checks to be made

Cool Socks needs to check a number of details on this advice against the sales documentation and the sales ledger account of the customer making payment. This is to make sure that there are no errors or discrepancies and that the right amount has been sent for the right transactions. This process is explained in full in the Case Study on pages 116-119.

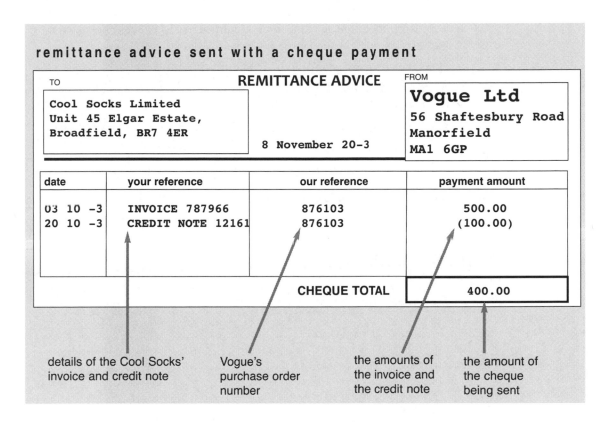

**remittance advice sent with a cheque**

- this remittance advice is for a payment from Vogue Limited – a cheque for £400 – sent together through the post to Cool Socks
- the advice shows the amounts of an invoice (£500) and a credit note (£100) taken account of when calculating the £400 payment
- these details will help Cool Socks in their checking process which will involve the sales documentation and the sales ledger account for Vogue Limited
- at the time of writing, cheques are becoming a less common means of settling customer accounts, but they are still popular with smaller and more traditional businesses
- if a customer's cheque is received in payment, it will need to be checked carefully to make sure it is correctly written out and has all the necessary details on it

**checking the cheque**

A **cheque** has to be in writing and signed by the person or organisation paying the money. All the details on a cheque have to be accurate and correct for it to be acceptable as a means of payment.

There are therefore a number of important basic checks that need to be carried out on a cheque before it can be paid in:

■ is the cheque signed? – it is invalid if it is not

■ is the name after the word 'pay' correct? – the bank will not accept it if it is not

■ is the cheque in date? – a cheque becomes invalid after six months

■ the amount in words and figures must be the same

The cheque below shows all these details:

is the cheque in date?

is the name of the person or business to whom the cheque is payable correct?

| Southern Bank PLC | | |
|---|---|---|
| Mereford Branch 16 Broad Street, Mereford MR1 7TR | date *8 November  20-3* | 97-76-54 |

Pay   *Cool Socks Limited* ——————————————  only

*Four hundred pounds only* ————

Account payee only

£ *400.00*

VOGUE  LTD

*Antonio Conti*
Director

123456     97 76 54     68384939

is the amount of the cheque in words and figures the same?

is the cheque signed?

If the business (Cool Socks) accepting payment by cheque does not 'check' these details before paying it in, Vogue Ltd's bank (Southern Bank) may refuse to pay it and will return it to Cool Socks' bank. But if everything is in order, the amount will be deducted from Vogue Ltd's bank account.

Now read the Case Study which follows. Note the internal checks that are made by Cool Socks when Trends settles its account.

## Case Study

# COOL SOCKS – PROCESSING THE PAYMENT

### situation

Cool Socks Limited, a manufacturer of fashion socks, supplies Trends, a fashion store in Broadfield. In this Case Study, Trends sends a payment and remittance advice, which is checked by Cool Socks for errors and discrepancies.

The financial documents issued so far by Cool Socks are an invoice for socks supplied (see next page), a credit note for £28.32 (not illustrated) for some faulty socks returned and a statement of account sent to Trends at the end of the month (see page 118).

The amount due is £283.20 (invoice amount) minus £28.32 (credit note amount)  = £254.88.

# INVOICE

## COOL SOCKS LIMITED

Unit 45 Elgar Estate, Broadfield, BR7 4ER
Tel 01908 765314  Fax 01908 765951  Email toni@cool.u-net.com
VAT Reg GB 0745 4672 76

invoice to

Trends
1 Friar Street
Broadfield
BR1 3RF

| | |
|---|---|
| invoice no | 787923 |
| account | 3993 |
| your reference | 47609 |
| date/tax point | 02 10 20-3 |

deliver to

as above

| product code | description | quantity | price | unit | total | discount % | net |
|---|---|---|---|---|---|---|---|
| 45B | Blue toebar socks | 100 | 2.36 | pair | 236.00 | 0.00 | 236.00 |

terms
Net monthly
Carriage paid
E & OE

| | |
|---|---|
| **goods total** | 236.00 |
| **VAT** | 47.20 |
| **TOTAL** | 283.20 |

STATEMENT OF ACCOUNT

## COOL SOCKS LIMITED

Unit 45 Elgar Estate, Broadfield, BR7 4ER
Tel 01908 765314  Fax 01908 765951  Email toni@cool.u-net.com
VAT REG GB 0745 4672 76

TO

| Trends |
| 4 Friar Street |
| Broadfield |
| BR1 3RF |

account    3993

date    31 10 20-3

| date | details | debit £ | credit £ | balance £ |
|------|---------|---------|----------|-----------|
| 01 10 20-3 | Balance b/f | 150.00 | | 150.00 |
| 02 10 20-3 | Faster payment 170961 | | 150.00 | 00.00 |
| 02 10 20-3 | Invoice 787923 | 283.20 | | 283.20 |
| 10 10 20-3 | Credit note 12157 | | 28.32 | 254.88 |

Pay Cool Socks Ltd at Albion Bank, Account 11451226, Sort code 904717

| TOTAL | 254.88 |
|-------|--------|

**Notes on the statement and the ledger account**

The statement of account illustrated above has four entries. The first two relate to full payment of last month's account (£150), and can be ignored. The last two relate to this Case Study and are highlighted by the grey boxes:

- the third entry is the invoice for £283.20 issued on 2 October to Trends
- the last entry is the credit note for £28.32 issued on 10 October to Trends

The amount owed by Trends to Cool Socks (the account balance) is £254.88.

These entries have also been entered by Cool Socks in the double-entry accounting system, in the **sales ledger account** for Trends shown below.

| Debit | Sales Ledger: Trends Account | | | | | Credit | |
|-------|------|------|---|------|------|------|---|
| 20-3 | Details | £ | p | 20-3 | Details | £ | p |
| 1 Oct | Balance b/d | 150 | 00 | 2 Oct | Bank | 150 | 00 |
| 2 Oct | Sales | 283 | 20 | 10 Oct | Sales returns | 28 | 32 |
| | | | | | | | |

**receipt of the remittance advice**

On 6 November Cool Socks received a remittance advice by email (see below) from Trends stating that £254.88 has been paid into the bank account of Cool Socks Limited by using a Faster Payments transfer.

What checks should Cool Socks make to make sure the payment of £254.88 is correct and valid?

---

# REMITTANCE ADVICE

FROM: Trends
4 Friar Street
Broadfield BR1 3RF

TO
Cool Socks Limited
Unit 45 Elgar Estate, Broadfield, BR7 4FR

06 11 20 3

| Your ref | Our ref | | Amount |
|---|---|---|---|
| 787923 | 47609 | FASTER PAYMENTS TRANSFER | 254.88 |

TOTAL   254.88

THIS HAS BEEN PAID BY FASTER PAYMENTS TRANSFER DIRECTLY INTO YOUR BANK ACCOUNT AT ALBION BANK NO 11451226 SORT CODE 90 47 17

---

**solution**

The following checks could be made by the accounts staff of Cool Socks.

**Question**  Are the remittance advice references correct?

**Answer**  Check the original documentation. The answer is 'Yes'.

- invoice number 787923 (see page 117) agrees with the 'Your ref 787923' of the remittance advice
- the Trends purchase order number 47609 (to be found in the Cool Socks filing system) is quoted on the remittance advice

**Question**  Is the remittance advice amount of £254.88 correct? Answer is 'Yes'.

**Answer**  Invoice value £283.20 minus credit note value £28.32 = £254.88

This can be verified from the statement issued by Cool Socks on 31 October and also from the sales ledger account of Trends in the books of Cool Socks. Both (see opposite page) show the two figures (£283.20 and £28.32) which result in the total owing figure of £254.88.

Note that Cool Socks would not need to carry out <u>all</u> these checks, but a minimum requirement is likely to be:
- a check of the documentation references (especially the invoice number), <u>and</u>
- a calculation of the amount paid – from figures obtained from the customer statement issued <u>or</u> from the sales ledger account

## DEALING WITH DISCREPANCIES

The Case Study on the previous four pages has explained the checks that should be made by the seller when a remittance advice is received from a credit customer. In this example, all was correct. Normally this is the case, but there are situations where references do not tie up or, more often, the amount is wrong. These **discrepancies** can occur when:

■ there is an **underpayment** – not enough money has been received

■ there is an **overpayment** – too much money has been received

■ the buyer has made a mistake in deducting **prompt payment discount**

We will deal with each of these in turn.

### underpayments

There are number of reasons why a credit customer may not send enough money when settling an account. These are described below, together with the action that should be taken in each case by the seller.

**reason**       the customer has made a genuine mistake with the figures

**solution**     the seller should contact the customer (by telephone or email), and politely explain the problem; the customer should be asked for an adjusting payment or advised that it will be adjusted for in the next statement

**reason**       the customer has not paid all the due invoices because there is a dispute over one of them

**solution**     the seller should contact the customer and attempt to resolve the problem; if necessary the matter may have to be referred to a line manager

### overpayments

There are a number of reasons why a credit customer may send too much money when settling an account. This is not a common experience! These reasons are described below and appropriate solutions are suggested.

**reason**       the customer has made a genuine mistake with the figures

**solution**     the seller should contact the customer and explain the situation; the ideal solution for the seller is to keep the extra money and wait for the next statement to make the necessary adjustment; it is possible that the customer may want the money (it may be a large amount), in which case an adjusting payment may need to be made

**reason**     the customer has ignored a credit note or has paid an invoice twice in error

**solution**   the seller should contact the customer and explain the situation; the ideal solution for the seller is to retain the extra money and wait for the next statement to make the necessary adjustment, unless the customer urgently needs the money, in which case an adjusting payment will need to be made promptly

## discrepancies with prompt payment discount

**Prompt payment discount** is an 'early payment discount' where a seller allows a customer to deduct a percentage discount from the invoice total if payment is made within a specified period of time, eg seven days.

Prompt payment discount is explained on pages 30-31. The main problem with prompt payment discount is that the amount is not stated on the invoice itself – just the discount percentage – and the calculation is left to the customer. This is where errors can occur as the customer can get it wrong.

When a business offers prompt payment discount, it is set out in the 'Terms' section at the bottom of the invoice, eg:

*prompt payment discount of 2.5% for payment within 7 days of the invoice date.*

If the goods total before VAT is £100, the discount available if the invoice is paid within 7 days of the invoice is (£100 x 2.5)/100 = £2.50.

The correct total amount actually payable is therefore:

| | |
|---|---|
| £100 minus £2.50 | = £97.50 |
| plus VAT @ 20% on £97.50 | = £19.50 |
| | = £117.00 |

As you can see from this, there is plenty of room for customer error:

■ the amount of discount calculated by the customer may be incorrect

■ the customer may take the discount after the seven days has elapsed

■ the customer may take a discount when it is not being offered at all

In each of these three cases, the seller will have to contact the customer and explain the nature of the discrepancy.

Examples of these errors are shown in the Case Study which follows on the next page.

# PROMPT PAYMENT DISCOUNT DISCREPANCIES

## situation

You work in the accounts department of Cool Socks Limited. The company offers to some (but not all) customers a prompt payment discount of 2.5% on invoices which are paid within 7 days of the invoice date.

When prompt payment discount is made available, the 'Terms' section at the bottom of the invoice always states.

*"Prompt payment discount of 2.5% for payment within 7 days of the invoice date."*

The date is 25 November and you have to check three invoices which have had prompt payment discount deducted by the customer. Your line manager asks you to report and correct any discrepancies you can find. The current VAT rate is 20%.

---

**Invoice 1 – payment amount received £1,140**

Dated 22 November. Terms indicate that 2.5% prompt payment discount is available for payment within 7 days. Goods total is £1,000, VAT £200 and discount of £60 (including VAT) deducted.

---

**Invoice 2 – payment amount received £468**

Dated 8 November. Terms indicate that 2.5% prompt payment discount is available for payment within 7 days. Goods total is £400, VAT £80 and discount of £12 (including VAT) is deducted.

---

**Invoice 3 – payment amount received £292.50**

Dated 22 November. There is no mention of a 2.5% prompt payment discount in the 'Terms' section of the invoice. Goods total is £250 and VAT is £50. Cash discount of £7.50 has been taken by the customer.

---

## solution

**Answers**

**Invoice 1**: the discount deducted is calculated at 5% (£60 including VAT) and should be at 2.5% (£30 including VAT). The payment should have been £975 + VAT £195 = £1,170.

**Invoice 2**: the 7 day period for deduction of prompt payment discount has expired and therefore no discount should be deducted. The payment should have been £400 + VAT of £80 = £480.

**Invoice 3**: there is no prompt payment discount available on this invoice but, despite this, the customer has taken 2.5% (£7.50). The payment should have been £300.

<table>
<tr><td>

**Chapter Summary**

</td><td>

■ When a customer who has bought goods or services on credit makes payment of the account, the customer will send a **remittance advice** to the seller.

■ Payment may be received by cheque or by electronic bank transfer (eg BACS or Faster Payments).

■ When a remittance advice is received it must be checked carefully against the sales documentation held by the seller and the customer's account in the seller's sales ledger. The amount received must be the correct amount. The documentation checked includes invoices, credit notes and the remittance advice itself.

■ If a cheque is received it must be checked to ensure that it is valid.

■ If payment is made by electronic bank transfer (eg BACS or Faster Payments), the bank statement must be checked in due course to confirm that the payment has been received.

■ Discrepancies relating to payments received can be caused by:

– **underpayments** – a disputed invoice may not have been included

– **overpayments** – a credit note may have been ignored or an invoice paid twice

– problems with **prompt payment discount** – discount rate incorrect, discount period expired, no discount available

■ In all cases the discrepancies must be communicated to the customer so that an appropriate adjustment can be made.

</td></tr>
</table>

| **Key Terms** | | |
|---|---|---|
| | **remittance advice** | an advice received from a customer telling the seller that a payment has been made |
| | **BACS** | Bankers Automated Clearing Services – an electronic bank transfer system which makes payment direct from one bank account to another – often used for bulk payments |
| | **Faster Payments** | an electronic bank transfer system which makes payment direct from one bank account to another – often used for individual payments |
| | **prompt payment discount** | a percentage reduction in the selling price given to the buyer if the buyer pays within a specified short space of time |

# Activities

**5.1** A business which receives a remittance advice from a customer is likely to check it against the following documents or accounts:

| | |
|---|---|
| (a) Delivery note, invoice, customer statement | |
| (b) Delivery note, invoice, sales ledger account | |
| (c) Invoice, purchase order, customer statement | |
| (d) Invoice, sales ledger account, customer statement | |

Which **one** of the above options is correct?

**5.2** On an invoice which offers prompt payment discount:

| | |
|---|---|
| (a) The prompt payment discount calculation is always shown | |
| (b) The prompt payment discount percentage is shown | |
| (c) The VAT (sales tax) is worked out on the goods total after the prompt payment discount is deducted | |
| (d) The final invoice total takes into account the prompt payment discount deducted | |

Which **one** of the above options is correct?

**5.3** On the next three pages are set out remittance advices and associated documents.

**You are to** check the remittance advices against the documents and:

1  Identify and describe any discrepancies that you find.

2  Suggest the action that could be taken by the supplier in each case.

**(a)**   **remittance advice sent to the seller**

REMITTANCE ADVICE

FROM: Trends
4 Friar Street
Broadfield BR1 3RF

TO
Cool Socks Limited
Unit 45 Elgar Estate, Broadfield, BR7 4ER

06 12 20-3

| Your ref | Our ref | | Amount |
|---|---|---|---|
| 788101 | 47645 | FASTER PAYMENT TRANSFER | 490.00 |

TOTAL   490.00

THIS HAS BEEN PAID BY FASTER PAYMENT TRANSFER DIRECTLY INTO YOUR BANK
ACCOUNT AT ALBION BANK NO 11451226 SORT CODE 90 47 17

**statement sent by the seller to the customer**

─────── **STATEMENT OF ACCOUNT** ───────

# COOL SOCKS LIMITED

Unit 45 Elgar Estate, Broadfield, BR7 4ER
Tel 01908 765314  Fax 01908 765951  Email toni@cool.u-net.com
VAT REG GB 0745 4672 76

TO

Trends
4 Friar Street
Broadfield
BR1 3RF

account   **3993**

date   **30 11 20-3**

| Date | Details | Debit £ | Credit £ | Balance £ |
|---|---|---|---|---|
| 01 11 20-3 | Balance b/f | 249.57 | | 249.57 |
| 02 11 20-3 | Payment received | | 249.57 | 00.00 |
| 02 10 20-3 | Invoice 788101 | 490.00 | | 490.00 |
| 10 10 20-3 | Credit note 12189 | | 49.00 | 441.00 |
| | TOTAL | | | 441.00 |

**(b)** **remittance advice sent to the seller**

| TO | REMITTANCE ADVICE | FROM |
|---|---|---|
| Cool Socks Limited<br>Unit 45 Elgar Estate,<br>Broadfield, BR7 4ER | 8 December 20-3 | **Vogue Ltd**<br>56 Shaftesbury Road<br>Manorfield<br>MA1 6GP |

| Date | Your reference | Our reference | Payment amount |
|---|---|---|---|
| 03 11 -3 | INVOICE 788106 | 876213 | 500.00 |
| 15 11 -3 | INVOICE 788256 | 876287 | 220.10 |
| 20 11 -3 | CREDIT NOTE 12218 | 876287 | (22.01) |
| | | **TOTAL** | 698.09 |

**sales ledger account of the customer in the accounting records of the seller**

| Debit | | | | Vogue Limited | | | Credit |
|---|---|---|---|---|---|---|---|
| 20-3 | Details | £ | p | 20-3 | Details | £ | p |
| 3 Nov | Sales | 500 | 00 | 10 Oct | Sales returns | 22 | 01 |
| 15 Nov | Sales | 220 | 10 | | | | |
| 17 Nov | Sales | 625 | 85 | | | | |

**(c)** remittance advice sent to the seller

---

# REMITTANCE ADVICE

FROM:
RTC Fashions
85 Fish Street
Stourminster ST1 8RT

*TO*
Chico Importers
34 Oldfield Street, London EC1 6TR

03 12 20-3

| Your ref | Our ref | | Amount |
|---|---|---|---|
| 10956 | 1078 | FASTER PAYMENTS TRANSFER<br>Invoice 10956 less 5% prompt payment discount | 638.40 |
| | | TOTAL | 638.40 |

THIS HAS BEEN PAID BY FASTER PAYMENT DIRECTLY INTO YOUR BANK ACCOUNT
AT HRBC BANK ACCOUNT NO xxxx6534 SORT CODE 40 47 17

---

invoice sent by the seller

---

# INVOICE

## CHICO IMPORTERS

34 Oldfield Street, London EC1 6TR
Tel 0208765322  Fax 0208765564  Email sales@chicoimporters.com
VAT Reg GB 0745 4672 76

invoice to

RTC Fashions
85 Fish Street
Stourminster
ST1 8RT

| | |
|---|---|
| invoice no | 10956 |
| account | 834 |
| your reference | 1078 |
| date/tax point | 5 11 20-3 |

| Product code | Description | Quantity | Price | Unit | Total | Discount % | Net |
|---|---|---|---|---|---|---|---|
| 5674R | T shirts (red) | 200 | 3.50 | each | 700.00 | 20.00 | 560.00 |

**terms**
Net monthly
Carriage paid

| | |
|---|---|
| **Goods total** | 560.00 |
| **VAT** | 112.00 |
| **TOTAL** | 672.00 |

# 6 Process documents from suppliers

## this chapter covers...

*In Chapter 2 we described the financial documents prepared by a **seller** of goods and services on credit. This chapter looks at the situation from the purchaser's point of view and describes the procedures and documents involved when goods and services are **bought** on credit.*

*The chapter covers the following areas:*

■ *the use of financial documents for the purchase of goods and services – quotation, purchase invoice, delivery note, goods received note, goods returns note, credit note*

■ *the checking of the supplier's documents received against the purchaser's documents*

■ *the calculation of document totals, including discounts and VAT*

■ *the coding and filing of documents*

■ *the checking and authorisation of documents*

■ *dealing with discrepancies*

*This chapter covers the treatment of documents until payment is made. The processes of calculating and making payment are covered in Chapter 8.*

## BUSINESS DOCUMENTS – THE PURCHASER'S POINT OF VIEW

When a business **sells** goods and services its main concern is that it provides what has been ordered and that it gets paid on time. When a business **orders** goods and services, on the other hand, it will want to ensure that:

■ the correct goods and services are provided – on time

■ they are charged at the right price

The traditional procedure is for the purchaser to accumulate on file – often stapled together – a series of documents which will be checked against each other as they are produced or come into the office, eg copy purchase order, delivery note, goods received note, invoice, credit note, statement, and so on. These will often be kept in a 'pending invoices' file until payment is made, when they will go into a 'paid invoices' file - as shown in the diagram below.

This chapter covers the treatment of documents until payment is made. Calculating and making payment is covered in Chapter 8.

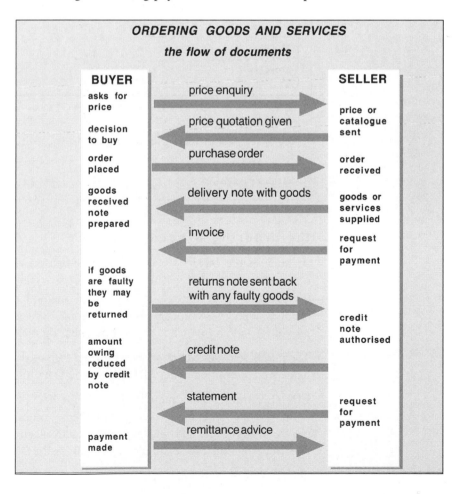

## ORDERING PROCEDURES

### getting prices and requesting quotations

When ordering goods or services a business will need to know the price that will be charged. The business is likely to 'shop around' to get the best price available. Enquiries can be made by telephone, looking at catalogues and price lists and very commonly by looking at and comparing website price lists and product descriptions.

Another way of getting a good price is by asking for a written (or emailed) quotation from the seller. The format of a quotation given by Cool Socks to its customer 'Trends' is shown below.

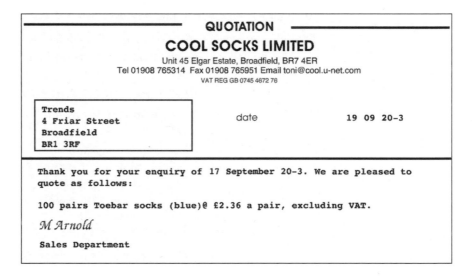

```
─────────────────  QUOTATION  ─────────────────
                COOL SOCKS LIMITED
             Unit 45 Elgar Estate, Broadfield, BR7 4ER
       Tel 01908 765314  Fax 01908 765951 Email toni@cool.u-net.com
                     VAT REG GB 0745 4672 78

 ┌──────────────────────────────┐
 │ Trends                       │      date           19 09 20-3
 │ 4 Friar Street               │
 │ Broadfield                   │
 │ BR1 3RF                      │
 └──────────────────────────────┘

  Thank you for your enquiry of 17 September 20-3. We are pleased to
  quote as follows:

  100 pairs Toebar socks (blue)@ £2.36 a pair, excluding VAT.

  M Arnold

  Sales Department
```

### the ordering process

As soon as the buyer is happy with the price provided on a quotation, or obtained from a price list, the ordering process can begin. The diagram on the previous page shows the traditional method of ordering goods and services: a purchase order is issued, the goods (or services) are delivered (or provided) and an invoice is sent for payment by the customer.

The purchase order can be in paper format (see next page) or it can be made by/carried out online using EDI (Electronic Data Interchange).

**EDI** (Electronic Data Interchange) is a method of connecting businesses online so that documents such as purchase orders and invoices can be electronically generated and payments made electronically when they are due. Supermarkets, for example, commonly use EDI.

### documents for purchases

This chapter concentrates on the traditional method of purchasing using paper documents. This is not to say that electronic methods are any different; they are very much based on the same principles. The documents we will now describe are:

- purchase order
- delivery note
- goods received note
- purchase invoice

When a business purchases goods, it is important that the accounting system includes checks and controls to ensure that:

- the correct goods have been received in an acceptable condition
- the correct terms (including discounts) and price have been applied
- the goods are paid for once only (paying for goods twice does occur!)

## PURCHASE ORDER

A purchaser, when the price of the product has been obtained or agreed, normally issues a **purchase order**. It is essential that this purchase order is **authorised** by the appropriate person who signs and dates the form. A business keeps a copy of every purchase order it issues and often files them in numerical order (each order has a numerical code).

The purchase order for Blue Toebar socks from the Cool Socks Case Study in Chapter 2 is shown below.

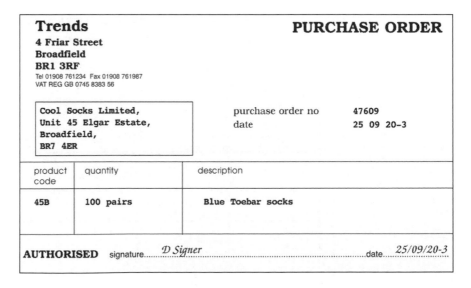

| **Trends** | | **PURCHASE ORDER** |
|---|---|---|
| 4 Friar Street | | |
| Broadfield | | |
| BR1 3RF | | |
| Tel 01908 761234  Fax 01908 761987 | | |
| VAT REG GB 0745 8383 56 | | |

| Cool Socks Limited,<br>Unit 45 Elgar Estate,<br>Broadfield,<br>BR7 4ER | purchase order no | 47609 |
|---|---|---|
| | date | 25 09 20-3 |

| product code | quantity | description |
|---|---|---|
| 45B | 100 pairs | Blue Toebar socks |

**AUTHORISED**   signature.......*D Signer*...................................................date.....*25/09/20-3*......

## DELIVERY NOTE

When the goods ordered are despatched by the seller they will normally be accompanied by a **delivery note**.

The delivery note shown below was described in the Cool Socks Case Study in Chapter 2. The main features are as follows:

■ the delivery note has a numerical reference (here it is 68873), useful for filing and later reference if there is a query

■ the method of delivery is stated – here the delivery is by parcel carrier

■ the delivery note quotes the purchase order number – 47609 – this enables the buyer to 'tie up' the delivery with the original purchase order

■ the delivery note quotes:

– Cool Socks' catalogue reference 45B as the product code

– the quantity supplied

– the description of the goods, but no price – it is not needed at this stage

These details will be checked against the goods themselves straightaway so that any discrepancies can be reported without delay.

If the business purchasing the goods uses a **goods received note** (see next page) this will also be completed at this stage

■ the delivery note will be signed and dated by the person receiving the goods as proof of delivery. This signature process can also be carried out electronically – the person receiving the goods will be asked to sign a portable electronic device

---

**DELIVERY NOTE**

## COOL SOCKS LIMITED

Unit 45 Elgar Estate, Broadfield, BR7 4ER
Tel 01908 765314  Fax 01908 765951  Email toni@cool.u-net.com
VAT REG GB 0745 4672 76

| Trends<br>4 Friar Street<br>Broadfield<br>BR1 3RF | delivery note no<br>delivery method<br>your order<br>date | 68873<br>Lynx Parcels<br>47609<br>02 10 20-3 |
|---|---|---|

| product<br>code | quantity | description |
|---|---|---|
| 45B | 100 pairs | Blue Toebar socks |

**Received**

signature.......... *V Williams* ..........name (capitals). *V WILLIAMS* ..........date. *05/10/20-3*

## GOODS RECEIVED NOTE

Some businesses use an internal document known as a **goods received note** (**GRN**). The buyer records on this document the receipt of the goods and the details set out on the delivery note or advice note sent by the supplier.

The GRN is essentially a checklist on which is recorded:

- the name of the supplier
- the quantity and details of the goods ordered
- the purchase order number
- the name of the carrier and any carrier reference number

As the goods are received and checked in, the GRN is ticked and signed to indicate that the right quantity and description of goods has been received.

The GRN forms part of the payment authorisation process: only when a completed and correct GRN is approved by the Accounts Department can the relevant invoice be paid.

Shown below is the goods received note relating to the Case Study in Chapter 2 in which the shop 'Trends' ordered some fashion socks from Cool Socks Limited.

Note that the receipt of the 100 pairs of socks has been recorded, and also the fact that 10 pairs are damaged.

| **Trends** | | **GOODS RECEIVED NOTE** | |
|---|---|---|---|
| **Supplier** | | | |
| Cool Socks Limited, Unit 45 Elgar Estate, Broadfield, BR7 4ER | | GRN no          1871 date          05 10 20-3 | |
| quantity | description | | order number |
| 100 pairs | Blue Toebar socks | | 47609 |
| **carrier**     Lynx Parcels | | consignment no   8479347 | |
| **received by**     *V Williams* | | checked by     *R Patel* | |
| **condition of goods** (please tick and comment) | good condition damaged  ✔ (10 pairs) shortages | | **copies to** Buyer          ✔ Accounts     ✔ Stockroom    ✔ |

## PURCHASE INVOICE

You will already be very familiar with the **purchase invoice** because it is the **sales invoice** sent out by the person selling the goods or services. In the Chapter 2 Case Study the sales invoice sent out by Cool Socks becomes the purchase invoice received by Trends, the buyer:

---

## ═══ INVOICE ═══

## COOL SOCKS LIMITED

Unit 45 Elgar Estate, Broadfield, BR7 4ER
Tel 01908 765314  Fax 01908 765051  Email toni@cool u-net.com
VAT Reg GB 0745 4672 76

invoice to

| |
|---|
| Trends |
| 4 Friar Street |
| Broadfield |
| BR1 3RF |

| | |
|---|---|
| invoice no | 787923 |
| account | 3993 |
| your reference | 47609 |
| date/tax point | 02 10 20-3 |

deliver to

as above

| product code | description | quantity | price | unit | total | discount % | net |
|---|---|---|---|---|---|---|---|
| 45B | Blue toebar socks | 100 | 2.36 | pair | 236.00 | 0.00 | 236.00 |

**terms**
Net monthly
Carriage paid
E & OE

| | |
|---|---|
| **goods total** | 236.00 |
| **VAT** | 47.20 |
| **TOTAL** | 283.20 |

## CHECKING INVOICE, DELIVERY NOTE AND PURCHASE ORDER

Now that you are familiar with all the purchase documents we will explain the checking process that will need to be made by the purchaser. This involves two separate procedures carried out in the Accounts Department:

- checking the documents – the invoice, delivery note (or GRN) and copy purchase order – with each other
- checking the calculations on the invoice

We will deal with these in separate stages, starting with the checking of the documents:

### check 1 – goods received and delivery note

When the goods are received they should be checked against the delivery note – the quantities should be counted and the condition of the goods checked and noted on a GRN if required. Any discrepancies or damage should be notified immediately to the supplier so that replacements can be sent or the buyer credited with the value of the missing or damaged goods (ie the amount due reduced by the issue of a credit note).

### check 2 – delivery note and purchase order

The delivery note should then be checked in the Accounts Department against a copy of the original purchase order (see illustration on page 131):

- supplier catalogue number – has the right type of goods been delivered?
- quantity – has the right number been delivered?
- specifications – are the goods delivered to the same specifications as those ordered?
- purchase order reference number – do the goods relate to the purchase order being examined?

If all is in order, the delivery note will be filed with the copy purchase order under the purchase order reference number, ready for checking against the invoice when it arrives.

### check 3 – invoice, delivery note and purchase order

When the invoice eventually arrives from the supplier, it should be checked against the delivery note and the purchase order (which should be filed together). The specific points to look at are:

- **invoice and delivery note**
  Are the details of the goods on the invoice and delivery note the same? The product code, description and quantity of the goods should agree.

■ **invoice and purchase order**

Has the correct price been charged? The unit price quoted by the supplier or obtained from the supplier's catalogue will be stated on the purchase order, and should agree with the unit price stated on the invoice. If there is a difference, it should be queried with the supplier.

**task**

Look at the invoice below and the purchase order and delivery note on the next page. They all relate to the same transaction. Can you spot any discrepancies? The answers are set out at the bottom of this page.

**———— INVOICE ————**

### Stourford Office Supplies
Unit 12, Avon Industrial Estate, Stourford, SF5 6TD
Tel 01807 765434  Fax 01807 765123  Email stourford@stourford.co.uk
VAT Reg GB 0745 4001 76

invoice to

| Martley Machine Rental Limited |
| 67 Broadgreen Road |
| Martley |
| MR6 7TR |

| invoice no | 652771 |
| account | MAR435 |
| your reference | 47780 |
| date/tax point | 31 03 20-3 |

deliver to

as above

| product code | description | quantity | price | unit | total | discount % | net |
|---|---|---|---|---|---|---|---|
| 3564748 | 80gsm white Supalaser | 15 | 3.50 | ream | 52.00 | 0.00 | 52.00 |

**terms**
Net monthly
Carriage paid
E & OE

| goods total | 52.00 |
| VAT | 10.04 |
| TOTAL | 41.96 |

The purchase order and delivery note agree, but the invoice has a number of discrepancies:
• the order reference differs (47700 and 47780)
• the product code differs (3564749 and 3564748)
• the product description differs (100 gsm and 80 gsm)
• the price differs (£4.00 and £3.50 per ream)

## Martley Machine Rental

67 Broadgreen Road
Martley
MR6 7TR
Tel 01908 546321  Fax 01908 546335
VAT REG GB 0745 8383 56

## PURCHASE ORDER

Stourford Office Supplies
Unit 12
Avon Industrial Estate
Stourford SF5 6TD

purchase order no     47700
date                  13 03 20-3

| product code | quantity | description | |
|---|---|---|---|
| 3564749 | 15 reams | 100gsm white Supalaser paper @ £4.00 per ream | |

**AUTHORISED**   signature............ *C Farmer* ..........................................date......... *13 March 20-3*

| catalogue number | quantity | order specifications | purchase order reference number |

---

## DELIVERY NOTE

### Stourford Office Supplies

Unit 12, Avon Industrial Estate, Stourford, SF5 6TD
Tel 01807 765434  Fax 01807 765123  Email stourford@stourford.co.uk
VAT Reg GB 0745 4001 76

Martley Machine Rental Ltd
67 Broadgreen Road
Martley
MR6 7TR

delivery note no      26754
delivery method       Puma Express
your order            47700
date                  27 03 20-3

| product code | quantity | description | |
|---|---|---|---|
| 3564749 | 15 reams | 100gsm white Supalaser paper | |

**Received**
signature............... *G Hughes* .......................print name (capitals)... *G.HUGHES* ...............date: *31.03.20-3*

*details to check on the purchase order and delivery note*

## CHECKING THE CALCULATIONS ON THE INVOICE

Another important step is for the Accounts Department to check the calculations on the invoice. If any one of these calculations is incorrect, the final total will be wrong, and the invoice will have to be queried with the supplier, so accurate checking is essential. The checks to be made are:

**quantity x unit price**   The quantity of the items multiplied by the unit price must be correct. The result – the total price or 'price extension' – is used for the calculation of any trade discount applicable.

**trade or bulk discount**   Any trade or bulk discount – allowances given to approved trade customers or for bulk purchases – must be deducted from the total price worked out. Trade or bulk discount is calculated as a percentage of the total price, eg a trade discount of 20% on a total price of £150 is calculated:

$$£150 \text{ x } \frac{20}{100} = £30$$

The net price charged (before VAT) is therefore

$$£150 - £30 = £120 = \text{net total}$$

**prompt payment discount**   Any prompt payment discount – an allowance sometimes given for quick payment – should be deducted from the full amount due on the invoice by the purchaser after the invoice has been received and within the time limit stipulated. No deductions will have been made from the invoice by the seller. The invoice will show the full amount due and any reduction will then be documented by a credit note issued by the seller.

**VAT**   Value Added Tax (a sales tax) in this book is calculated at 20%. To calculate VAT, the total after the deduction of any bulk or trade discount is treated as follows:

$$\text{Total x } \frac{20}{100} = \text{VAT amount}$$

Use a calculator and multiply the total by 0.2 to give the VAT, which is then added to the total.

Note that fractions of a penny are ignored. If the total price is £55.78, the VAT will be:

£55.78  x  0.2  =  £11.156

£11.156 then loses the last digit – the fraction of a penny – to become £11.15.

For the purpose of your studies you must assume that the calculations on all invoices must be checked. In practice, computerised invoicing performs the calculations automatically, and in principle should be correct.

Now check the calculations on the invoice on page 136. You should be able to detect a large number of errors:

■ quantity  x  unit price should be £52.50, not £52.00

■ the VAT is wrongly calculated £52.00  x  0.2  =  £10.40,  not £10.04 (it would be £10.50 on £52.50)

■ the VAT has been deducted instead of added: the total should be £52.50 + £10.50 = £63.00

## GOODS RETURNS – CHECKING CREDIT NOTES

A purchaser will sometimes have to return faulty or incorrect goods or claim for prompt payment discount which is due. In these cases the purchaser will request a credit note from the seller to reduce the amount owed. In no circumstances should the invoice itself be changed – this would create havoc with the accounting records!

If faulty or incorrect goods are sent back they are normally sent with a **goods returns note** which sets out the details of the goods. See the example below.

| **Trends** | | **GOODS RETURNS NOTE** | |
|---|---|---|---|
| 4 Friar Street | | | |
| Broadfield | | | |
| BR1 3RF | | | |
| Tel 01908 761234  Fax 01908 761987 | | | |
| VAT REG GB 0745 8383 56 | | | |
| Cool Socks Limited, Unit 45 Elgar Estate, Broadfield, BR7 4ER | | returns note no  **2384** | |
| | | date  **08 10 20-3** | |
| product code | quantity | description | |
| 45B | 10 pairs | Blue Toebar socks | |
| REASON FOR RETURN: *faulty goods, credit requested* | | | |
| **SIGNATURE**   *R SINGH* | | DATE   *10 10 20-3* | |

When the goods are received back by the seller and checked, a **credit note** will be issued to reduce the amount owing. The credit note from the Cool Socks Case Study is illustrated at the bottom of this page.

## CHECKING THE CREDIT NOTE

When the **credit note** is received by the purchaser it will have to be checked carefully to make sure that the quantity of goods, the price, discount and VAT are correctly calculated. It will be checked against the **goods received note** if one has been issued (not all businesses do), or the **goods returns note** or other internal records to make sure that the discrepancy has been properly resolved – ie has full credit been given for damaged/missing/incorrect goods? In the case of the example below it is £28.32 for damaged socks.

If the credit note is correct, the document will be entered into the accounting records and then filed with the copy purchase order, delivery note, invoice, GRN or copy returns note, awaiting the arrival of the statement.

---

### ———— CREDIT NOTE ————

# COOL SOCKS LIMITED

Unit 45 Elgar Estate, Broadfield, BR7 4ER
Tel 01908 765314  Fax 01908 765951  Email toni@cool.u-net.com
VAT REG GB 0745 4672 76

to

| | |
|---|---|
| **Trends**<br>**4 Friar Street**<br>**Broadfield**<br>**BR1 3RF** | |

| | |
|---|---|
| credit note no | 12157 |
| account | 3993 |
| your reference | 47609 |
| our invoice | 787923 |
| date/tax point | 13 10 20–3 |

| product code | description | quantity | price | unit | total | discount % | net |
|---|---|---|---|---|---|---|---|
| 45B | Blue Toebar socks | 10 | 2.36 | pair | 23.60 | 0.00 | 23.60 |

**Reason for credit**
**10 pairs of socks received damaged**
**(Your returns note no. R/N 2384)**

| | |
|---|---|
| GOODS TOTAL | 23.60 |
| VAT | 4.72 |
| TOTAL | 28.32 |

---

**Trends**                          **GOODS RECEIVED NOTE**

**Supplier**

| Cool Socks Limited,<br>Unit 45 Elgar Estate,<br>Broadfield,<br>BR7 4ER | GRN no<br>date | 1871<br>05 10 20-3 |
|---|---|---|

| quantity | description | order number |
|---|---|---|
| 100 pairs | Blue Toebar socks | 47609 |

**carrier**   Lynx Parcels          consignment no   8479347

**received by**   *V Williams*          checked by   *R Patel*

| **condition of goods**<br>(please tick and<br>comment) | good condition<br>damaged ✔ (10 pairs)<br>shortages | **copies to**<br>Buyer ✔<br>Accounts ✔<br>Stockroom ✔ |
|---|---|---|

---

### goods received note – details to check

If you compare the **credit note** on the opposite page and the **goods received note** shown above you will see that the following details can be checked:

- the identity of the goods returned – here it is blue Toebar socks
- the quantity returned – ten pairs of socks in this case
- the purchase order reference number – here it is 47609

As you will see, all is correct and so it is in order for Trends to make payment for this transaction on the due date.

The processes for preparing for payment of purchasers' accounts will be dealt with in full in Chapter 8.

## CODING PURCHASES INVOICES AND CREDIT NOTES

### the need to code

When a business processes invoices and credit notes received from suppliers it will usually code them so that they can be entered into the accounting system quickly and easily. This will be very useful, for example, if a computer accounting system is used. Normally two different sets of codes will be used:

- a **supplier account** code which will identify the supplier of the goods or services – this code may be alphabetic, alpha-numeric or numeric; if letters are involved they usually relate to the first few letters of the name of the supplier

- a **general ledger account** code which will identify the account which will be debited in the accounting system – it normally relates to the type of purchases made or expenses paid; it may be alpha-numeric or numeric

You will see from the purchases invoice and credit note on the opposite page that the codes may be entered in boxes imprinted onto the document by a rubber stamp used by the buyer (see the grey arrows indicating the boxes).

### using the account code lists

The business will keep account lists to hand so that accounts staff can quickly look up the appropriate code. As noted above, these will be for:

- supplier accounts

- general ledger accounts, eg categories of purchases

Extracts from these two types of account lists are shown below, Note that the account names are sorted in alphabetical order:

| Supplier | Supplier code |
|---|---|
| Jarma Supplies | JA006 |
| John Taylor Limited | JO004 |
| Labtech Limited | LA001 |
| Liverpool Kitware | LI001 |

| Item | General Ledger code |
|---|---|
| Shades | 5045 |
| T-shirts | 5060 |
| Trainers | 5100 |
| Trousers | 5210 |

The **invoice** on the next page has therefore been given the following codes:

Supplier code JA006 for Jarma Supplies

General ledger code 5060 for Max T-shirts purchased

The **credit note** on the next page has been given the following codes:

Supplier code LA001 for Labtech Limited

General ledger code 5045 for Monaco shades purchased

# INVOICE

**JARMA SUPPLIES**

Advent House, Otto Way
New Milton, SR1 6TF
Tel 01722 295875  Fax 01722 295611  Email sales@johnsonthreads.co.uk
VAT Reg GB 01982 6865 06

invoice to

RT Fashionware
34, Tennyson High Road
Maidstone
ME4 5EW

| | |
|---|---|
| invoice no | 7736 |
| account | 94122 |
| your reference | 675 |
| date/tax point | 01 04 20-7 |

| description | quantity | price | unit | total |
|---|---|---|---|---|
| Max T-shirts (red) | 200 | 3.00 | each | 600.00 |

**terms**
30 days
Carriage paid
E & OE

| Supplier a/c reference | general ledger a/c number |
|---|---|
| JA006 | 5060 |

| | |
|---|---|
| **goods total** | 600.00 |
| VAT | 120.00 |
| TOTAL | 720.00 |

---

**coding details entered on sellers' documents by the purchaser, RT Fashionware**

---

# CREDIT NOTE

**LABTECH LIMITED**

Unit 7 Roughway Estate,
Martley Road, Cookford, CO1 9GH
Tel 01843 265432  Fax 01843 265439  Email accounts@fabtech.co.uk
VAT Reg GB 0877 9333 06

to

RT Fashionware
34, Tennyson High Road
Maidstone
ME4 5EW

| | |
|---|---|
| credit note no | 976 |
| account | 94122 |
| your reference | 47601 |
| date/tax point | 12 04 20-7 |

| description | quantity | price | unit | total |
|---|---|---|---|---|
| Monaco shades 2744 | 5 | 30.00 | each | 150.00 |

**reason for credit:**
lenses damaged

| supplier a/c reference | general ledger a/c number |
|---|---|
| LA001 | 5045 |

| | |
|---|---|
| **goods total** | 150.00 |
| VAT | 30.00 |
| TOTAL | 180.00 |

## Chapter Summary

■ A business ordering goods or services will need to obtain the best price for goods and services, either from catalogues and online price lists or by requesting a quotation.

■ When a business places orders for goods or services on credit, it may do so using a paper-based system or by ordering online.

■ When a business orders goods on credit using a manual paper-based system it is likely to deal with a number of financial documents: quotation, purchase order, purchase invoice, delivery note, goods received note, goods returns note, credit note.

■ It is important that a series of checks are made to the financial documents to ensure that the goods or services provided are the correct ones, charged at the right price. The checks will involve calculations and references.

■ If a discrepancy is found, it should be noted and the seller contacted so that the account of the purchaser can be credited and the amount owing reduced accordingly.

■ Purchases invoices and credit notes should be coded with the supplier account and general ledger account codes for types of purchases so that they can easily be entered into the accounting system.

## Key Terms

| | |
|---|---|
| **quotation** | a document requested by the purchaser and issued by the seller stating the cost of goods or services to be provided |
| **EDI** | Electronic Data Interchange (EDI) is an electronic system of ordering goods and services using secure private computer links |
| **purchase order** | a document issued and authorised by the buyer of goods and services, sent to the seller, indicating the goods or services required |
| **purchases invoice** | a document issued by the seller of goods or services to the purchaser indicating the amount owing and the required payment date |
| **delivery note** | a document listing and accompanying the goods sent to the purchaser |
| **goods received note** | a document used by purchasers to record receipt of goods and documenting any returns made |
| **goods returns note** | a document sent to the supplier with faulty goods |
| **credit note** | a document issued by the seller of goods or services to the purchaser reducing the amount owing |

# Activities

**6.1**  What type of business document would normally be used when goods are bought on credit?

**(a)**  To order the goods from the seller?

**(b)**  To accompany goods sent from the seller?

**(c)**  To record the receipt and any discrepancies relating to the goods at the buyer's premises?

**(d)**  To advise the buyer in the first instance of the amount of money due?

**(e)**  To advise the buyer that a reduction is being made in the buyer's account for faulty goods supplied?

**6.2**  What is the difference between a delivery note and a goods received note?

**6.3**  Which documents would normally be checked by the buyer against the purchase order? Select **one** option.

| | |
|---|---|
| (a)  The delivery note and the invoice | |
| (b)  The invoice and the returns note | |
| (c)  The goods received note and the returns note | |
| (d)  The returns note and the delivery note | |

**6.4**  What document would a buyer expect to receive from a seller if goods which were delivered in a damaged condition have been returned to the seller?

**6.5**  Eduservice, an educational consultancy business, ordered some USB sticks from Compusupply Limited on purchase order 53659 for the IT Department at Martley College in Broadfield. The goods were delivered to the Eduservice office at 45 The Ridings, Broadfield on 3 February.

You work in the Eduservice office as an accounts assistant. Part of your job is to deal with all the documents.

You have today (5 February 20-3) received an invoice from Compusupply. You are not happy with the service you are receiving from this company and are thinking of going elsewhere for a supplier.

Shown on the next two pages are:

• an extract from an email from Compusupply agreeing the level of trade discount given

• the original purchase order

• the invoice you receive

**You are to** write an email to Compusupply setting out the errors that have been made. Address the email to sales@compusupply.co.uk and sign it off with your own name as an accounts assistant. The date is 5 February 20-3.

---

**Extract of email dated 1 November 20-02 from Compusupply to Eduservice**

"In view of our long-standing trading relationship we are happy to increase the trade discount we allow your company from 10% to 15% from 1 November 20-2.

Kind regards

James Watts
Credit Controller
Compusupply"

---

# EDUSERVICE                    *PURCHASE ORDER*

45 The Ridings
Broadfield
BR2 3TR
Tel 01908 333691

### TO

| Compusupply Limited<br>Unit 17 Elgar Estate,<br>Broadfield, BR7 4ER | purchase order no   53659<br><br>date          27 January 20-3 |
|---|---|

| Product code | Quantity | Description |
|---|---|---|
| 4573 | 1 | Opus 1GB USB sticks @ £95 per box of ten<br><br>Please deliver to:<br>J Wales, IT Department<br>Martley College, Fairacre, Broadfield  BR5 7YT |

Authorised    signature....*J Wales*................................date....*27.1.20-3*...............

# INVOICE

**COMPUSUPPLY LIMITED**
Unit 17 Elgar Estate, Broadfield, BR7 4ER
Tel 01908 765756  Fax 01908 765777  Email sales@compusupply.co.uk
VAT Reg GB 0745 4689 13

invoice to

Eduservice
45 The Ridings
Broadfield
BR2 3TR

| | |
|---|---|
| invoice no | 20424 |
| account | 242 |
| your reference | 53659 |
| date/tax point | 30.01.20-3 |

deliver to

as above

| Product code | Description | Quantity | Price | Unit | Total | Discount % | net |
|---|---|---|---|---|---|---|---|
| 4574 | Opus 2GB USB sticks | 1 | 125.00 | (box of 10) | 125.00 | 10 | 112.50 |

| | |
|---|---|
| **Goods total** | 112.50 |
| **VAT** | 22.50 |
| **TOTAL** | 135.00 |

**terms**
Net monthly
Carriage paid
E & OE

**6.6**    **(a)**    John Smith & Co, a stationery shop, ordered 20 boxes of gel pens from Helicon Stationery Supplies on purchase order 17643 (see below).

The goods were delivered to John Smith & Co on 4 December 20-4, but the order was short by 2 boxes and only 18 boxes were delivered. This was noted in a goods received note (see the next page). The problem was advised to Helicon Supplies by email on 4 December and a credit note requested. The credit note was issued on 10 December and sent to John Smith & Co. (see the next page).

**You are to** check the three documents and write the text of an email from John Smith & Co to Helicon pointing out any discrepancies you find. Use your own name. The date is 12 December.

**(b)**    John Smith & Co code all purchase invoices and credit notes with a supplier code and a general ledger code. Extracts from the two coding lists are shown below.

**You are to** state the supplier and general ledger codes which are to be used on the credit note on the next page.

| Supplier | Supplier code |
|---|---|
| French & Co | FR002 |
| Gemax Supplies | GE004 |
| Helicon Stationery | HE001 |
| JSTAT Ltd | JS001 |

| Item | General Ledger code |
|---|---|
| Paper | 5005 |
| Pens | 5010 |
| Pension costs | 5201 |
| Power costs | 7210 |

---

## John Smith & Co                              PURCHASE ORDER

7 Buttermere Road
Broadfield  BR6 3TR
Tel 01908 761234  Fax 01908 761987
email info@johnsmith&co.co.uk
VAT REG GB 0745 8383 56

| Helicon Stationery Supplies 91 High Street, Broadfield, BR7 4ER | purchase order no    **17643** date    **25 11 20-4** |
|---|---|

| Product code | Quantity | Description |
|---|---|---|
| **919BK** | **20 boxes of 10** | **Gel Pens (Black)** |

**AUTHORISED**  signature......*D.Smith*................................................date...*25/11/20-4*...

# John Smith & Co          GOODS RECEIVED NOTE

GRN no.      302

supplier     Helicon Stationery Supplies

date         4 December 20-4

| Order ref. | Quantity | Description |
|---|---|---|
| 17643 | 20 boxes of 10 | Gel pens (black) |

**received by**......*D Patel*............................................checked by......*R T Fraser*..............

**condition of goods**        condition - *good*

                              damages - *none*

                              shortages √ *18 out of 20 boxes received*

---

# CREDIT NOTE                  HELICON STATIONERY SUPPLIES

**to**

91 HIGH STREET, BROADFIELD, BR7 4ER

Tel 01908 129426  Fax 01908 129919

email  sales@heliconstationery.co.uk

VAT REG GB 0622 838370

| John Smith & Co |
|---|
| 7 Buttermere Road |
| Broadfield  BR6 3TR |

credit note no      234672

account             2984

your reference      17644

date/tax point      10 December 20-4

| Product code | Description | Quantity | Price | Unit | Total | Discount % | Net |
|---|---|---|---|---|---|---|---|
| 909BK | Rollerball pens (black) | 3 | 8.00 | box | 24.00 | 10 | 19.20 |

**reason for credit**

Shortages

supplier a/c reference    general ledger a/c number

| | |
|---|---|
| **Goods total** | 19.20 |
| **VAT @ 20%** | 3.84 |
| **TOTAL** | 23.04 |

# 7 Accounting for purchases, returns, and discounts

## this chapter covers...

*This chapter focuses on using the accounting system to record the details of purchases, purchases returns, and discounts received (using the credit note system – see pages 30-31).*

*Having looked in the previous chapter at the documents and procedures involved in buying on credit we will now take the financial documents of purchases invoices and credit notes for purchases returns and discounts received and record them in books of prime entry (day books) and in the bookkeeping system of general ledger and purchases ledger.*

*We will be using three books of prime entry:*

- *purchases day book*
- *purchases returns day book*
- *discounts received day book*

*Information from these day books will then be transferred into the bookkeeping system using accounts in general ledger and purchases ledger.*

***Notes:***

- *in this chapter we focus on accounting for credit purchases, purchases returns, and discounts received. Cash purchases transactions will be seen when we study the cash book in Chapter 9*
- *we use the international standards term 'trade payable' to mean a person who is owed money by a business; normally this is a supplier. In your studies you may also come across the traditional term 'creditor' which means exactly the same thing*

## THE ACCOUNTING SYSTEM

We have seen in Chapter 1 (page 4) that the accounting system comprises a number of stages of recording and presenting financial transactions:

- financial documents
- books of prime entry (eg day books)
- double-entry bookkeeping
- trial balance

In this chapter we look at how financial documents for credit purchases, purchases returns, and discounts received transactions are recorded in the books of prime entry, together with the entries to be made in the double-entry bookkeeping accounts. Later in the book we will see how a list of the balances of the double-entry accounts is used to form the initial trial balance (Chapter 11).

## ACCOUNTING FOR CREDIT PURCHASES, PURCHASES RETURNS, AND DISCOUNTS RECEIVED

In accounting, the term 'purchases' means **the purchase of goods with the intention that they should be resold at a profit**.

This means that an office stationery shop will record as purchases those items – such as photocopier paper, ring binders – which it buys with the intention of resale at a profit. Such purchases – together with the running costs of the business, eg wages, heating and lighting, telephone – are described as **revenue expenditure**. Other asset items purchased in connection with the running of the business – eg buildings, shop fittings – are recorded not as purchases but, instead, are accounted for as the purchase of an asset, ie buildings, shop fittings – such expenditure is described as **capital expenditure**.

'Purchases returns' are when goods previously bought on credit are returned by the buyer to the supplier.

'Discounts received' (or **prompt payment discount**) is a discount offered by a supplier to customers in order to encourage customers to settle up straightaway or in a short time from the invoice date; it is discounts received in the accounting system of the buyer.

The diagram on the next page shows the order in which the accounting records are prepared for credit purchases, purchases returns, and discounts received transactions. You will see that the steps are:

■ start with a **financial document**, either a purchases invoice (for purchases) or a credit note received (for purchases returns and discounts received)

■ enter it in the appropriate **book of prime entry** (the first accounting book in which the financial document is recorded and summarised), purchases day book, purchases returns day book, or discounts received day book

■ transfer the information from the book of prime entry into the double-entry accounts in the **general ledger**

■ transfer the information from the book of prime entry into the subsidiary accounts of trade payables in the **purchases ledger**

## accounting for credit purchases and purchases returns transactions

**financial documents**
- purchases invoices
- credit notes received for purchases returns and discounts received

**books of prime entry**
- purchases day book
- purchases returns day book
- discounts received day book

**general ledger**

*double-entry accounts*
- purchases account
- purchases returns account
- discounts received account
- purchases ledger control account
- Value Added Tax account

**purchases ledger**

*subsidiary accounts*
- accounts of trade payables (suppliers)

We will now look in more detail at the use of the books of prime entry and the double-entry bookkeeping system for credit purchases, purchases returns, and discounts received. These are very similar to the system already used for credit sales, sales returns, and discounts allowed in Chapter 4 and you may wish to refer to the sections of Chapter 4 which cover books of prime entry (pages 77-78), and methods of coding in accounting systems (page 94).

## ACCOUNTING SYSTEM FOR CREDIT PURCHASES

The accounting system for credit purchases fits together in the following way:

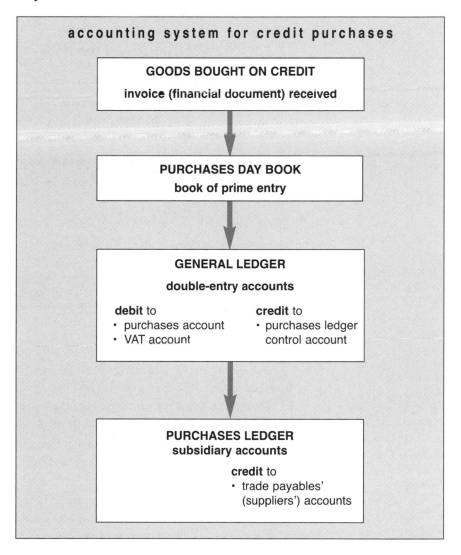

We will now look in more detail at the purchases day book and the accounting system for credit purchases.

In the examples which follow we will assume that the business is registered for Value Added Tax and that VAT is charged on invoices received from suppliers.

The VAT rate used in the examples is 20%.

## PURCHASES DAY BOOK

The purchases day book is a collection point for accounting information on the credit purchases of a business and is set out in the following way (with sample entries shown):

| Purchases Day Book | | | | | | PDB57 |
|---|---|---|---|---|---|---|
| **Date** | **Details** | **Invoice number** | **Account code** | **Total** | **VAT\*** | **Net** |
| 20-4 | | | | £ | £ | £ |
| 5 Jan | P Bond Ltd | 1234 | PL125 | 96 | 16 | 80 |
| 9 Jan | D Webster | A373 | PL730 | 144 | 24 | 120 |
| 16 Jan | P Bond Ltd | 1247 | PL125 | 48 | 8 | 40 |
| 20 Jan | Sanders & Sons | 5691 | PL495 | 192 | 32 | 160 |
| 31 Jan | Totals for month | | | 480 | 80 | 400 |
| | | | | GL2350 | GL2200 | GL5100 |

\* VAT = 20 per cent

**Notes:**

- Purchases day book is prepared from financial documents – purchases invoices received from suppliers. The invoice number used is either that of the supplier's invoice (as above) or is a unique number given to each invoice by the buyer's accounts department

- the code 'PDB57' is used for cross-referencing to the bookkeeping system: here it indicates that this is page 57 of the purchases day book (PDB)

- the **account code** column cross-references here to 'PL' – the Purchases Ledger – followed by the account number of the trade payable (supplier)

- the **total** or **gross** column records the amount of each financial document, ie after VAT has been included

- the code 'GL' beneath the totals amounts refers to the account numbers in General Ledger

- Purchases day book is totalled at appropriate intervals – daily, weekly or monthly (as here) – and the total of the **net** column tells the business the amount of credit purchases for the period

- the amounts from purchases day book are recorded in the ledger accounts

In order to write up the purchases day book, we take purchases invoices – that have been checked and authorised – for the period and enter the details:

- ▇ date of invoice
- ▇ name of supplier
- ▇ purchase invoice number, using either the supplier's invoice number, or a unique number given to each invoice by the buyer's accounts department
- ▇ cross-reference to the supplier's account number in the purchases ledger, eg 'PL125'
- ▇ enter the total amount of the invoice into the 'total' column
- ▇ enter the VAT amount shown on the invoice – don't be concerned with any adjustments to the VAT for the effect of any settlement (cash) discounts, simply record the VAT amount shown
- ▇ enter the net amount of the invoice (often described as 'goods or services total'), before VAT is added

## BOOKKEEPING FOR CREDIT PURCHASES

After the purchases day book has been written up and totalled, the information from it is transferred to the double-entry system in general ledger. The accounts in general ledger to record the transactions from the purchases day book on the previous page are as follows:

### GENERAL LEDGER

| Dr | Value added tax account (GL2200) | | Cr |
|---|---|---|---|
| 20-4 | £ | 20-4 | £ |
| 31 Jan  Purchases Day Book | | | |
| PDB57 | 80 | | |

| Dr | Purchases ledger control account (GL2350) | | Cr |
|---|---|---|---|
| 20-4 | £ | 20-4 | £ |
| | | 31 Jan    Purchases Day Book | |
| | | PDB57 | 480 |

| Dr | Purchases account (GL5100) | | Cr |
|---|---|---|---|
| 20-4 | £ | 20-4 | £ |
| 31 Jan  Purchases Day Book | | | |
| PDB57 | 400 | | |

Note that from the purchases day book:

■ total of the total column, £480, has been credited to purchases ledger control account (which records the liability to trade payables)

■ the total of the VAT column, £80, has been debited to VAT account (which has gained value)

■ the total of the net column, £400, has been debited to purchases account (which has gained value)

■ each entry in general ledger is cross-referenced back to the page number of the purchases day book; here the reference is to 'PDB57'

The last step is to record the amount of purchases made from each individual trade payable. We do this by recording the purchases invoices in the purchases ledger as follows:

**PURCHASES LEDGER**

| Dr | | **P Bond Limited (PL125)** | | Cr |
|---|---|---|---|---|
| 20-4 | £ | 20-4 | | £ |
| | | 5 Jan | Purchases PDB57 | 96 |
| | | 16 Jan | Purchases PDB57 | 48 |

| Dr | | **Sanders & Sons (PL495)** | | Cr |
|---|---|---|---|---|
| 20-4 | £ | 20-4 | | £ |
| | | 20 Jan | Purchases PDB57 | 192 |

| Dr | | **D Webster (PL730)** | | Cr |
|---|---|---|---|---|
| 20-4 | £ | 20-4 | | £ |
| | | 9 Jan | Purchases PDB57 | 144 |

**Notes:**

■ the purchases day book incorporates a reference column, used to cross-reference each transaction to the account of each supplier in the purchases ledger (PL); this enables a particular transaction to be traced from financial document (invoice received), through the book of prime entry (purchases day book), to the supplier's account

■ each entry in the purchases ledger is cross-referenced back to the page number of the purchases day book; here the reference is 'PDB57'

### subsidiary accounts

The accounts in purchases ledger are prepared following the principles of double-entry bookkeeping. However, they are **subsidiary accounts** which means they are used to provide a note of how much each trade payable is owed by the business.

Subsidiary accounts are not part of double-entry but are represented in the general ledger by purchases ledger control account. This means that, here, the £480 credit entry is split up in the purchases ledger between the three suppliers' subsidiary accounts. Note that subsidiary accounts are often referred to as **memorandum accounts**.

## ACCOUNTING SYSTEM FOR PURCHASES RETURNS

**Purchases returns** (or returns out) are when goods previously bought on credit are returned by the business to its suppliers. A credit note (see page 26) is requested and, when received, it is entered in the accounting system to reduce the amount owing to the trade payable.

The accounting procedures for purchases returns involve:

■ **financial documents** – credit notes received from suppliers

■ **book of prime entry** – purchases returns day book

■ **double-entry accounts** – general ledger (purchases returns account, which records the total net amount of credit notes received, Value Added Tax account, which records the VAT amount of purchases returns, and purchases ledger control account, which records the liability to trade payables)

■ **purchases ledger** – the subsidiary accounts for each individual trade payable of the business

The way in which the accounting system for purchases returns fits together is shown in the diagram on the next page.

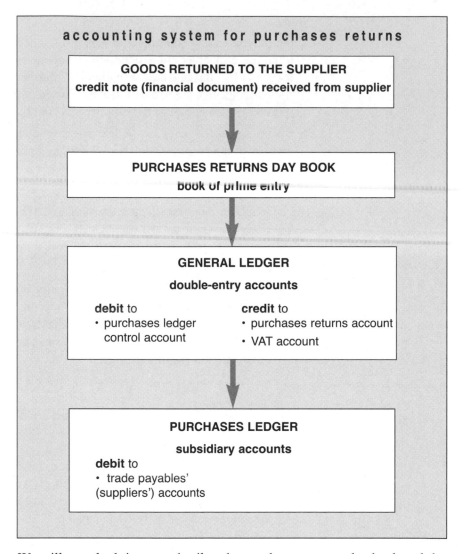

We will now look in more detail at the purchases returns day book and the double-entry accounts for purchases returns. Note that the business is registered for Value Added Tax.

## PURCHASES RETURNS DAY BOOK

The purchases returns day book uses virtually the same layout as the purchases day book seen earlier in this chapter. It operates in a similar way, storing up information about purchases returns transactions until such time as a transfer is made into the double-entry accounts system. The prime documents for purchases returns day book are credit notes received from suppliers.

The purchases returns day book is written up as follows, with sample entries:

| Purchases Returns Day Book | | | | | | PRDB3 |
|---|---|---|---|---|---|---|
| **Date** | **Details** | **Credit note no** | **Account code** | **Total** | **VAT*** | **Net** |
| 20-4 | | | | £ | £ | £ |
| 20 Jan | D Webster | 123 | PL730 | 48 | 8 | 40 |
| 27 Jan | Sanders & Sons | 406 | PL495 | 96 | 16 | 80 |
| | | | | | | |
| 31 Jan | Totals for month | | | 144 | 24 | 120 |
| | | | | GL2350 | GL2200 | GL5110 |

\* VAT = 20 per cent

**Notes:**

■ the purchases returns day book is prepared from credit notes received from suppliers. The credit note number used is either that of the supplier's credit note (as above) or is a unique number given to each credit note by the buyer's accounts department

■ the day book is totalled at appropriate intervals – weekly or monthly

■ the VAT-inclusive amounts from the total column are debited to the trade payables' individual accounts in the purchases ledger

■ the total of the VAT column is transferred to the credit of the VAT account in the general ledger

■ the total of the net column tells the business the amount of purchases returns for the period. This amount is transferred to the credit of purchases returns account in the general ledger

■ the total or gross column records the amount of each credit note received, ie after VAT has been included. This amount is transferred to the debit of purchases ledger control account in general ledger

## BOOKKEEPING FOR PURCHASES RETURNS

After the purchases returns day book has been written up and totalled, the information from it is transferred into the double-entry system. The accounts in the general ledger to record the transactions from the above purchases returns day book (including any other transactions already recorded on these accounts) are as follows:

## GENERAL LEDGER

| Dr | Value added tax account (GL2200) | | | | Cr |
|---|---|---|---|---|---|
| 20-4 | | £ | 20-4 | | £ |
| 31 Jan | Purchases Day Book PDB57 | 80 | 31 Jan | Purchases Returns Day Book PRDB3 | 24 |

| Dr | Purchases ledger control account (GL2350) | | | | Cr |
|---|---|---|---|---|---|
| 20-4 | | £ | 20-4 | | £ |
| 31 Jan | Purchases Returns Day Book PRDB3 | 144 | 31 Jan | Purchases Day Book PDB57 | 480 |

| Dr | Purchases returns account (GL5110) | | | | Cr |
|---|---|---|---|---|---|
| 20-4 | | £ | 20-4 | | £ |
| | | | 31 Jan | Purchases Returns Day Book PRDB3 | 120 |

The last step is to record the amount of purchases returns made to each trade payable. We do this by recording the purchases returns in the subsidiary accounts for each trade payable in the purchases ledger as follows:

## PURCHASES LEDGER

| Dr | Sanders & Sons (PL495) | | | | Cr |
|---|---|---|---|---|---|
| 20-4 | | £ | 20-4 | | £ |
| 27 Jan | Purchases Returns PRDB3 | 96 | 20 Jan | Purchases PDB57 | 192 |

| Dr | D Webster (PL730) | | | | Cr |
|---|---|---|---|---|---|
| 20-4 | | £ | 20-4 | | £ |
| 20 Jan | Purchases Returns PRDB3 | 48 | 9 Jan | Purchases PDB57 | 144 |

## ACCOUNTING SYSTEM FOR DISCOUNTS RECEIVED

We have already seen, on pages 30-31, the two methods permitted by HM Revenue & Customs to account for the Value Added Tax when a prompt payment discount (PPD) is offered by the supplier.

In this section we see how the accounting for PPD in the customer's (buyer's) books, ie discounts received, is carried out using the method where a credit note is issued by the supplier. Note that this method is used by AAT to assess PPD transactions.

When accounting for discounts received by using credit notes, a Discounts Received Day Book (DRDB) is used to record credit notes issued by the supplier for PPD and received by the customer. The accounting system is shown below.

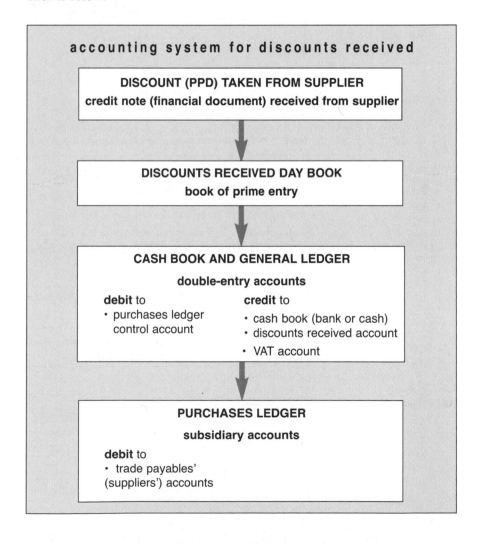

We will now look in detail at the discounts received day book and the double-entry accounts to record prompt payment discount in the books of the customer (buyer). Note that the business is registered for Value Added Tax.

## DISCOUNTS RECEIVED DAY BOOK

Discounts received day book (DRDB) uses virtually the same layout as the purchases day book seen on page 154.

In order to see how the discounts received day book and the bookkeeping entries are recorded we will use the following purchases invoice received by Lea Ltd from the supplier, Bialas & Co:

| | |
|---|---|
| **INVOICE** | |
| **Number 2120** | |
| From Bialas & Co | 4 April 20-4 |
| To Lea Ltd | |

| | £ |
|---|---|
| Goods Net | 500.00 |
| VAT | 100.00 |
| Total | 600.00 |

Terms: 5 per cent prompt payment discount for payment within ten days

**Note:** if the supplier is paid after ten days, the payment will be for £600 and no PPD entries will be required.

If the supplier is paid within ten days, the payment will be net £475, VAT £95, total £570. The supplier will issue a credit note for £30 (ie £25 + VAT £5) which will be recorded by the customer in the discounts received day book as follows:

| Discounts Received Day Book | | | | | | DRDB1 |
|---|---|---|---|---|---|---|
| **Date** | **Details** | **Credit note no** | **Account code** | **Total** | **VAT** | **Net** |
| 20-4 | | | | £ | £ | £ |
| 10 April | Bialas & Co | CN42* | PL204 | 30 | 5 | 25 |
| 30 April | Totals for month | | | 30 | 5 | 25 |
| | | | | GL2350 | GL2200 | GL3490 |

*Note that the credit note received from the supplier is recorded here as a CN, using the supplier's credit note number – 'CN 42' used as an example.

**Notes:**

- the discounts received day book is prepared from credit notes for PPD received from suppliers

- the day book is totalled at appropriate intervals – weekly or monthly (only one transaction in the example on the previous page)

- the VAT-inclusive amounts from the total column are debited to the trade payables' individual subsidiary accounts in the purchases ledger

- the total of the VAT column is transferred to the credit of the VAT account in the general ledger

- the total of the net column tells the business the amount of discounts received for the period. This amount is transferred to the credit of discounts received account in the general ledger

- the total column records the amount of each credit note received, ie after VAT has been included. This amount is transferred to the debit of purchases ledger control account in the general ledger

## BOOKKEEPING FOR DISCOUNTS RECEIVED

After the discounts received day book has been written up and totalled, the information from it is transferred into the double-entry system as follows:

| Cash Book* (credit side) | | | | | | | | CB025 |
|---|---|---|---|---|---|---|---|---|
| Date | Details | Account code | Cash | Bank | VAT | Cash purchases | Trade payables | Other expenses |
| 20-4 | | | £ | £ | £ | £ | £ | £ |
| 10 April | Bialas & Co | PL204 | | 570 | | | 570 | |

*The layout of the cash book is explained fully in Chapter 9.

**GENERAL LEDGER**

| Dr | Discounts received account (GL3490) | | Cr |
|---|---|---|---|
| 20-4 | £ | 20-4 | £ |
| | | 10 April   Discounts Received | |
| | | Day Book DRDB1 | 25 |

| Dr | Value added tax account (GL2200) | | Cr |
|---|---|---|---|
| 20-4 | £ | 20-4 | £ |
| | | 10 April   Discounts Received | |
| | | Day Book DRDB1 | 5 |

| Dr | Purchases ledger control account (GL2350) | | Cr |
|---|---|---|---|
| 20-4 | | £ | 20-4 | £ |
| 10 April | Bank   CB025 | 570 | |
| 10 April | Discounts Received | | |
| | Day Book DRDB1 | 30 | |

The last step is to record the amount of discounts received in the subsidiary account of the trade payable in the purchases ledger as follows:

**PURCHASES LEDGER**

| Dr | Bialas & Co (PL204) | | Cr |
|---|---|---|---|
| 20-4 | | £ | 20-4 | | £ |
| 10 April | Bank   CB025 | 570 | 4 April | Purchases   PDB | 600 |
| 10 April | Discounts Received | | | | |
| | Day Book DRDB1 | 30 | | | |

# THE USE OF ANALYSED PURCHASES DAY BOOKS

Businesses use analysed day books whenever they wish to analyse purchases and purchases returns between different categories of purchases:

- goods bought for resale, often split between types of goods purchased, eg in a clothes shop between ladies wear and mens wear

- purchases made by different departments, eg within a department store

For example, a business with two different types of purchases – purchases type 1 and purchases type 2 – will write up its purchases day book as follows:

| Purchases Day Book | | | | | | | | PDB86 |
|---|---|---|---|---|---|---|---|---|
| Date | Details | Invoice number | Account code | Total | VAT* | Net | Purchases type 1 | Purchases type 2 |
| 20-4 | | | | £ | £ | £ | £ | £ |
| 2 Sep | Fashions Limited | 1401 | PL087 | 144 | 24 | 120 | 70 | 50 |
| 4 Sep | Eastern Telephones | 1402 | PL061 | 240 | 40 | 200 | – | 200 |
| 8 Sep | Mercian Models | 1403 | PL102 | 336 | 56 | 280 | 280 | – |
| 12 Sep | Media Advertising | 1404 | PL092 | 720 | 120 | 600 | – | 600 |
| 15 Sep | Style Limited | 1405 | PL379 | 480 | 80 | 400 | 100 | 300 |
| 19 Sep | Wyvern Motors | 1406 | PL423 | 192 | 32 | 160 | – | 160 |
| 30 Sep | Totals for month | | | 2,112 | 352 | 1,760 | 450 | 1,310 |
| | | | | GL2350 | GL2200 | | GL5160 | GL5190 |

* VAT = 20 per cent

Analysed purchases day books and purchases returns day books can be adapted to suit the particular needs of a business. Thus there is not a standard way in which to present the books of prime entry – the needs of the user of the information are all important. By using analysed day books, the owner of the business can see how much has been bought by types of purchases, or by departments.

**Notes:**

- in this purchases day book each purchases invoice has been given a unique number (starting at 1401) by the buyer's accounts department

- the account code column is to 'PL' (Purchases Ledger) and the supplier's account number

- the code 'GL' beneath the totals amounts refers to the account numbers in General Ledger

■ the analysis columns – here purchases type 1 and purchases type 2 – show the amount of purchases net of VAT (ie before VAT is added)

■ the analysis columns analyse the net amount – by type of expenditure – from purchases invoices

# WYVERN TRADERS – PURCHASES AND RETURNS

This Case Study shows how credit purchases and purchases returns are recorded in the accounting system of a business. The Case Study makes use of:

- **books of prime entry**
  - purchases day book
  - purchases returns day book
- **general ledger accounts**
  - purchases account
  - purchases returns account
  - Value Added Tax account
  - purchases ledger control account
- **purchases ledger accounts**
  - trade payables' subsidiary accounts

The Chapter Summary (pages 169-171) includes diagrams which summarise the procedures for recording credit purchases and purchases returns transactions in the accounting system.

## situation

Wyvern Traders is a wholesaler of stationery and office equipment. The business is registered for VAT. The VAT rate is 20%. The following are the credit purchases and purchases returns transactions for April 20-4:

| 20-4 | |
|---|---|
| 1 Apr | Purchased goods from Midland Supplies, £120.00 + VAT, their invoice no 12486 |
| 9 Apr | Returned goods to Midland Supplies, £40.00 + VAT, credit note no 104 received |
| 14 Apr | Purchased goods from Swan Equipment, £80.00 + VAT, their invoice no P076 |
| 26 Apr | Purchased goods from Swan Equipment, £160.00 + VAT, their invoice no P102 |
| 30 Apr | Returned goods to Swan Equipment, £80.00 + VAT, credit note no X102 received |

The day books, general ledger and purchases ledger accounts are illustrated on the next two pages: arrows indicate the transfers from the day books to the individual accounts. Note that some accounts have been repeated on both pages in order to show, on the same page, the accounts relating to a particular day book: in practice a business would keep all the transactions together in one account.

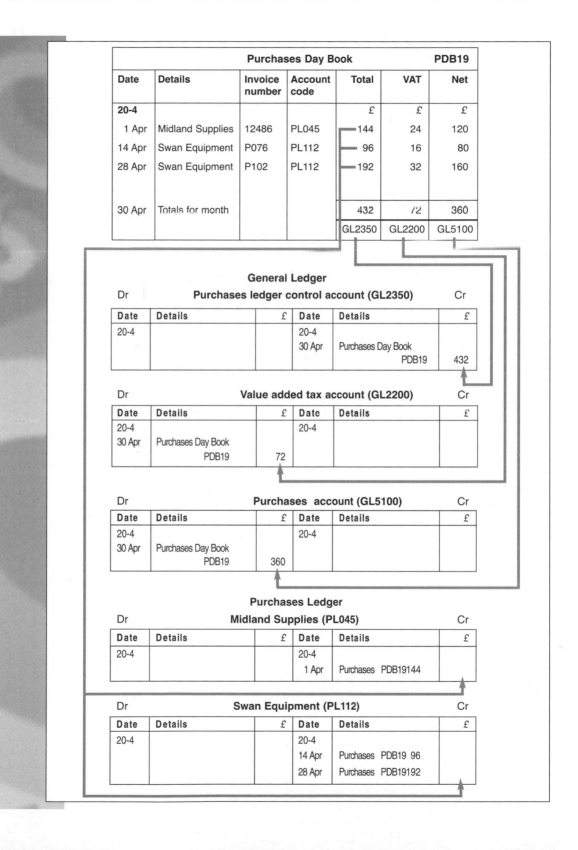

**Purchases Day Book**      **PDB19**

| Date | Details | Invoice number | Account code | Total | VAT | Net |
|------|---------|----------------|--------------|-------|-----|-----|
| **20-4** | | | | £ | £ | £ |
| 1 Apr | Midland Supplies | 12486 | PL045 | 144 | 24 | 120 |
| 14 Apr | Swan Equipment | P076 | PL112 | 96 | 16 | 80 |
| 28 Apr | Swan Equipment | P102 | PL112 | 192 | 32 | 160 |
| 30 Apr | Totals for month | | | 432 | 72 | 360 |
| | | | | GL2350 | GL2200 | GL5100 |

**General Ledger**

Dr      **Purchases ledger control account (GL2350)**      Cr

| Date | Details | £ | Date | Details | £ |
|------|---------|---|------|---------|---|
| 20-4 | | | 20-4 | | |
| | | | 30 Apr | Purchases Day Book PDB19 | 432 |

Dr      **Value added tax account (GL2200)**      Cr

| Date | Details | £ | Date | Details | £ |
|------|---------|---|------|---------|---|
| 20-4 | | | 20-4 | | |
| 30 Apr | Purchases Day Book PDB19 | 72 | | | |

Dr      **Purchases  account (GL5100)**      Cr

| Date | Details | £ | Date | Details | £ |
|------|---------|---|------|---------|---|
| 20-4 | | | 20-4 | | |
| 30 Apr | Purchases Day Book PDB19 | 360 | | | |

**Purchases Ledger**

Dr      **Midland Supplies (PL045)**      Cr

| Date | Details | £ | Date | Details | £ |
|------|---------|---|------|---------|---|
| 20-4 | | | 20-4 | | |
| | | | 1 Apr | Purchases  PDB19 | 144 |

Dr      **Swan Equipment (PL112)**      Cr

| Date | Details | £ | Date | Details | £ |
|------|---------|---|------|---------|---|
| 20-4 | | | 20-4 | | |
| | | | 14 Apr | Purchases  PDB19 | 96 |
| | | | 28 Apr | Purchases  PDB19 | 192 |

| Purchases Returns Day Book | | | | Total | VAT | PRDB7 Net |
|---|---|---|---|---|---|---|
| Date | Details | Credit note number | Reference | Total | VAT | Net |
| 20-4 | | | | £ | £ | £ |
| 9 Apr | Midland Supplies | 104 | PL045 | 48 | 8 | 40 |
| 30 Apr | Swan Equipment | X102 | PL112 | 96 | 16 | 80 |
| | | | | | | |
| 30 Apr | Totals for month | | | 144 | 24 | 120 |
| | | | | GL2350 | GL2200 | GL5110 |

### General Ledger

Dr          **Purchases ledger control account (GL2350)**          Cr

| Date | Details | £ | Date | Details | £ |
|---|---|---|---|---|---|
| 20-4 | | | 20-4 | | |
| 30 Apr | Purchases Returns Day Book PRDB7 | 144 | 30 Apr | Purchases Day Book PDB19 | *432 |

Dr          **Value added tax account (GL2200)**          Cr

| Date | Details | £ | Date | Details | £ |
|---|---|---|---|---|---|
| 20-4 | | | 20-4 | | |
| 30 Apr | Purchases Day Book PDB19 | *72 | 30 Apr | Purchases Returns Day Book PRDB7 | 24 |

Dr          **Purchases returns account (GL5110)**          Cr

| Date | Details | £ | Date | Details | £ |
|---|---|---|---|---|---|
| 20-4 | | | 20-4 | | |
| | | | 30 Apr | Purchases Returns Day Book PRDB7 | 120 |

### Purchases Ledger

Dr          **Midland Supplies (PL045)**          Cr

| Date | Details | £ | Date | Details | £ |
|---|---|---|---|---|---|
| 20-4 | | | 20-4 | | |
| 9 Apr | Purchases Returns PRDB7 | 48 | 1 Apr | Purchases PDB19 | *144 |

Dr          **Swan Equipment (PL112)**          Cr

| Date | Details | £ | Date | Details | £ |
|---|---|---|---|---|---|
| 20-4 | | | 20-4 | | |
| 30 Apr | Purchases Returns PRDB7 | 96 | 14 Apr | Purchases PDB19 | *96 |
| | | | 28 Apr | Purchases PDB19 | *192 |

*transactions entered previously

**Chapter Summary**

The diagrams on the next two pages summarise the material we have studied in this chapter. They show the procedures for recording transactions in the accounting system for credit purchases, purchases returns, and discounts received.

Further chapter summary points follow on page 172.

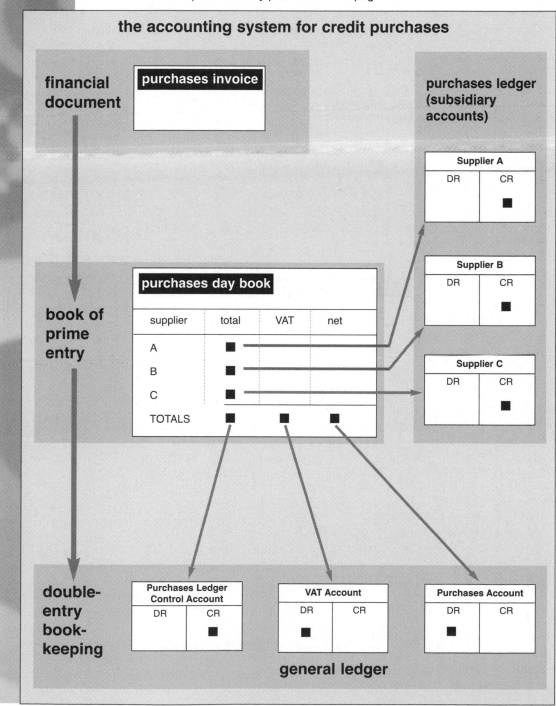

# the accounting system for credit purchases

**financial document**

**purchases invoice**

**book of prime entry**

**purchases day book**

| supplier | total | VAT | net |
|----------|-------|-----|-----|
| A | ■ | | |
| B | ■ | | |
| C | ■ | | |
| TOTALS | ■ | ■ | ■ |

**purchases ledger (subsidiary accounts)**

| Supplier A | |
|-----|-----|
| DR | CR |
| | ■ |

| Supplier B | |
|-----|-----|
| DR | CR |
| | ■ |

| Supplier C | |
|-----|-----|
| DR | CR |
| | ■ |

**double-entry book-keeping**

| Purchases Ledger Control Account | |
|-----|-----|
| DR | CR |
| | ■ |

| VAT Account | |
|-----|-----|
| DR | CR |
| ■ | |

| Purchases Account | |
|-----|-----|
| DR | CR |
| ■ | |

**general ledger**

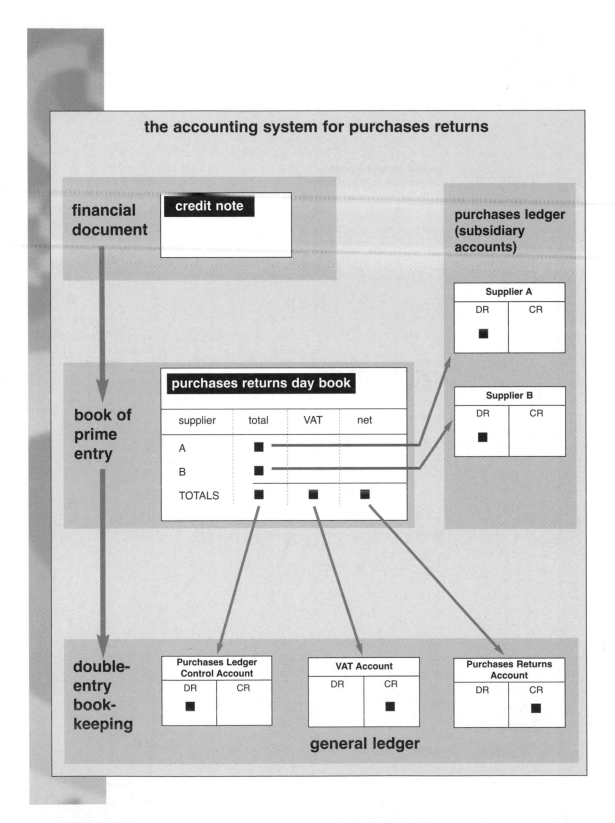

## the accounting system for purchases returns

**financial document**

credit note

**purchases ledger (subsidiary accounts)**

Supplier A

| DR | CR |
|----|----|
| ■  |    |

Supplier B

| DR | CR |
|----|----|
| ■  |    |

**book of prime entry**

**purchases returns day book**

| supplier | total | VAT | net |
|----------|-------|-----|-----|
| A | ■ | | |
| B | ■ | | |
| TOTALS | ■ | ■ | ■ |

**double-entry book-keeping**

Purchases Ledger Control Account

| DR | CR |
|----|----|
| ■  |    |

VAT Account

| DR | CR |
|----|----|
|    | ■  |

Purchases Returns Account

| DR | CR |
|----|----|
|    | ■  |

**general ledger**

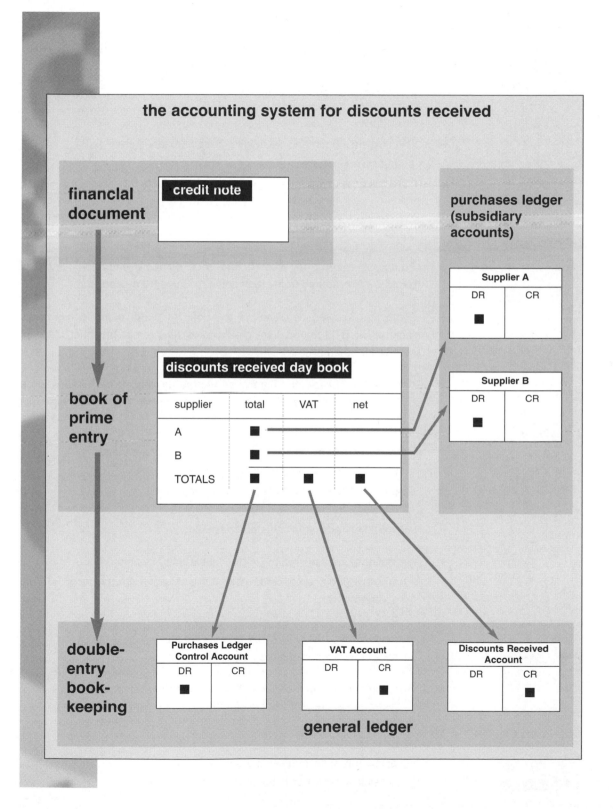

## the accounting system for discounts received

**financial document**

credit note

**purchases ledger (subsidiary accounts)**

| Supplier A | |
|---|---|
| DR | CR |
| ■ | |

| Supplier B | |
|---|---|
| DR | CR |
| ■ | |

**book of prime entry**

### discounts received day book

| supplier | total | VAT | net |
|---|---|---|---|
| A | ■ | | |
| B | ■ | | |
| TOTALS | ■ | ■ | ■ |

**double-entry book-keeping**

| Purchases Ledger Control Account | |
|---|---|
| DR | CR |
| ■ | |

| VAT Account | |
|---|---|
| DR | CR |
| | ■ |

| Discounts Received Account | |
|---|---|
| DR | CR |
| | ■ |

**general ledger**

■ The accounting system comprises a number of specific stages of recording and presenting financial transactions:
  - financial documents
  - books of prime entry (eg day books)
  - double-entry bookkeeping
  - trial balance

■ The financial documents relating to credit purchases are:
  - purchases invoices
  - credit notes for purchases returns and discounts received

■ Purchases day book is the book of prime entry for credit purchases. It is prepared from purchases invoices received from suppliers.

■ Purchases returns day book is the book of prime entry for purchases returns. It is prepared from credit notes received from suppliers.

■ Discounts received day book is the book of prime entry for discounts received. It is prepared from credit notes for prompt payment discount received from suppliers.

■ Analysed purchases and purchases returns day books are used when a business wishes to analyse its purchases between different types of expenditure.

■ Recording credit purchases in the double-entry system uses:
  - financial documents, purchases invoices
  - book of prime entry, purchases day book
  - double-entry accounts in the general ledger
  - subsidiary accounts in the purchases ledger

■ Recording purchases returns in the double-entry system uses:
  - financial documents, credit notes for purchases returns received from suppliers
  - book of prime entry, purchases returns day book
  - double-entry accounts in the general ledger
  - subsidiary accounts in the purchases ledger

■ Recording discounts received in the double-entry system uses:
  - financial documents, credit notes for prompt payment discount received from suppliers
  - book of prime entry, discounts received day book
  - double-entry accounts in the general ledger
  - subsidiary accounts in the purchases ledger

| **Key Terms** | | |
|---|---|---|
| | **purchases** | the purchase of goods with the intention that they should be resold at a profit |
| | **revenue expenditure** | the cost of purchases and running costs of the business |
| | **capital expenditure** | the cost of asset items other than for resale, purchased in connection with the running of the business, eg buildings, shop fittings |
| | **purchases day book** | book of prime entry prepared from purchases invoices |
| | **purchases returns** | goods purchased on credit which are returned to the supplier |
| | **discounts received** | prompt payment discount offered by a supplier to customers in order to encourage customers to settle up straightaway or in a short time from the invoice date; it is discounts received in the accounting system of the buyer |
| | **purchases returns day book** | book of prime entry prepared from credit notes received from suppliers |
| | **discounts received day book** | book of prime entry prepared from credit notes for prompt payment discount received from sellers |
| | **analysed day books** | day books which incorporate analysis columns, for example between<br>– goods bought for resale, often split between different types of goods<br>– purchases made by different departments |
| | **general ledger** | ledger section which includes<br>– purchases account<br>– purchases returns account<br>– discounts received account<br>– purchases ledger control account<br>– Value Added Tax account |
| | **purchases ledger** | subsidiary ledger section which contains the subsidiary accounts of the trade payables (suppliers) |
| | **subsidiary account** | a subsidiary ledger (eg purchases ledger) account which provides a record of individual amounts (eg owing by the business to trade payables) |

# Activities

**7.1**   Which **one** of the following is a book of prime entry?

| | |
|---|---|
| (a)   Purchases account | |
| (b)   Value Added Tax account | |
| (c)   Purchases returns day book | |
| (d)   Purchases ledger account of M Ostrowski | |

**7.2**   Which **one** of the following is in the right order?

| | |
|---|---|
| (a)   Purchases returns day book; purchases ledger control account; credit note issued; purchases returns account; supplier's account | |
| (b)   Purchases returns account; supplier's account; purchases ledger control account; purchases returns day book; credit note issued | |
| (c)   Purchases returns day book; purchases returns account; purchases ledger control account; supplier's account; credit note issued | |
| (d)   Credit note issued; purchases returns day book; purchases returns account; purchases ledger control account; supplier's account | |

**7.3**   Which **one** of the following is the correct general ledger entries for a discounts received transaction?

| | |
|---|---|
| (a)   Debit purchases ledger control; debit VAT; credit discounts received | |
| (b)   Debit purchases ledger control; credit discounts received; credit VAT | |
| (c)   Debit discounts received; debit VAT; credit purchases ledger control | |
| (d)   Debit discounts received; credit purchases ledger control; credit VAT | |

**7.4**   Explain in note format:

   **(a)**   The principles of recording a credit purchases transaction in the accounting system.

   **(b)**   The principles of recording a purchases returns transaction in the accounting system.

For Activities 7.5 and 7.6:

- work in pounds and pence, where appropriate
- the rate of Value Added Tax is to be calculated at 20% (when calculating VAT amounts, you should ignore fractions of a penny, ie round down to a whole penny)
- use a coding system incorporating the following:

| | | | |
|---|---|---|---|
| *purchases day book* | *– PDB36* | | |
| *purchases returns day book* | *– PRDB11* | *general ledger account numbers* | |
| | | *purchases ledger control account* | *– GL2350* |
| *purchases ledger account numbers* | | *purchases account* | *– GL5100* |
| *AMC Enterprises* | *– PL520* | *purchases returns account* | *– GL5110* |
| *S Green* | *– PL574* | *Value Added Tax account* | *– GL2200* |
| *I Johnstone* | *– PL604* | | |
| *Mercia Manufacturing* | *– PL627* | | |
| *L Murphy* | *– PL659* | | |
| *Severn Supplies* | *– PL721* | | |

**7.5**  During April 20-5, Wyvern Wholesalers had the following credit transactions:

20-5

2 Apr   Purchased goods from Severn Supplies £250 + VAT, invoice no 6789

5 Apr   Purchased goods from I Johnstone £210 + VAT, invoice no  A241

9 Apr   Purchased goods from L Murphy £185 + VAT, invoice no 2456

15 Apr   Purchased goods from Mercia Manufacturing £180 + VAT, invoice no X457

19 Apr   Purchased goods from AMC Enterprises £345 + VAT, invoice no AMC 456

26 Apr   Purchased goods from S Green £395 + VAT, invoice no 2846

**You are to:**

**(a)**   Enter the above transactions in Wyvern Wholesaler's purchases day book for April 20-5, using the format shown on the next page.

**(b)**   Record the accounting entries in Wyvern Wholesaler's general ledger and purchases ledger.

(Note that you will need to retain these ledger accounts for use with Activity 7.6)

| Purchases Day Book | | | | | | PDB36 |
|---|---|---|---|---|---|---|
| Date | Details | Invoice number | Account code | Total £ | VAT £ | Net £ |
| | | | | | | |
| | | | | | | |
| | | | | | | |
| | | | | | | |
| | | | | | | |
| | | | | | | |
| | | | | | | |
| | | | | | | |
| | | | | | | |
| | | | | | | |

**7.6**    The following are the purchases returns of Wyvern Wholesalers for April 20-5. They are to be:

**(a)**    Entered in the purchases returns day book for April 20-5, using the format shown below.

**(b)**    Recorded in the general ledger and purchases ledger (use the ledgers already prepared in the answer to Activity 7.5).

20-5

| | |
|---|---|
| 7 Apr | Returned goods to Severn Supplies £50 + VAT, credit note no 225 received |
| 14 Apr | Returned goods to L Murphy £80 + VAT, credit note no X456 received |
| 21 Apr | Returned goods to AMC Enterprises £125 + VAT, credit note no 3921 received |
| 29 Apr | Returned goods to S Green £68 + VAT, credit note no SG247 received |

| Purchases Returns Day Book | | | | | | PRDB11 |
|---|---|---|---|---|---|---|
| Date | Details | Credit note number | Account code | Total £ | VAT £ | Net £ |
| | | | | | | |
| | | | | | | |
| | | | | | | |
| | | | | | | |
| | | | | | | |
| | | | | | | |

**7.7** You are employed by Hussein Limited as an accounts assistant. The business has a manual accounting system. Double-entry takes place in the general ledger; individual accounts of trade payables are kept as subsidiary accounts in the purchases ledger. The VAT rate is 20%.

**Notes:**
- show your answer with a tick, words or figures, as appropriate
- coding is not required

**(a)** The following credit transactions all took place on 30 April 20-4 and have been entered into the purchases day book as shown below. No entries have yet been made into the ledger system.

**Purchases day book**

| Date 20-4 | Details | Invoice number | Total £ | VAT £ | Net £ |
|---|---|---|---|---|---|
| 30 April | Seng Ltd | 4517 | 1,152 | 192 | 960 |
| 30 April | Peall & Co | 2384 | 2,832 | 472 | 2,360 |
| 30 April | Knightons | A761 | 4,176 | 696 | 3,480 |
| 30 April | Galeazzi plc | 7248 | 1,488 | 248 | 1,240 |
| | Totals | | 9,648 | 1,608 | 8,040 |

What will be the entries in the general ledger?

**General ledger**

| Account name | Amount £ | Debit | Credit |
|---|---|---|---|
| | | | |
| | | | |
| | | | |

What will be the entries in the purchases ledger?

**Purchases ledger**

| Account name | Amount £ | Debit | Credit |
|---|---|---|---|
| | | | |
| | | | |
| | | | |
| | | | |

**(b)** The following credit transactions all took place on 30 April 20-4 and have been entered into the purchases returns day book as shown below. No entries have yet been made into the ledger system.

**Purchases returns day book**

| Date 20-4 | Details | Credit note number | Total £ | VAT £ | Net £ |
|-----------|---------|--------------------|---------|-------|-------|
| 30 April | Martin & Co | 381 | 1,056 | 176 | 880 |
| 30 April | Wentworth Stores | C48 | 672 | 112 | 560 |
| | Totals | | 1,728 | 288 | 1,440 |

What will be the entries in the general ledger?

**General ledger**

| Account name | Amount £ | Debit | Credit |
|--------------|----------|-------|--------|
| | | | |
| | | | |
| | | | |

What will be the entries in the purchases ledger?

**Purchases ledger**

| Account name | Amount £ | Debit | Credit |
|--------------|----------|-------|--------|
| | | | |
| | | | |

(c) The following discounts received transactions all took place on 30 April 20-4 and have been entered into the discounts received day book as shown below. No entries have yet been made into the ledger system.

**Discounts received day book**

| Date 20-4 | Details | Credit note number | Total £ | VAT £ | Net £ |
|---|---|---|---|---|---|
| 30 April | Kumar Ltd | CN070 | 12 | 2 | 10 |
| 30 April | Prior & Co | CN594 | 60 | 10 | 50 |
| | Totals | | 72 | 12 | 60 |

What will be the entries in the general ledger?

**General ledger**

| Account name | Amount £ | Debit | Credit |
|---|---|---|---|
| | | | |
| | | | |
| | | | |

What will be the entries in the purchases ledger?

**Purchases ledger**

| Account name | Amount £ | Debit | Credit |
|---|---|---|---|
| | | | |
| | | | |

**7.8** The following is taken from the coding lists used at a business called Fashion Trading.

| Supplier | Purchases ledger account code |
|---|---|
| Bingham Fashions | BIN001 |
| Bourne Stores | BOU002 |
| Elite Trading | ELI001 |
| Green Dragon | GRE001 |
| Guest & Co | GUE002 |
| High Society | HIG001 |
| Modes Ltd | MOD001 |
| Myers Trading | MYE002 |
| Treetop Stores | TRE001 |
| Wragby Ltd | WRA001 |
| Zeta & Co | ZET001 |

You are to set up the purchases ledger account codes for the new suppliers shown below.

| Supplier | Purchases ledger account code |
|---|---|
| Bridon Ltd | |
| Foster & Co | |
| Hirst & Co | |

**7.9** Purchases invoices have been prepared and partially entered in the purchases day book, as shown below.

(a) Complete the entries in the purchases day book by inserting the appropriate figures for each invoice.

(b) Total the last five columns of the purchases day book.

**Purchases day book**

| Date 20-4 | Details | Invoice number | Total £ | VAT £ | Net £ | Purchases type 1 £ | Purchases type 2 £ |
|---|---|---|---|---|---|---|---|
| 30 June | Canoy Ltd | C350 | 1,608 | | 1,340 | 1,340 | |
| 30 June | McVeigh & Co | 5148 | | 390 | | | 1,950 |
| 30 June | Robinsons | R/862 | 2,952 | | | 2,460 | |
| | **Totals** | | | | | | |

# 8 Prepare payments to suppliers

## this chapter covers...

In Chapter 6 'Process documents from suppliers' we described the financial documents dealt with by a purchaser of goods and services on credit. These documents included the purchase invoice, credit note, delivery note and goods received note.

In this chapter we describe the next stage in the process – the preparation of the documentation needed when payment is to be made for the goods or services purchased.

The chapter covers the following areas:

- a brief review of the purchasing process

- checking a statement of account received from a supplier against the transactions in the account of the supplier in the purchases ledger

- identifying any discrepancies between a statement of account and transactions in the account of the supplier in the purchases ledger

- calculating the amount due to each supplier on the correct payment date

- preparing remittance advices for making payment by cheque or by electronic bank transfer (eg BACS or Faster Payment)

This chapter will not go into detail about the various bank payment systems. These are fully explained in the Osborne Books text 'Bookkeeping Controls Tutorial'.

## A REVIEW OF THE PURCHASING PROCESS

When a business makes a purchase of goods on credit it deals with a number of financial documents. These were covered in Chapter 5 and include:

■ **purchase order** – issued by the buyer ordering the goods

■ **delivery note** – sent with the goods by the supplier

■ **goods received note** – details of goods received and any discrepancies

■ **purchase invoice** – received from the supplier, setting out what is owed

■ **purchase credit note** – any refund to the buyer's account for missing, damaged or incorrect goods or any mistakes on the invoice

The next stage – dealt with in this chapter – is:

■ the receipt of the supplier's **statement of account** setting out what is owed – the transactions on the statement should be checked with the supplier's account in the purchases ledger of the buyer

■ the preparation of a **remittance advice** by the buyer, advising the supplier that payment is being made and the method of payment

This stage, and its place in the process, is shown at the bottom of the diagram below.

## RECONCILING THE SUPPLIER STATEMENT OF ACCOUNT

Chapter 6 described the processes of checking all the purchases documentation to identify and deal with any discrepancies. The documents involved in the checking process are:

■ the delivery note and the actual goods received (possibly using a goods received note)

■ the supplier invoices and credit notes for calculation errors

■ the supplier invoices and credit notes against the purchase order

By the time that all these checks have been made and the invoices and credit notes have been authorised, the buyer should settle up and pay the **supplier's account in the purchases ledger**. This account will contain details of all the transactions such as payments, purchases and purchases returns. The account should in fact mirror all the items which will appear in the supplier's **statement of account**. See the next page for an example of a statement of account and the supplier account in the purchases ledger. Compare the two. This process is known as **reconciliation**, which basically means 'tying up' the transactions.

This is all illustrated in the Case Study which follows.

**Case Study**

## KNITWICK – SUPPLIER STATEMENT RECONCILIATION

### situation

Knitwick Traders is a clothing company which specialises in fashion wear. It has a regular trading relationship with Medici Importers (based in London) which supplies it with high quality Italian clothes.

Medici Importers sends statements of account to Knitwick at the end of each month and Knitwick normally settles the account at the beginning of the next month. During the month of November 20-5 the following documents were sent to Knitwick by Medici Importers. They were checked by Knitwick and were found to be correct.

| 2 invoices: | 8 November | Ref 4312 | £850.00 |
| | 14 November | Ref 4367 | £120.00 |
| 1 credit note: | 20 November | Ref 534 | £85.00 |

In addition, Knitwick sent £674.50 in settlement of October's account to Medici Importer's bank account by electronic bank transfer in the first week of November.

In the first week of December, Knitwick received the statement of account shown on the next page. You have been asked to reconcile the statement with the purchases ledger account for Medici Importers also shown on the next page.

**STATEMENT OF ACCOUNT**

# MEDICI IMPORTERS

8 San Marco Avenue, Broadfield, BR2 8DC
Tel 01908 765101  Fax  01908 765109  Email info@medicimporters.co.uk
VAT REG GB 0532 4672 21

TO

```
Knitwick Traders
Unit 14 Landseer Estate
Hull
HU9 6CV
```

account        2894

date          30 11 20-5

| Date | Details | Debit £ | | Credit £ | | Balance £ |
|------|---------|---------|--|----------|--|-----------|
| 01 11 20-5 | Balance b/f | 674.50 | ✓ | | | 674.50 |
| 05 11 20-5 | BACS payment | | | 674.50 | ✓ | 00.00 |
| 08 11 20-5 | Invoice 4312 | 850.00 | ✓ | | | 850.00 |
| 14 11 20-5 | Invoice 4367 | 120.00 | ✓ | | | 970.00 |
| 20 11 20-5 | Credit note 534 | | | 85.00 | ✓ | 885.00 |

Electronic bank transfer: pay Medici Importers at National
Bank, Account 76528607, Sort code 54 12 33

**TOTAL**                          885.00

| Debit | Purchases Ledger: Medici Importers Account | | | | | | | Credit | |
|-------|--------|--|------|----|------|---------|--|------|----|
| **20-5** | **Details** | | **£** | **p** | **20-5** | **Details** | | **£** | **p** |
| 5 Nov | Bank | ✓ | 674 | 50 | 1 Nov | Balance b/d | ✓ | 674 | 50 |
| 20 Nov | Purchases returns | ✓ | 85 | 00 | 8 Nov | Purchases | ✓ | 850 | 00 |
| | | | | | 14 Nov | Purchases | ✓ | 120 | 00 |

## solution

Knitwick will compare the two documents and tick off the items which appear in both documents. These are shown here in the two different grey boxes for purposes of illustration only.

All the transactions are accounted for – there are no unticked amounts which might indicate some form of discrepancy.

This means that the two documents have now been 'reconciled' – ie they both tie up with each other and payment of the account – the £885.00 owing – will be authorised and made on the due date.

## DEALING WITH DISCREPANCIES

The Case Study on the previous two pages has shown a situation where all the documentation is correct and has been reconciled; all is well and payment can then be authorised and paid on the due date.

It is assumed here that the relevant financial documents – eg invoices and credit notes – have already been checked for accuracy and are free from any discrepancies.

But there may sometimes be discrepancies between the **supplier's statement of account** and the supplier's account kept in the buyer's **purchases ledger**. These will need to be sorted out before payment can be made.

These problems may be sorted out at accounts assistant level, or if the problem is more serious, by a line manager. Examples include:

■ **an invoice or credit note which appears on the supplier's statement, but for the wrong amount**

– the document will be held by the buyer and the amount can be verified, so this is likely to be an error made by the supplier when entering the amount in the accounts; it will need to be queried by the buyer and investigated and put right by the supplier

■ **an invoice or credit note is on the supplier's statement and not in the buyer's purchases ledger**

– this could be an invoice or credit note not posted to the buyer's purchases ledger, or to the wrong supplier's account, by the buyer; this should be investigated and if there is an error by the buyer, included in the payment of account

■ **an invoice or credit note is in the buyer's purchases ledger and not on the supplier's statement**

– this could be an invoice or credit note not posted to the supplier's accounts, or posted to the wrong customer account by the supplier; this item should be queried by the buyer and, if there is an error made by the supplier, included in the payment of account

■ **an invoice or credit note which appears twice on the supplier's statement**

– this is an obvious duplication of an invoice or credit note by the supplier (it does happen!); the supplier should be notified of the error and the amount not included in the payment of account

The lesson here is that accurate reconciliation of the supplier statement and purchases ledger account is very important: if a payment is made and there is an undetected discrepancy, it can be very difficult to put things right.

## INVOICE AUTHORISATION AND DISPUTED INVOICES

### statement or no statement?

It has been assumed in this chapter so far that suppliers will send out statements as a matter of course.

If statements are issued, businesses generally pay regularly on receipt of the statement, as this is an easier way of calculating payment. This is the situation set out in the Case Study earlier in this chapter (see pages 184 185).

In commercial practice, however, **statements are not always sent out by suppliers**. Some suppliers rely instead on each customer making payment of invoices when they are due, adjusting for any credit notes issued.

Whatever method is used by a buyer for sorting out the payment of the account, certain principles remain the same:

■ invoices should be paid by the due date, which can be calculated from the terms of the invoice

■ invoices should be **checked** and **authorised** before the payment date

### invoice authorisation

In most organisations invoices that have been checked are passed to the person in the Accounts Department who deals with making payments to suppliers. These invoices will then have to be **authorised** for payment.

When an invoice is checked and found to be correct, the person carrying out the check will usually mark the document and authorise it for payment. This authorisation can take a number of forms:

■ the checker can initial and date the invoice, and tick it or write 'pay' as an authorisation

■ the organisation may have a special rubber stamp which can be used in the authorisation process – this stamp may also provide space for **coding**, eg the cost code (the account number for the type of expense) and the purchase order reference number which can be entered in the purchases day book and also used for internal filing purposes; it may also contain the signature or initials of the person who has authority to authorise the invoice for payment

This procedure of authorisation helps the efficiency of the organisation:

■ the checker's initials will be there in case of any future query on the invoice, eg an undetected error

■ the invoice will be in the system for payment on the due date

### disputed invoices

In this chapter so far we have assumed that a business:

■ will pay the total amount shown on the statement

■ will pay all the invoices that are due and authorised for payment

There are times, however, when a buyer might decide that an invoice on a statement should not be paid. Normally in an accounts office you will be able to see this on the statement because the invoice will not be ticked, or you may get a note from your line manager telling you not to pay certain items. The invoice may be **disputed** with the supplier: for example, your business may claim that the goods supplied are incorrect.

Now read the following Case Study which explains how to calculate a payment which involves a disputed invoice.

**Case Study**

# ALDERSGATE SUPPLIES – PAYMENT OF ACCOUNT

### situation

You work in the Accounts Department of Krumm & Co which is supplied with electrical equipment by Aldersgate Supplies.

It is your job to prepare the payments for all suppliers at the beginning of each month. The latest statement from Aldersgate Supplies is shown on the next page and an email dated 4 December from your supervisor is set out below.

The ticks on the statement indicate the items that are recorded in the purchases ledger and will have to be taken into account when payment is made.

| email | |
|---|---|
| from | henry@krumm.co.uk |
| subject | Aldersgate Supplies account - disputed invoice |
| date | 4 December 20-5 12:01:11 GMT |
| to | a.student@krumm.co.uk |

Hi Aslam
Please note that Invoice 16700 for £450 is in dispute. Aldersgate clearly misread our purchase order and sent the wrong equipment, but still claim that they sent us the right stuff. On no account should this invoice be paid until the dispute is settled. Thanks.

Regards
Henry

| | STATEMENT OF ACCOUNT |
|---|---|

# STATEMENT OF ACCOUNT
# ALDERSGATE SUPPLIES
10 Aldersgate Street, London EC1A 7GH
Tel 0207 7051017  Fax  0207 7051231  Email sales@aldersgatesupplies.co.uk
VAT REG GB 6733 8372 99

TO

Krumm & Co
56 Eccles Road
Bolton
BL7 4DF

account    26742

date    30 11 20-5

| Date | Details | Debit £ | Credit £ | Balance £ |
|---|---|---|---|---|
| 01 11 20-5 | Balance b/f | 1250.70 ✓ | | 1250.70 |
| 04 11 20-5 | BACS payment | | 1250.70 ✓ | 00.00 |
| 08 11 20-5 | Invoice 16700 | 450.00 | | 450.00 |
| 14 11 20-5 | Invoice 16810 | 790.00 ✓ | | 1240.00 |
| 20 11 20-5 | Credit note 534 | | 79.00 ✓ | 1161.00 |
| 27 11 20-5 | Invoice 16985 | 800.00 ✓ | | 1961.00 |

Electronic bank transfer: pay Aldersgate Supplies at HRBC Bank, Account  79001875, Sort code 41 22 01

**TOTAL**    1961.00

## solution

The payment amount is worked out as follows:

*calculation (£)*

1 The first two items represent the balance outstanding at the beginning of November and then the payment made by Krumm & Co. They are the same amount (a debit and a credit) and therefore cancel each other out.    0

2 Invoice 16700 for £450 is in dispute and so is not included    0

3 Invoice 16810 for £790 is added on    + 790.00

4 Credit note 534 for £79 is deducted    − 79.00

5 Invoice 16985 for £800 is added on    + 800.00

The total payment to be made to Aldersgate Supplies is £1511    = £1511.00

The next step is to prepare a remittance advice note to advise Aldersgate Supplies of the payment being made by electronic bank transfer.

## PREPARING REMITTANCE ADVICES

### definition

As we saw in Chapter 6, a **remittance advice** is a document which can be posted, faxed or emailed, stating that a certain amount of money is being sent by a credit customer to a supplier in settlement of an account. A remittance advice is used:

- **to accompany a cheque** – a practice which is decreasing in use as fewer cheques are now used to make payment
- to advise the sending of a payment **direct to the seller's bank account** through **BACS** or **Faster Payments** electronic bank transfer systems

### completing the remittance advice

A remittance advice normally takes one of two forms:

- **a list of all the items which make up the payment**

  This is very useful for the supplier as it will enable the supplier's accounts department to reconcile the incoming payment with the customer's account in the sales ledger by ticking off all the items. Sometimes, if the account is very active and a computer accounting system is used, the remittance advice may contain hundreds of items and take up a number of pages. To make things simple in this text and in your studies, remittance advices are normally restricted to just a few items.

- **notification of the total amount**

  This is the simplest form of remittance advice: it sets out the fact that a payment for a certain amount is being made by cheque or electronically.

A cheque remittance advice listing individual transactions is shown below.

An explanation of the details that have to be completed on a remittance advice for an electronic bank transfer is given on the next page.

| TO | **REMITTANCE ADVICE**FROM | | |
|---|---|---|---|
| Cool Socks Limited<br>Unit 45 Elgar Estate,<br>Broadfield, BR7 4ER | 31 October 20-3 | **Trends**<br>4 Friar Street<br>Broadfield<br>BR1 3RF | |

| date | your reference | our reference | payment amount |
|---|---|---|---|
| 01 10 20-3 | INVOICE 787923 | 47609 | 283.20 |
| 10 10 20-3 | CREDIT NOTE 12157 | 47609 | (28.32) |
| | | | |
| | | **CHEQUE TOTAL** | 254.88 |

<table>
<tr><td>**Case Study**</td></tr>
</table>

# ALDERSGATE SUPPLIES – REMITTANCE ADVICE

## situation – continued

You work in the Accounts Department of Krumm & Co which has a supplier, Aldersgate Supplies. You are asked to complete the remittance advice advising that a Faster Payment is being sent direct to the bank account of Aldersgate Supplies.

## solution

The completed document is shown below.

---

**REMITTANCE ADVICE**

FROM.
Krumm & Co
56 Eccles Road
Bolton BL7 4DF

**TO**
Aldersgate Supplies **1**
10 Aldersgate Street, London EC1A 7GH

03 12 20-5 **2**

| date **3** | your reference **4** | our reference **5** | payment amount £ **6** |
|---|---|---|---|
| 17 11 20-5 | Invoice 16810 | PO98756 | 790.00 |
| 24 11 20-5 | Credit note 534 | PO98756 | (79.00) |
| 30 11 20-5 | Invoice 16985 | PO98792 | 800.00 |
| | | TOTAL | 1511.00 **7** |

**8**
THIS AMOUNT HAS BEEN PAID BY FASTER PAYMENT DIRECTLY INTO YOUR BANK ACCOUNT AT HRBC BANK ACCOUNT NO 79001875 SORT CODE 41 22 01

---

The following details have been completed by Krumm & Co:

1    at the top left, the name and address of the supplier – Aldersgate Supplies

2    at the top right, the date of the transfer of the money – 3 December 20-5

3    'date' – the dates of each of the documents listed

4    'your reference' – the description and supplier reference numbers of the invoices and credit note listed

5    'our reference' – Krumm & Co's purchase order numbers relating to the listed documents

6    'payment amount' – the amounts of the invoices and the credit note; note that the credit note amount is in brackets because it is deducted and not added

7    'total' – the amount being transferred to Aldersgate Supplies' bank account

8    at the bottom – details of the bank account number and sort code number of Aldersgate Supplies' bank (HRBC)

## Chapter Summary

- When a business ordering goods on credit from a supplier has checked all the financial documents – invoice, delivery note, credit note – it will then be in a position to settle up the supplier's account in the purchases ledger.

- A common practice is for the supplier to send a **statement of account** to each customer, listing all the transactions – sales, returns, payments – which will then be recorded in the **purchases ledger account**.

- It is important that the customer checks that the items on the supplier's statement of account 'tie up' with the items in the supplier's account in the purchases ledger. This process is known as a **reconciliation**.

- If there are any **discrepancies** between the supplier's statement of account and the purchases ledger account they must be identified and investigated. They will affect the amount of money that will be paid to the supplier.

- When payment of the account is made by the buyer, the amount is calculated by totalling **authorised invoices** due for payment and deducting any **authorised credit notes** and **discrepancies** that have been found.

- Payment on the due date is advised to the supplier by completing and sending a **remittance advice**, with details of an electronic bank transfer made to the supplier's bank account, or by enclosing a cheque.

## Key Terms

**statement of account**  document issued by a supplier listing all the payments, invoices and credit notes on the account, providing a total of the amount due

**purchases ledger account**  the account of the supplier in the accounting records of the buyer; it will also list the transactions on the account

**reconciliation**  a comparison and 'tying up' of transactions in two documents – in this case the statement of account and purchase ledger – in order to check for any discrepancies

**discrepancy**  a difference between the transactions recorded in two separate documents – for example a wrong figure highlighting an error or even a 'wrong' document such as a disputed invoice

**remittance advice**  an advice sent to a supplier advising the sending of an amount of money, either by cheque or direct to their account using an electronic bank transfer

# Activities

**8.1**    The two documents that have to be reconciled to work out the amount owing to a supplier are:

| (a) | The invoice and the remittance advice | |
|---|---|---|
| (b) | The supplier statement and the remittance advice | |
| (c) | The supplier statement and the supplier's purchases ledger account in the books of the buyer | |
| (d) | The remittance advice and the supplier's purchases ledger account in the books of the buyer | |

State which **one** of these four options is the correct answer.

**8.2**    The following must be checked and authorised for payment before a supplier payment can be prepared by a business that has received goods on credit terms:

| (a) | Supplier invoice | |
|---|---|---|
| (b) | Delivery note | |
| (c) | Remittance advice | |
| (d) | Supplier account in the purchases ledger | |

State which **one** of these four options is the correct answer.

**8.3**    If you found two purchases invoices for £250 with the same date and invoice number listed in a supplier statement you would need to query it and:

| (a) | Add £250 to the amount owing to the supplier as shown on the statement | |
|---|---|---|
| (b) | Deduct £250 from the amount owing to the supplier as shown on the statement | |
| (c) | Enter the invoice amount in the supplier's account in the purchases ledger | |
| (d) | Pay the total amount owing as shown on the supplier statement | |

State which **one** of these four options is the correct answer.

**8.4**    A remittance advice is used:

| (a) | Instead of a cheque when paying a supplier | |
|---|---|---|
| (b) | Instead of an electronic bank transfer when paying a supplier | |
| (c) | To accompany a cheque when paying a supplier | |
| (d) | To request payment when returning goods | |

State which **one** of these four options is the correct answer.

**8.5** You work in the Accounts Department of Hemsley Ltd. One of your routine tasks is to reconcile the supplier statements of account with the supplier accounts in the purchases ledger.

**You are to** reconcile the statement of account and purchases ledger account of your supplier Luxon Traders shown below. If you find any discrepancies:

- explain what the error could be
- suggest what you would do to resolve the problem
- state the amount you think the payment should be

| STATEMENT OF ACCOUNT | | | | |
|---|---|---|---|---|

**LUXON TRADERS**
56 High Street, Fowey, Cornwall, TR4 9DS
info@luxontraders.co.uk

TO

Hemsley Limited
6 Enterprise Park
Luton
LU7 3BN

account    9133

date    31 03 20-1

| Date | Details | Debit £ | Credit £ | Balance £ |
|---|---|---|---|---|
| 01 03 20-1 | Balance b/f | 156.00 | | 156.00 |
| 05 03 20-1 | BACS payment | | 156.00 | 00.00 |
| 08 03 20-1 | Invoice 76333 | 150.00 | | 150.00 |
| 08 03 20-1 | Invoice 76333 | 150.00 | | 300.00 |
| 20 03 20-1 | Credit note 923 | | 50.00 | 250.00 |
| | **TOTAL** | | | **250.00** |

| Debit | Purchases Ledger: Luxon Traders Account | | | | | | Credit | |
|---|---|---|---|---|---|---|---|---|
| 20-1 | Details | £ | p | 20-1 | Details | £ | p | |
| 5 Mar | Bank | 156 | 00 | 1 Mar | Balance b/d | 156 | 00 | |
| 20 Mar | Purchases returns | 50 | 00 | 8 Mar | Purchases | 150 | 00 | |

**8.6** You work in the Accounts Department of R J Powell Ltd. One of your routine tasks is to reconcile the supplier statements of account with the supplier accounts in the purchases ledger.

**You are to** reconcile the statement of account and purchases ledger account of your supplier A Krauss Limited shown below. If you find any discrepancies:

- explain what the error could be

- suggest what you would do to resolve the problem

- state the amount you think the payment should be

# STATEMENT OF ACCOUNT
# A Krauss Limited

213 Farringdon Road, Latcham, LA4 5FG
sales@akrausstrading.co.uk

TO
R J Powell Limited
48,Heathside Street
Broadheath
WR2 8NB

account  32123

date  30 04 20-1

| Date | Details | Debit £ | Credit £ | Balance £ |
|------|---------|---------|----------|-----------|
| 01 04 20-1 | Balance b/f | 990.00 | | 990.00 |
| 07 04 20-1 | BACS payment | | 990.00 | 00.00 |
| 09 04 20-1 | Invoice 12856 | 233.25 | | 233.25 |
| 19 04 20-1 | Invoice 12932 | 109.50 | | 342.75 |
| | **TOTAL** | | | 342.75 |

| Debit | | | | | Purchases Ledger: A Krauss Limited Account | | | Credit | |
|-------|---------|---|---|---|---------|---------|---|---|---|
| **20-1** | **Details** | £ | p | **20-1** | **Details** | | £ | p |
| 7 Apr | Bank | 990 | 00 | 1 Apr | Balance b/d | | 990 | 00 |
| 22 Apr | Purchases returns | 72 | 90 | 9 Apr | Purchases | | 233 | 25 |
| | | | | 19 Apr | Purchases | | 109 | 50 |

**8.7** Complete the remittance advice on the bottom of the page, using the details and the ticked items on the statement shown below. The purchase order number for the invoices are PO85262 and PO85271 and for credit note PO85248. The bank details are on the advice. The date is 3 October.

# STATEMENT OF ACCOUNT
# ALDERSGATE SUPPLIES

10 Aldersgate Street, London EC1A 7GH
Tel 0207 7051017  Fax  0207 7051231  Email sales@aldersgatesupplies.co.uk
VAT REG GB 6733 8372 99

TO

Hetherington Limited
Unit 23 Wessex Estate
Langborne Road
Seatown SE8 5VZ

| account | 26742 |
| date | 30 09 20-5 |

| Date | Details | Debit £ | Credit £ | Balance £ |
|---|---|---|---|---|
| 01 09 20-5 | Balance b/f | 550.00 ✓ | | 550.00 |
| 04 09 20-5 | BACS payment | | 550.00 ✓ | 00.00 |
| 08 09 20-5 | Invoice 10945 | 120.75 ✓ | | 120.75 |
| 14 09 20-5 | Invoice 10963 | 380.25 ✓ | | 501.00 |
| 20 09 20-5 | Credit note 109 | | 46.00 ✓ | 455.00 |

Electronic payments: pay Aldersgate Supplies at
HRBC Bank, Account  79001875, Sort code 41 22 01

| TOTAL | 455.00 |

## BACS REMITTANCE ADVICE

TO

FROM:
Hetherington Limited
Unit 23 Wessex Estate
Langborne Road
Seatown SE8 5VZ

date:

| date | your reference | our reference | payment amount £ |
|---|---|---|---|
| | | | |
| | | | |

| | TOTAL | |

THIS AMOUNT HAS BEEN PAID BY BACS CREDIT TRANSFER DIRECTLY INTO YOUR BANK
ACCOUNT AT HRBC BANK ACCOUNT NO 79001875, SORT CODE 41 22 01

**8.8**   Hetherington Limited also sends out cheques with some remittance advices.

Complete the cheque remittance advice and cheque set out below. You should not sign the cheque as only a director has authority to do so. The settlement details are as follows:

Date:  5 June 20-5

Supplier: Sutherland & Co, 67 Great March Street, Eastwick, EA3 9JN

Invoice 7856 for £345.90 dated 23 May 20-5, purchase order 472984

Credit note 4562 for £87.50 dated 29 May 20-5, purchase order 472975

---

## REMITTANCE ADVICE

TO

FROM:
Hetherington Limited
Unit 23 Wessex Estate
Langborne Road
Seatown SE8 5VZ

date:

| date | your reference | our reference | payment amount £ |
|------|----------------|---------------|------------------|
|      |                |               |                  |

CHEQUE TOTAL

---

**Southern Bank PLC**
Mereford Branch
16 Broad Street, Mereford MR1 7TR

date                                            97-76-54

Pay _____

_____   only

Account payee only

£

HETHERINGTON  LTD

123456      97 76 54      68384939                    Director

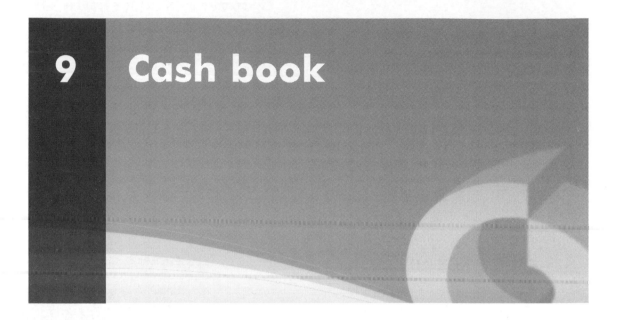

# 9 Cash book

## this chapter covers...

*Cash book records the money transactions of the business, such as receiving payments from customers, and making payments to suppliers and for other expenses. Such money transactions are received and paid either in cash, by cheque, BACS (the bank computer payment transfer system), debit or credit card, and Faster Payments.*

*In this chapter:*

- *we look at how financial transactions are recorded in a two column cash book with money columns for bank and cash*

- *we extend the money columns of the cash book to include analysis between VAT, trade receivables, trade payables, cash sales, cash purchases, income and expenses*

- *we see how cash book is written up from financial transactions, is totalled and balanced*

*The cash book of a business is usually controlled by the cashier. Entries made in cash book must be transferred to the general ledger, sales ledger and purchases ledger, for example transfers in respect of:*

- *cash sales*

- *cash purchases*

- *receipts from credit customers*

- *payments to credit suppliers*

- *other payments and receipts, eg non-current assets, expenses paid, loans received and repaid*

*There are two Case Studies in this chapter. The first is for a business that is just setting up using a two column cash book; the second is for an established business using an analysed cash book. In both Case Studies we examine how the financial transactions are transferred from cash book to the ledgers.*

# LAYOUT OF THE TWO COLUMN CASH BOOK

Although a cash book can be set out in many formats to suit the requirements of a particular business, a common format is the two column cash book – so called because it has two money columns on each side. This is set out in the same way as a double-entry account, with debit and credit sides, but with two money columns on each side, as shown below:

| Dr | | | | | Cash Book | | | | Cr |
|---|---|---|---|---|---|---|---|---|---|
| Date | Details | Account code | Cash £ | Bank £ | Date | Details | Account code | Cash £ | Bank £ |
| | | money in | | | | | money out | | |

**Note** the following points:

- this layout includes both the bank account and the cash account (used for cash kept on the business premises)
- the cash and bank columns on the debit side are used for money in, ie receipts
- the cash and bank columns on the credit side are used for money out, ie payments
- the account code column is used to code or cross-reference to the other entry in the ledger system

The Case Study which follows shows the use of the cash and bank columns of a two column cash book, and also how data is transferred from cash book into the double-entry bookkeeping system.

**Case
Study**

# CASH BOOK FOR A NEW BUSINESS

## situation

Jayne Hampson sets up a new business on 1 June 20-8. The following transactions of her business take place during the first month and are to be entered in her two column cash book:

1 June    Started in business with capital of £10,000 paid into the bank

4 June    Bought a delivery van for £7,500 paying by cheque

7 June    Paid rent for the month of £500 by cheque

12 June   Transferred £1,000 from bank to cash

18 June   Paid wages £500 in cash

20 June   Received a loan from the bank of £2,000

26 June   Jayne Hampson took drawings of £200 in cash

Note that Jayne Hampson's business is not registered for Value Added Tax.

## solution

The cash book is written up as follows.

| Dr | | | | | Cash Book | | | CB52 | | Cr |
|---|---|---|---|---|---|---|---|---|---|---|
| Date | Details | Account code | Cash £ | Bank £ | Date | Details | Account code | Cash £ | Bank £ |
| 20-8 | | | | | 20-8 | | | | |
| 1 Jun | Capital | GL3100 | | 10,000 | 4 Jun | Delivery van | GL0750 | | 7,500 |
| 12 Jun | Bank | C | 1,000 | | 7 Jun | Rent | GL6350 | | 500 |
| 20 Jun | Bank loan | GL2140 | | 2,000 | 12 Jun | Cash | C | | 1,000 |
| | | | | | 18 Jun | Wages | GL6380 | 500 | |
| | | | | | 26 Jun | Drawings | GL3200 | 200 | |
| | | | | | 30 Jun | Balances c/d | | 300 | 3,000 |
| | | | 1,000 | 12,000 | | | | 1,000 | 12,000 |
| 1 Jul | Balances b/d | | 300 | 3,000 | | | | | |

**Notes:**

- money in – eg capital introduced – has been recorded on the debit side, ie the business has gained value

- money out – eg rent and wages paid – has been recorded on the credit side, ie the business has given value

- the balance of the cash and bank columns has been calculated as the difference between money in and money out (receipts minus payments equals the balance). Balancing of accounts is usually carried out at the end of each month where the balances are *carried down (c/d)* to the first day of the next month where they are *brought down (b/d)*. We will look in more detail at balancing the cash book later in this chapter

From the completed cash book, we need to transfer the data into the double-entry system. To do this we need to:

- identify on which side of the cash book the transaction has been recorded – debit (money in), or credit (money out)
- record the other double-entry transaction on the opposite side of the appropriate account

The other accounts from this cash book can now be recorded and, over the next few pages, we will look at each transaction and see how each is recorded in the double-entry bookkeeping system. Note that the transaction on 12 June (transferred £1,000 from bank to cash) involves both a receipt and a payment within the cash book; it is usual to indicate both of them in the account code column with a 'C' – this stands for 'contra' and shows that both parts of the transaction are in the same book, ie no further accounting transactions are needed.

The page of the cash book is coded CB52 and this will be the cross-reference for the other ledger accounts.

## TRANSFERS TO THE DOUBLE-ENTRY SYSTEM

### capital

Capital is the amount of money invested in the business by the owner. A capital account records the amount paid into the business; the accounting entries are:

- debit cash book bank or cash column
- credit capital account

The capital transaction from Jayne Hampson's cash book is entered in capital account as follows:

**GENERAL LEDGER**

| Dr | | | Capital account (GL3100) | | | Cr |
|----|----|----|----|----|----|----|
| 20-8 | | £ | 20-8 | | | £ |
| | | | 1 Jun | Bank | CB52 | 10,000 |

**Note:** the introduction of capital into a business is often the very first business transaction entered into the double-entry system.

## non-current assets

**Non-current assets** are items purchased by a business for use on a long-term basis. Examples are premises, vehicles, machinery and office equipment.

When non-current assets are purchased, a separate account for each type of non-current asset is used in general ledger, eg premises account, vehicles account, machinery account, etc. The bookkeeping entries are:

– debit non-current asset account (using the appropriate account)

– credit cash book bank or cash column

The non-current asset transaction in Jayne Hampson's cash book is entered in vehicles account as follows:

**GENERAL LEDGER**

| Dr | | | | Vehicles account (GL0750) | | Cr |
|---|---|---|---|---|---|---|
| 20-8 | | | £ | 20-8 | | £ |
| 4 Jun | Bank | CB52 | 7,500 | | | |

## payments for expenses

Businesses pay various day-to-day expenses – revenue expenditure – such as rent, wages, electricity, telephone, vehicle running expenses, etc. A separate account is used in general ledger for each main class of revenue expenditure, eg rent account, wages account, etc.

The accounting entries are:

– debit expense account (using the appropriate account)

– credit cash book bank or cash column

The two expenses transactions in Jayne Hampson's cash book are entered in the expenses accounts as follows:

**GENERAL LEDGER**

| Dr | | | | Rent account (GL6350) | | Cr |
|---|---|---|---|---|---|---|
| 20-8 | | | £ | 20-8 | | £ |
| 7 Jun | Bank | CB52 | 500 | | | |

| Dr | | | | Wages account (GL6380) | | Cr |
|---|---|---|---|---|---|---|
| 20-8 | | | £ | 20-8 | | £ |
| 18 Jun | Cash | CB52 | 500 | | | |

## loans

*loan received*

When a business receives a loan, eg from the bank, it is the bank column of cash book which is debited, while a loan account (in the name of the lender) is credited:

- – debit cash book bank column
- – credit loan account (in the name of the lender)

The loan transaction from Jayne Hampson's cash book is entered in loan account as follows:

**GENERAL LEDGER**

| Dr | | | Bank loan account  (GL2140) | | Cr |
|---|---|---|---|---|---|
| 20-8 | | £ | 20-8 | | £ |
| | | | 20 Jun   Bank | CB52 | 2,000 |

*loans repaid*

A loan repayment, on the other hand (not shown in the Case Study), is recorded the opposite way round to a loan received because money is being paid from the bank to repay the lender.  Therefore loan account is debited and the bank column of cash book is credited:

- – debit loan account
- – credit cash book bank column

Note that loans are not usually received or repaid in cash, so it is the cash book bank column that records the transaction.

## drawings

Drawings is the term used when the owner takes money from the business for personal use. A drawings account is used to record such amounts; the accounting entries for withdrawal of money are:

- – debit drawings account
- – credit cash book bank or cash column

The transaction in Jayne Hampson's cash book is entered in drawings account as follows:

**GENERAL LEDGER**

| Dr | | | Drawings account  (GL3200) | Cr |
|---|---|---|---|---|
| 20-8 | | £ | 20-8 | £ |
| 26 Jun   Cash | CB52 | 200 | | |

## BALANCING THE CASH BOOK

The cash book – like the other accounts in the double-entry system – needs to be balanced in order to show the running total of the account. For cash book, the cash and bank columns are separately balanced in order to show:

- the amount of cash held by the business
- the amount of money in the bank or an overdraft

The cash book is balanced in the following way (using the cash book from the Case Study on page 202, as an example):

### cash columns

- add the two cash columns and subtotal in pencil (ie £1,000 in the debit column, and £700 in the credit column); remember to erase the subtotals afterwards
- deduct the lower total from the higher (payments from receipts) to give the balance of cash remaining (ie £1,000 – £700 = £300)
- the higher total is recorded at the bottom of both cash columns in a totals 'box' (£1,000)
- the balance of cash remaining (£300) is entered as a balancing item above the totals box (on the credit side), and is brought down underneath the total on the debit side as the opening balance for next month (£300)

### bank columns

- add the two bank columns and sub-total in pencil giving £12,000 on the debit side and £9,000 on the credit side
- deducting the lower from the higher total gives £12,000 – £9,000 = £3,000
- the bank balance of £3,000 is entered on the side with the lower sub-total – here the credit side – as balance carried down and then brought down on the debit side, below the totals line, to indicate money in the bank

Note that a cash balance can be brought down on the debit side only, indicating the amount of cash held. A bank balance can be brought down on either debit or credit side – a debit balance indicates money in the bank, while a credit balance indicates a bank overdraft.

It is very important to appreciate that the bank columns of cash book represent a business' own records of bank transactions and the balance at bank. The bank keeps its own records of the business' bank transactions – as shown by the bank statement.

## ANALYSED CASH BOOK

Many businesses use an analysed cash book to provide more information. As well as the columns for cash and bank which we have seen earlier in this chapter, an analysed cash book divides receipts and payments between a number of analysis columns, such as:

- receipts
  - cash sales
  - VAT on cash sales and other income
  - receipts from trade receivables in the sales ledger
  - other income

- payments
  - cash purchases
  - VAT on cash purchases and other expenses
  - payments to trade payables in the purchases ledger
  - other expenses

A business will use whatever analysis columns suit it best: the cash book should be adapted to meet the needs of the business in the best possible way.

**Case Study**

# ANALYSED CASH BOOK

### situation

Wyvern Auto Spares buys car parts from manufacturers, and sells to local garages and to members of the public. The business is registered for VAT.

The business uses a cash book which analyses receipts and payments as follows:

| RECEIPTS | PAYMENTS |
|---|---|
| bank | bank |
| cash | cash |
| VAT | VAT |
| cash sales | cash purchases |
| trade receivables | trade payables |
| other income | other expenses |

The following transactions are to be entered for the first week of December 20-7:

| | |
|---|---|
| 1 Dec | Balances from previous week: cash £255, bank £875 |
| 1 Dec | Sales for cash £240 + VAT |
| 1 Dec | Commission received by cheque, £40 + VAT |
| 1 Dec | A customer, Main Street Garage, settles an invoice for £195, paying by bank transfer |
| 2 Dec | Paid rent on premises £325 (no VAT) by cheque |
| 2 Dec | Sales for cash £160 + VAT |
| 2 Dec | Paid an invoice for £250 from Boxhall Supplies Ltd (a supplier) by bank transfer for £240, £10 being deducted for prompt payment discount* |
| 3 Dec | Transferred £500 of cash into the bank |
| 3 Dec | Paid for office stationery in cash, £40 + VAT |
| 3 Dec | A45 Service Station, settles an invoice for £143, paying £140 by cheque and is allowed £3 for prompt payment discount* |
| 4 Dec | Sales £320 + VAT, received half in cash, and half by cheque |
| 4 Dec | Paid for urgently needed spares in cash, £80 + VAT |
| 5 Dec | Paid an invoice for £150 from Vord Supplies (a supplier) by bank transfer |
| 5 Dec | Sales for cash £200 + VAT |
| 5 Dec | Paid wages £385 in cash |
| 5 Dec | Balanced the cash book at the end of the week |

As cashier to Wyvern Auto Spares Limited, you are to:

• write up the analysed cash book for the week commencing 1 December 20-7

• balance the cash book at 5 December 20-7

The rate of Value Added Tax is 20%. All cheques are banked on the day of receipt.

*Prompt payment discount (PPD) for the transactions on 2 December and 3 December is not recorded in cash book; instead, a credit note will be issued by the supplier to the customer (see Chapters 4 and 7).

## solution

**Dr (Receipts)**

| Date | Details | Account code | Cash | Bank | VAT | Cash sales | Trade receivables | Other income |
|---|---|---|---|---|---|---|---|---|
| 20-7 | | | £ | £ | £ | £ | £ | £ |
| 1 Dec | Balances b/d | | 255 | 875 | | | | |
| 1 Dec | Sales | GL | 288 | | 48 | 240 | | |
| 1 Dec | Commission | GL | | 48 | 8 | | | 40 |
| 1 Dec | Main Street Garage | SL | | 195 | | | 195 | |
| 2 Dec | Sales | GL | 192 | | 32 | 160 | | |
| 3 Dec | Cash | C | | 500 | | | | |
| 3 Dec | A45 Service Station | SL | | 140 | | | 140 | |
| 4 Dec | Sales | GL | 192 | 192 | 64 | 320 | | |
| 5 Dec | Sales | GL | 240 | | 10 | 200 | | |
| | | | 1,167 | 1,950 | 192 | 920 | 335 | 40 |
| 6 Dec | Balances b/d | | 138 | 1,235 | | | | |

**Cr (Payments)**

| Date | Details | Account code | Cash | Bank | VAT | Cash purchases | Trade payables | Other expenses |
|---|---|---|---|---|---|---|---|---|
| 20-7 | | | £ | £ | £ | £ | £ | £ |
| 2 Dec | Rent | GL | | 325 | | | | 325 |
| 2 Dec | Boxhall Supplies Ltd | PL | | 240 | | | 240 | |
| 3 Dec | Bank | C | 500 | | | | | |
| 3 Dec | Office stationery | GL | 48 | | 8 | | | 40 |
| 4 Dec | Purchases | GL | 96 | | 16 | 80 | | |
| 5 Dec | Vord Supplies | PL | | 150 | | | 150 | |
| 5 Dec | Wages | GL | 385 | | | | | 385 |
| 5 Dec | Balances c/d | | 138 | 1,235 | | | | |
| | | | 1,167 | 1,950 | 24 | 80 | 390 | 750 |

**Note the following points:**

• the analysed cash book analyses each receipt and payment between a number of headings. A business will adapt the cash book and use whatever analysis columns suit it best

• for transactions involving receipts from trade receivables and payments to trade payables, no amount for VAT is shown in the VAT columns. This is because VAT has been charged on invoices issued and received and was recorded in the VAT account (via the day books) when the sale or purchase was made

• the cash and bank columns are balanced as described earlier (page 206)

• the column for account codes indicates the ledger section for completing double-entry. The transaction on 3 December of the transfer of cash to bank is coded 'C' and is shown on both sides of the cash book – no further entries need to be made

# LEDGER TRANSFERS FROM THE ANALYSED CASH BOOK

Set out over the next few pages are the entries from the analysed cash book in the Case Study of Wyvern Auto Spares as they are transferred to the double-entry system. These transfers are for:

- VAT
- cash sales
- cash purchases
- receipts from trade receivables
- payments to trade payables
- other income
- other expenses

The entries for general ledger, sales ledger and purchases ledger are as follows (note that these transfers are described in more detail earlier in this chapter):

| Dr | | **Sales ledger control account** | | Cr |
|---|---|---|---|---|
| 20-7 | £ | 20-7 | | £ |
| | | 5 Dec Cash Book | | *335 |

| Dr | | **Purchases ledger control account** | | Cr |
|---|---|---|---|---|
| 20-7 | £ | 20-7 | | £ |
| 5 Dec Cash Book | *390 | | | |

**\*Note** how only the total of the analysis column for trade receivables and trade payables from the cash book is entered in the appropriate control account.

| Dr | | **Sales account** | | Cr |
|---|---|---|---|---|
| 20-7 | £ | 20-7 | | £ |
| | | 5 Dec Cash Book | | **920 |

| Dr | | **Purchases account** | | Cr |
|---|---|---|---|---|
| 20-7 | £ | 20-7 | | £ |
| 5 Dec Cash Book | **80 | | | |

\*\*Total of the analysis column from the analysed cash book

| Dr | | | **Value added tax account** | | Cr |
|---|---|---|---|---|---|
| 20-7 | | £ | 20-7 | | £ |
| 5 Dec | Cash Book | ***24 | 5 Dec  Cash Book | | ***192 |

*** Total of the analysis column from the analysed cash book.

| Dr | | | **Commission received account** | | Cr |
|---|---|---|---|---|---|
| 20-7 | | £ | 20-7 | | £ |
| | | | 1 Dec  Bank | | 40 |

| Dr | | | **Rent paid account** | | Cr |
|---|---|---|---|---|---|
| 20-7 | | £ | 20-7 | | £ |
| 2 Dec | Bank | 325 | | | |

| Dr | | | **Office stationery account** | | Cr |
|---|---|---|---|---|---|
| 20-7 | | £ | 20-7 | | £ |
| 3 Dec | Cash | 40 | | | |

| Dr | | | **Wages account** | | Cr |
|---|---|---|---|---|---|
| 20-7 | | £ | 20-7 | | £ |
| 5 Dec | Cash | 385 | | | |

Note that, in the above accounts, the term 'Cash Book' is used as the cross-reference when the total of an analysis column is recorded. This is because transactions will often be a mix of cash and bank items. Where the receipt or payment can be identified to 'Cash' of 'Bank' – as with the income and expenses here – then the cross-reference is to the appropriate word.

### SALES LEDGER

| Dr | | | **Main Street Garage** | | Cr |
|---|---|---|---|---|---|
| 20-7 | | £ | 20-7 | | £ |
| | | | 1 Dec  Bank | | 195 |

| Dr | | | **A45 Service Station** | | Cr |
|---|---|---|---|---|---|
| 20-7 | | £ | 20-7 | | £ |
| | | | 3 Dec  Bank | | 140 |

**PURCHASES LEDGER**

| Dr | **Boxhall Supplies Ltd** | | Cr |
|---|---|---|---|
| 20-7 | £ | 20-7 | £ |
| 2 Dec   Bank | 240 | | |

| Dr | **Vord Supplies** | | Cr |
|---|---|---|---|
| 20-7 | £ | 20-7 | £ |
| 5 Dec   Bank | 150 | | |

Note that the transactions recorded in sales ledger and purchases ledger are – as totals – recorded in sales ledger control account and purchases ledger control account.

## HOW THE CASH BOOK FITS INTO THE ACCOUNTING SYSTEM

We have looked at a number of bank and cash receipts and payments which are recorded firstly in the cash book and secondly in the ledger system of the general ledger, sales ledger and purchases ledger. As the cash book is the first place in the accounting system to record bank transactions, it is the **book of prime entry** for bank and cash receipts and payments.

There are two ways in which the cash book can fit into the accounting system:

■ as well as being a book of prime entry the cash book can perform the function of being a double-entry account, ie a debit entry made in cash book is recorded on the credit side of another double-entry account

■ the cash book is treated solely as a book of prime entry, in which case separate double-entry accounts – called **cash account** and **bank account** – are used in the general ledger

The diagram on the next page shows how the cash book performs the functions of a book of prime entry and a double-entry account. The diagram shows the flow involving:

■ financial documents – primary records for bank receipts and payments

■ the cash book as a book of prime entry

■ double-entry bookkeeping, involving the cash book and other ledgers

In accounting systems where the cash book is used as a book of prime entry only, separate accounts for cash and bank are used in the general ledger. These are shown on page 214.

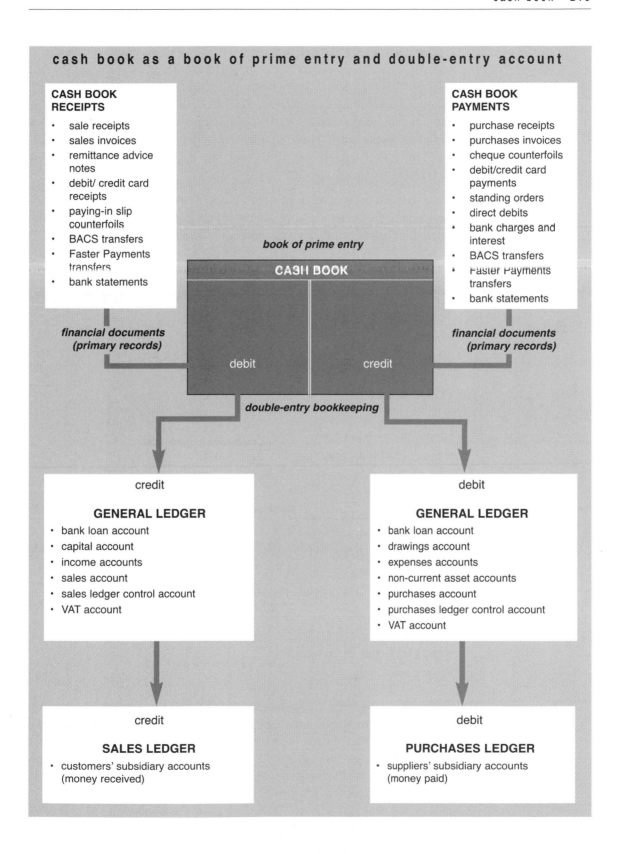

# cash book as a book of prime entry and double-entry account

**CASH BOOK RECEIPTS**

- sale receipts
- sales invoices
- remittance advice notes
- debit/ credit card receipts
- paying-in slip counterfoils
- BACS transfers
- Faster Payments transfers
- bank statements

**CASH BOOK PAYMENTS**

- purchase receipts
- purchases invoices
- cheque counterfoils
- debit/credit card payments
- standing orders
- direct debits
- bank charges and interest
- BACS transfers
- Faster Payments transfers
- bank statements

*book of prime entry*

**CASH BOOK**

debit | credit

*financial documents (primary records)*

*financial documents (primary records)*

*double-entry bookkeeping*

credit

**GENERAL LEDGER**

- bank loan account
- capital account
- income accounts
- sales account
- sales ledger control account
- VAT account

debit

**GENERAL LEDGER**

- bank loan account
- drawings account
- expenses accounts
- non-current asset accounts
- purchases account
- purchases ledger control account
- VAT account

credit

**SALES LEDGER**

- customers' subsidiary accounts (money received)

debit

**PURCHASES LEDGER**

- suppliers' subsidiary accounts (money paid)

## CASH AND BANK ACCOUNT

Where an accounting system treats the cash book solely as a book of prime entry, a cash account and a bank account are used in the general ledger to complete double-entry. These accounts show the total receipts and payments made in cash or through the bank during the period, together with opening and closing balances.

From the cash book of Wyvern Auto Spares, in the Case Study on page 207, the totals of the receipts and payments from the cash and bank columns are entered in cash account and bank account as shown below.

### GENERAL LEDGER

| Dr | | | Cash account | | Cr |
|---|---|---|---|---|---|
| 20-7 | | £ | 20-7 | | £ |
| 1 Dec | Balance b/d | 255 | 5 Dec | Cash Book | **1,029 |
| 5 Dec | Cash Book | *912 | 5 Dec | Balance c/d | 138 |
| | | 1,167 | | | 1,167 |
| 6 Dec | Balance b/d | 138 | | | |

\* £288 + £192 + £192 + £240        see cash book on page 209

\*\* £500 + £48 + £96 + £385

| Dr | | | Bank account | | Cr |
|---|---|---|---|---|---|
| 20-7 | | £ | 20-7 | | £ |
| 1 Dec | Balance b/d | 875 | 5 Dec | Cash Book | **715 |
| 5 Dec | Cash Book | *1,075 | 5 Dec | Balance c/d | 1,235 |
| | | 1,950 | | | 1,950 |
| 6 Dec | Balance b/d | 1,235 | | | |

\*£48 + £195 + £500 + £140 + £192        see cash book on page 209

\*\*£325 + £240 + £150

Note that the amounts shown as Cash Book on the debit sides of the two control accounts are the total receipts from the cash book, excluding balances brought down (and, if applicable, carried down). Likewise, the amounts shown on the credit sides are the total payments from the cash book, excluding balances brought down (if applicable) and carried down.

## CHECKING THE CASH BOOK

As the cash book forms such an integral part of a business double-entry system, it is essential that transactions are recorded accurately and that balances are calculated correctly at regular intervals, eg weekly or monthly – depending on the needs of the business. How can the cash book be checked for accuracy?

### cash columns

To check the cash columns is easy. It is simply a matter of counting the cash in the cash till, cash box, or safe, and agreeing it with the balance shown by the cash book. In the example from the cash book of Wyvern Auto Spares, in the Case Study on page 207, there should be £138 in the cash till at 6 December 20-7. If the cash cannot be agreed in this way, the discrepancy needs to be investigated urgently.

### bank columns

How are these to be checked? We could, perhaps, enquire at the bank and ask for the balance at the month-end, or we could arrange for a bank statement to be sent to us, or we could use internet banking to print off a statement. However, the balance of the account at the bank may well not agree with that shown by the bank columns of the cash book. There are several reasons why there may be a difference: for example, a cheque that has been written out recently to pay a bill may not yet have been recorded on the bank statement, ie it has been entered in the cash book, but is not yet on the bank statement. To agree the bank statement and the bank columns of the cash book, it is usually necessary to prepare a bank reconciliation statement, and this topic is dealt with fully in Chapter 3 of *Bookkeeping Controls Tutorial*.

**Chapter Summary**

■ The cash book records the money transactions of the business in the form of cash and bank receipts and payments.

■ Receipts are recorded on the debit side; payments are recorded on the credit side.

■ A common form of cash book is the two column cash book with columns for cash and bank.

■  Transactions recorded in the cash book include:

- cash sales
- cash purchases
- receipts from credit customers
- payments to credit suppliers
- other payments and receipts, eg non-current assets, expenses paid,
  loans received and repaid

■  An analysed cash book provides more information and divides receipts and
payments between a number of columns.

■  Analysis columns for receipts include:
- cash sales
- VAT on cash sales and other income
- receipts from trade receivables
- other income

■  Analysis columns for payments include:
- cash purchases
- VAT on cash purchases and other expenses
- payments to trade payables
- other expenses

■  In the accounting system cash book can combine the roles of:
- the book of prime entry for bank and cash receipts and payments
- the double-entry account for cash and bank

■  When the cash book is used solely as the book of prime entry, a cash
account and a bank account are used in general ledger to complete double-
entry bookkeeping.

| Key Terms | | |
|---|---|---|
| **cash book** | | records cash and bank receipts and payments; can combine the roles of the book of prime entry for bank receipts and payments and the double-entry account for cash and bank, or can be a book of prime entry only |
| **two column cash book** | | cash book with columns for cash and bank |

| | |
|---|---|
| **capital** | the amount of money invested in the business by the owner |
| **non-current assets** | items purchased by a business for use on a long-term basis |
| **drawings** | when the owner takes money from the business for personal use |
| **cash sales** | where a customer buys goods or services and pays in full immediately |
| **cash purchases** | where a business buys goods or services from a supplier and pays in full immediately |
| **analysed cash book** | a cash book which divides receipts and payments between a number of columns |
| **receipts analysis columns** | for example:<br>– cash sales<br>– VAT on cash sales and other income<br>– receipts from trade receivables<br>– other income |
| **payments columns** | for example:<br>– cash purchases<br>– VAT on cash purchases and other expenses<br>– payments to trade payables<br>– other expenses |
| **cash account and bank account** | double-entry accounts in the general ledger used when the cash book is treated solely as the book of prime entry; they show the total receipts and payments made in cash or through the bank during the period, together with the opening and closing balances |

# Activities

**9.1** The cash book is:

| | | |
|---|---|---|
| (a) | A financial document | |
| (b) | The account kept by the bank of its customer's bank receipts and payments | |
| (c) | A part of double-entry bookkeeping only | |
| (d) | The book of prime entry for bank receipts and payments | |

Which **one** of these options is correct?

**9.2** The following cash book shows a number of transactions of a new business set up by Hannah Wyrembak on 30 April 20-7:

| Dr | | | | | Cash Book | | CB70 | | Cr |
|---|---|---|---|---|---|---|---|---|---|
| Date | Details | Account Code | Cash | Bank | Date | Details | Account Code | Cash | Bank |
| 20-7 | | | £ | £ | 20-7 | | | £ | £ |
| 30 Apr | Capital | | 2,000 | 8,000 | 30 Apr | Rent | | | 1,000 |
| 30 Apr | Loan from bank | | | 5,000 | 30 Apr | Wages | | 800 | |
| | | | | | 30 Apr | Drawings | | | 500 |
| | | | | | 30 Apr | Vehicle | | | 10,000 |
| | | | | | 30 Apr | Balances c/d | | 1,200 | 1,500 |
| | | | 2,000 | 13,000 | | | | 2,000 | 13,000 |
| 1 May | Balances b/d | | 1,200 | 1,500 | | | | | |

Note that Hannah Wyrembak's business is not registered for Value Added Tax.

**You are to** transfer the data from the cash book into the double-entry system of Hannah Wyrembak.

**Note:** full account codes are not required.

**9.3** The following cash book shows a number of transactions of Teme Traders which all took place on 30 April 20-5:

| Dr | | | | | | | | Cash Book | | CB32 | | Cr |
|---|---|---|---|---|---|---|---|---|---|---|---|---|
| Date | Details | Account code | Cash | Bank | | Date | Details | | Account code | Cash | Bank |
| 20-5 | | | £ | £ | | 20-5 | | | | £ | £ |
| 30 Apr | Balances b/d | | 275 | 2,080 | | 30 Apr | Mereford Mills | | | | |
| 30 Apr | Cash sales | | 40 | | | | (trade payable) | | | | 3,200 |
| 30 Apr | Commission | | | | | 30 Apr | Cash purchases | | | | 96 |
| | received | | | 48 | | 30 Apr | Office equipment | | | | 2,600 |
| 30 Apr | Lindum Ltd | | | | | 30 Apr | Wages | | | | 1,550 |
| | (trade receivable) | | | 2,400 | | 30 Apr | General expenses | | | 80 | |
| 30 Apr | Loan from bank | | | 2,000 | | 30 Apr | Balance c/d | | | 235 | |
| 30 Apr | Balance c/d | | | 918 | | | | | | | |
| | | | 315 | 7,446 | | | | | | 315 | 7,446 |
| 1 May | Balance b/d | | 235 | | | 1 May | Balance b/d | | | | 918 |

Note that Teme Traders' business is not registered for Value Added Tax.

**(a)** The balance brought down of £2,080 on 30 April shows that, according to the cash book, the business has money in the bank. True or false?

**(b)** The balance brought down of £918 on 1 May shows that, according to the cash book, the business has money in the bank. True or false?

**(c)** You are to transfer the data from the cash book into the general ledger of Teme Traders.

**(d)** Show the entries in the sales ledger and purchases ledger of Teme Traders.
**Note:** full account codes are not required.

**9.4** Which **one** of the following transactions will not be recorded on the payments side of cash book?

| | | |
|---|---|---|
| (a) | Purchase of a vehicle for £10,000 paid for by cheque | |
| (b) | Cash purchase for £150 | |
| (c) | Bank transfer from a trade receivable for £1,350 | |
| (d) | BACS transfer to a supplier for £2,200 | |

**9.5** Which **one** of the following transactions will not be recorded on the receipts side of cash book?

| | | |
|---|---|---|
| (a) | Cheque to a trade payable for £870 | |
| (b) | Bank transfer from a trade receivable for £3,250 | |
| (c) | Debit card payment by a customer for £580 | |
| (d) | Cash sales of £195 | |

**9.6** Indicate whether the following statements are true or false by putting a tick in the relevant column of the table below.

| | True | False |
|---|---|---|
| **(a)** Cash book is the book of prime entry for bank and cash receipts and payments | | |
| **(b)** Cash book can be the double-entry account for bank and cash | | |
| **(c)** The VAT column total on the receipts side of an analysed cash book is debited to VAT account in general ledger | | |
| **(d)** The trade receivables column total from an analysed cash book is credited to sales ledger control account in general ledger | | |

**9.7** David Lewis runs a shop selling carpets to the public on cash terms and to trade customers on credit terms. He buys his carpets direct from manufacturers, who allow him credit terms.

David Lewis' business is registered for VAT. The VAT rate is 20%. He uses an analysed cash book, which is a book of prime entry and a double-entry account.

The following transactions take place during the week commencing 12 May 20-7 (all cheques are banked on the day of receipt):

| | |
|---|---|
| 12 May | Debit balances from previous week: cash £205, bank £825 |
| 12 May | Cash sales £600 (including VAT), cheque received |
| 12 May | Paid shop rent by bank transfer £255 (no VAT) |
| 13 May | Cash sales £180 (including VAT), cash received |
| 13 May | A trade receivable, T Jarvis, settles an invoice for £155 by bank transfer |
| 13 May | Paid an invoice for £363 from Terry Carpets (a trade payable) by cheque |
| 14 May | Cash sales £720 (including VAT), cheque received |
| 14 May | Paid an invoice for £145 from Trade Supplies (a trade payable), paying by cheque |
| 14 May | Purchases paid for in cash, £36 (including VAT) |
| 15 May | Transferred £250 of cash into the bank |
| 15 May | Cash sales £288 (including VAT), cash received |
| 15 May | Paid an invoice for £291 from Longlife Carpets (a trade payable), by bank transfer |
| 16 May | Cash purchases of £240 (including VAT) paid by BACS |
| 16 May | A trade receivable, Wyvern Council, settles an invoice for £560, paying by BACS |

**You are to:**

**(a)** Enter the transactions from the previous page in the analysed cash book of David Lewis shown below.

**(b)** Balance the cash book at 16 May 20-7, bringing down the balances at 17 May 20-7.

**(c)** Show the cash book transactions in the following accounts:

| sales ledger | – | T Jarvis |
| | – | Wyvern Council |
| purchases ledger | – | Terry Carpets |
| | – | Trade Supplies |
| | – | Longlife Carpets |

**Note:** full account codes are not required.

**Dr (Receipts)**

| Date | Details | Account code | Cash £ | Bank £ | VAT £ | Cash sales £ | Trade receivables £ | Other income £ |
|------|---------|--------------|--------|--------|-------|--------------|---------------------|----------------|
|      |         |              |        |        |       |              |                     |                |

**Cr (Payments)**

| Date | Details | Account code | Cash £ | Bank £ | VAT £ | Cash purchases £ | Trade payables £ | Other expenses £ |
|------|---------|--------------|--------|--------|-------|------------------|------------------|------------------|
|      |         |              |        |        |       |                  |                  |                  |

**9.8** You are an accounts assistant at Trafalgar Limited. One of your duties is to write-up the cash book. There are five payments to be entered in Trafalgar Limited's cash book.

**Receipts for cash payments**

| Received cash with thanks for goods bought. | Received cash with thanks for goods bought. |
|---|---|
| From Trafalgar Ltd, a customer without a credit account. | From Trafalgar Ltd, a customer without a credit account. |
| Net        £25 | Net        £80 |
| VAT        £5 | VAT        £16 |
| Total      £30 | Total      £96 |
| *Knowles & Co* | *S Goulding* |

**Bank payments**

| Liyan Ltd | Nelson Street Garage | Sandhu & Co |
|---|---|---|
| (Purchases ledger account PL320) | (No credit account with this supplier) | (Purchases ledger account PL540) |
| £920 | £132 including VAT | £645 |

**(a)** Enter the details from the two receipts for cash payments and the three bank payments into the credit side of the cash book shown below and total each column.

**Cash book – credit side**

| Details | Cash £ | Bank £ | VAT £ | Trade payables £ | Cash purchases £ | Vehicle expenses £ |
|---|---|---|---|---|---|---|
| Balance b/f | | | | | | |
| Knowles & Co | | | | | | |
| S Goulding | | | | | | |
| Liyan Ltd | | | | | | |
| Nelson Street Garage | | | | | | |
| Sandhu & Co | | | | | | |
| **Totals** | | | | | | |

There are three amounts received to be entered in Trafalgar Limited's cash book.

Cheques received from credit customers:

Watkin Ltd   £429

P Pandya   £1,522

Cash received:

£235 received from Matt Martin for rent of parking spaces (No VAT)

**(b)**   Enter the above details into the debit side of the cash book and total each column.

Cash book – debit side

| Details | Cash £ | Bank £ | Trade receivables £ | Other income £ |
|---|---|---|---|---|
| Balance b/f | 254 | 1,598 | | |
| Watkin Ltd | | | | |
| P Pandya | | | | |
| Matt Martin | | | | |
| Totals | | | | |

**(c)**   Using your answers to (a) and (b) above, calculate the cash balance.

£ [              ]

**(d)**   Using your answers to (a) and (b) above, calculate the bank balance.

£ [              ]

**(e)**   Will the bank balance calculated in (d) above be a debit or credit balance?

| Debit | |
|---|---|
| Credit | |

# 10 Petty cash book

## this chapter covers...

In this chapter we look at the petty cash book, which is used to record low-value cash payments for small purchases and expenses incurred by a business. Examples of these payments include the purchase of office stationery items, and the payment of travel expenses.

The way that the petty cash book works is that an amount of cash is handed by the cashier to a member of staff, the petty cashier, who:

■ is responsible for security of the petty cash money

■ makes cash payments against authorised petty cash vouchers

■ records the payments made, and analyses them, in a petty cash book

■ reconciles the petty cash book with the amount of cash held

We look at the layout of the petty cash book, with columns for expenses and see how it is written up by the petty cashier from authorised petty cash vouchers.

We see how a petty cash book is balanced and how the petty cashier claims reimbursement from the cashier of amounts of money paid out.

Towards the end of the chapter we will see how a petty cash book fits into the accounting system as the book of prime entry for low-value cash payments and as part of the double-entry system.

## THE PETTY CASH BOOK IN THE ACCOUNTING SYSTEM

The petty cash book is used to record low-value cash payments for purchases and expenses – such as small items of stationery, postages, etc. Items like these are not appropriate to enter in the cash book because they would 'clutter' it up with lots of small amounts. Instead a member of staff is given the responsibility of being the petty cashier.

Petty cash book is the book of prime entry for low-value cash payments.

## USES OF THE PETTY CASH BOOK

The petty cash book records the low-value cash payments for purchases and expenses of the business, such as:

– stationery items
– small items of office supplies
– casual wages
– window cleaning
– bus, rail and taxi fares incurred on behalf of the business
– meals and drinks incurred on behalf of the business
– post office (for postages)
– tips and donations

Petty cash payments are usually for amounts up to a maximum value, for example, up to £25 for any one expense item. The petty cashier of a business will be told the maximum amount that can be paid out on any one voucher.

As well as payments there may, from time-to-time, be small receipts of cash to be recorded. For example, if a member of staff purchases items such as postage stamps or stationery, they will pay the petty cashier who issues a receipt to record the details and the amount of money received.

The petty cash book is the responsibility of the petty cashier who:

■ receives an amount of money (known as the petty cash float) from the cashier to be used for petty cash payments
■ is responsible for security of the petty cash money
■ makes cash payments against authorised petty cash vouchers
■ records the payments made, and analyses them to expenses columns in a petty cash book
■ receives and records any small amounts of income, eg postage stamps sold to staff for their private use

- balances the petty cash book at regular intervals, usually weekly or monthly
- tops up the petty cash float by claiming reimbursement from the cashier of amounts paid out
- passes the completed petty cash book to the bookkeeper so that data can be transferred into the ledger system

## THE IMPREST SYSTEM

Petty cash books usually operate using the **imprest system**. With this system, the petty cashier starts each week (or month) with a certain amount of money – the imprest amount. As payments are made during the week (or month) the amount of money will reduce and, at the end of the period, the cash will be made up by a payment from bank account to restore the imprest amount. For example:

| | |
|---|---|
| Started week with imprest amount | £100.00 |
| Total of petty cash amounts paid out during week | £80.00 |
| Cash held at end of week | £20.00 |
| Amount drawn from bank to restore imprest amount | £80.00 |
| Cash at start of next week, ie imprest amount | £100.00 |

If, at any time, the imprest amount proves to be insufficient, further amounts of cash can be drawn from the cashier. Also, from time-to-time, it may be necessary to increase the imprest amount so that regular shortfalls of petty cash are avoided.

In contrast, the **non-imprest system** is where the petty cash supply is not topped up to the same value each time.

## PETTY CASH VOUCHERS – PURPOSE AND CONTENT

The purpose of petty cash vouchers is to enable payments to be made out of petty cash. They are the financial documents used by the petty cashier to write up the petty cash book.

Petty cash vouchers contain the following:

- the date, details and amount of expenditure
- the signature of the person making the claim and receiving the money
- the signature of the person authorising the payment, normally the petty cashier, or a manager if the amount is higher than the authorisation limit

- additionally, most petty cash vouchers are numbered, so that they can be controlled
- with the relevant documentation, such as a receipt from a shop or post office etc, attached to the petty cash voucher

An example petty cash voucher is as follows:

| petty cash voucher | | Number *47* |
|---|---|---|
| | date | *5 April 20-4* |

| description | | amount | |
|---|---|---|---|
| | | £ | p |
| *Photocopier paper* | | *3* | *20* |
| *VAT at 20%* | | *0* | *64* |
| *Total* | | *3* | *84* |

signature  *T Harris*

authorised  *R Singh*

## LAYOUT OF THE PETTY CASH BOOK

Petty cash book is usually set out as follows:

**Petty cash book**

| Date 20-4 | Details | Amount £ | Date 20-4 | Details | Amount £ | VAT £ | Motor expenses £ | Office expenses £ |
|---|---|---|---|---|---|---|---|---|
| | money in: debit side | | | | money out: credit side | | | |

The layout shows that:

- there are columns showing the date and details of all receipts and payments

- receipts are shown in the debit column on the left
- the amount column on the credit side records the amount paid out on each petty cash voucher
- then follow columns which analyse by expense each transaction entered in the amount column

A business will use whatever expenses columns are most suitable for it and, indeed, there may be more columns than shown in the example. It is important that expenses are recorded in the correct columns so that petty cash book shows a true picture of petty cash expenditure.

## PETTY CASH AND VAT

Value Added Tax is charged by VAT-registered businesses on their taxable supplies. Therefore, there will often be VAT included as part of the expense paid out of petty cash. Often the indication of the supplier's VAT registration number on a receipt or invoice will tell you that VAT has been charged on the items purchased.

Where VAT has been charged, the amount of tax might be indicated separately on the receipt or invoice. However, for small money amounts it is quite usual for a total to be shown without indicating the amount of VAT. An example of a receipt which does not show the VAT content is illustrated below. The receipt is for a box of envelopes purchased from Wyvern Stationers. It shows:

- the name and address of the retailer

- the date and time of the transaction

- the VAT registration number of the retailer

- the price of the item, £4.80

- the amount of money given, a £10 note

- the amount of change given, £5.20

| Wyvern Stationers |
| 25 High St Mereford |
| 08 10 -4   16.07 |
| VAT Reg 454 7106 34 |

| Salesperson Rashid | |
| Stationery | 4.80 |
| | |
| TOTAL | 4.80 |
| CASH | 10.00 |
| CHANGE | 5.20 |

What the receipt does not show, however, is the VAT content of the purchase price – it only shows the price after the VAT has been added on.

How do we calculate the purchase price before the VAT is added on?

The formula is:

$$\frac{amount\ paid\ x\ 100}{100 + VAT\ rate} = price\ before\ VAT\ is\ added\ on$$

If we assume that the VAT rate is 20%, the calculation is:

$$\frac{£4.80 \times 100}{100 + 20} \quad = \quad \frac{£480}{120} \quad = \quad £4.00$$

The VAT content is therefore:

$$£4.80 \text{ minus } £4.00 = 80p$$

In this case £0.80 will be entered in the VAT column in the petty cash book, £4.00 in the appropriate expense column, and the full £4.80 in the total amount column.

Remember when calculating VAT amounts that fractions of a penny are ignored, ie the tax is rounded down to a whole penny.

---

## Case Study

# PETTY CASH BOOK

This Case Study shows how a petty cash book is written up by the petty cashier from authorised petty cash vouchers. The petty cash float is reimbursed at the end of the week and the petty cash book is balanced. Voucher numbers have been recorded in the details column – note that in AAT Assessments voucher numbers may not need to be shown.

### situation

You work in the accounts office of Wyvern Traders. One of your tasks is to keep the petty cash book, which is operated using the imprest system. There are a number of transactions which have been authorised (all transactions, unless otherwise indicated, include VAT at 20%) to be entered for the week in the petty cash book (PCB30):

20-4

| | |
|---|---|
| 5 Apr | Started the week with an imprest amount of £100.00 |
| 5 Apr | Envelopes £3.84 on voucher no 47 |
| 5 Apr | Taxi fare £5.76 on voucher no 48 |
| 6 Apr | Received £10 in cash from Jo Lee for postage stamps purchased (receipt no 122 issued) |
| 6 Apr | Post office £2.75 (no VAT) on voucher no 49 |
| 7 Apr | Taxi fare £9.60 on voucher no 50 |
| 7 Apr | Paid J Jones, a trade payable (PL054), £15.00 (no VAT shown in petty cash book – amount will be on VAT account already) on voucher no 51 |
| 8 Apr | Marker pens £7.20 on voucher no 52 |
| 8 Apr | Post office £5.85 (no VAT) on voucher no 53 |
| 9 Apr | Taxi fare £12.00 on voucher no 54 |

The petty cash book is to be balanced on 9 April with reimbursement of the imprest amount from cash book (CB55). The balance is to be brought down on 10 April.

### solution

The following petty cash book is written up by the petty cashier of Wyvern Traders for the week ended 9 April 20-4 as follows:

| Petty Cash Book | | | | | | | | | | | PCB30 |

| Date 20-4 | Details | Amount £ | Date 20-4 | Details | | Amount £ | VAT £ | Postages £ | Stationery £ | Travel £ | Ledger £ |
|---|---|---|---|---|---|---|---|---|---|---|---|
| 5 Apr | Balance b/d | 100.00 | | | | | | | | | |
| | | | 5 Apr | Envelopes | 47 | 3.84 | 0.64 | | 3.20 | | |
| | | | 5 Apr | Taxi fare | 48 | 5.76 | 0.96 | | | 4.80 | |
| 6 Apr | J Lee 122 (postages) | 10.00 | | | | | | | | | |
| | | | 6 Apr | Post office | 49 | 2.75 | | 2.75 | | | |
| | | | 7 Apr | Taxi fare | 50 | 9.60 | 1.60 | | | 8.00 | |
| | | | 7 Apr | J Jones (PL054) | | 15.00 | | | | | 15.00 |
| | | | 8 Apr | Marker pens | 52 | 7.20 | 1.20 | | 6.00 | | |
| | | | 8 Apr | Post office | 53 | 5.85 | | 5.85 | | | |
| | | | 9 Apr | Taxi fare | 54 | 12.00 | 2.00 | | | 10.00 | |
| | | | | | | 62.00 | 6.40 | 8.60 | 9.20 | 22.80 | 15.00 |
| | | | | | | | GL2200 | GL6330 | GL6360 | GL6370 | GL2350 |
| 9 Apr | Bank CB55 | 52.00 | | | | | | | | | |
| | | | 9 Apr | Balance c/d | | 100.00 | | | | | |
| | | 162.00 | | | | 162.00 | | | | | |
| 10 Apr | Balance b/d | 100.00 | | | | | | | | | |

**Notes:**

- this petty cash book has been written up for the week. It is for a business to decide how often petty cash book is to be totalled and balanced – generally, though, this will be done either weekly or monthly

- this cash book starts each new week with a cash float of £100 – this is the imprest amount. The amount of the float at the start is for the business to decide based on the level of expenses regularly paid out in petty cash – £100 may be sufficient, but larger floats may be needed. In any case, if the petty cashier runs out of cash during the week or month, a top-up can be made from cash book

• the expenses columns are for a business to decide what is suitable for their circumstances. The ledger column is used for payments from petty cash to trade payables who have accounts in purchases ledger – these suppliers are more usually paid through the bank but, if the amount is small, they may be paid in cash from petty cash

We will now see in the main text below how the data is transferred into the double-entry bookkeeping system.

Note that the page of the petty cash book is coded PCB30 and this will be the cross-reference for the other ledger accounts.

## BALANCES

### 5 Apr  Balance b/d

The week commences with a petty cash book float of £100, described as 'balance b/d', ie brought down from the previous page of the petty cash book. (Note that this may also be written as 'balance b/f', ie brought forward from the previous page.) The imprest amount for this petty cash book is £100.

### 9 Apr  Balance c/d

The petty cashier has claimed reimbursement from the cashier of £52.00, ie petty cash paid out £62.00 less £10 received from Jo Lee for postage stamps. This restores the cash float to £100 which is now recorded as the balance c/d on the credit (payments) side. The receipts and payments columns are then both totalled to £162.00.

### 10 Apr  Balance b/d

To complete double-entry bookkeeping the balance of £100 is brought down on the debit side. Note that, here, the date used in the day following the balance carried down – this shows that the cash float of £100 is ready for the next week's transactions.

## TRANSFERRING THE EXPENSES COLUMNS

In order to complete double-entry the total of each of the expenses columns is transferred into the double-entry bookkeeping system:

■ payment of an expense
  – debit expense account (using the appropriate account)
■ payment to a supplier (from the 'ledger' column)
  – debit purchases ledger control account (in general ledger)
  – debit the trade payables' subsidiary account (in purchases ledger)

From the Case Study the general ledger accounts will be written up as follows at the end of the week (9 April):

## GENERAL LEDGER

| Dr | Value added tax account (GL2200) | | Cr | |
|---|---|---|---|---|
| 20-4 | | £ | 20-4 | £ |
| 9 Apr | Petty cash book PCB30 | 6.40 | | |

| Dr | Postages account (GL6000) | | Cr | |
|---|---|---|---|---|
| 20-4 | | £ | 20-4 | £ |
| 9 Apr | Petty cash book PCB30 | 8.60 | 6 Apr  Petty cash book PCB30 | *10.00 |

*cash received by the petty cashier from Jo Lee for postage stamps purchased

| Dr | Stationery account (GL6360) | | Cr | |
|---|---|---|---|---|
| 20-4 | | £ | 20-4 | £ |
| 9 Apr | Petty cash book PCB30 | 9.20 | | |

| Dr | Travel expenses account (GL6370) | | Cr | |
|---|---|---|---|---|
| 20-4 | | £ | 20-4 | £ |
| 9 Apr | Petty cash book PCB30 | 22.80 | | |

| Dr | Purchases ledger control account (GL2350) | | Cr | |
|---|---|---|---|---|
| 20-4 | | £ | 20-4 | £ |
| 9 Apr | Petty cash book PCB30 | 15.00 | | |

The above £15 payment ledger transaction will also be debited to the account of the trade payable – here J Jones – in the purchases ledger, as follows:

## PURCHASES LEDGER

| Dr | J Jones (PL054) | | Cr | |
|---|---|---|---|---|
| 20-4 | | £ | 20-4 | £ |
| 7 Apr | Petty cash book PCB30 | 15.00 | | |

## RESTORING THE CASH FLOAT

To restore the petty cash float to the imprest amount, the petty cashier completes a requisition form for a cash withdrawal from the bank. An example of a requisition is shown below:

**CASH REQUISITION**

| | |
|---|---|
| Amount | £52.00 |
| Date | 9 April 20-4 |
| Details | Reimbursement of petty cash |
| Signature | Jane Watkins, petty cashier |
| Authorised by | Natalie Wilson, supervisor |

*requisition form*

The double-entry bookkeeping entries to record this reimbursement are:
- *debit* petty cash book
- *credit* cash book, ie the payments side

The amount of £52.00 cash paid from the bank to the petty cashier is recorded in the cash book as follows:

| Dr | | | | | | Cash Book | | CB55 | | Cr |
|---|---|---|---|---|---|---|---|---|---|---|
| Date 20-4 | Details | Account code | Cash £ | Bank £ | Date 20-4 | Details | Account code | Cash £ | Bank £ |
| | | | | | 9 Apr | Petty cash | PCB30 | | 52.00 |

After this reimbursement, the petty cash float is restored and the petty cash book has a balance brought down of £100.00 on 9 April. The petty cash book is now ready for next week's transactions.

## CONTROL OF PETTY CASH

The petty cashier is usually responsible to the accounts supervisor for control of the petty cash and for correct recording of authorised petty cash transactions.

Most businesses set out in writing the procedures to be followed by the petty cashier. This is of benefit not only for the petty cashier to know the extent of his or her duties, but also to help the person who takes over at holiday or other times. The main procedures for the operation and control of petty cash are as follows:

1    On taking over, the petty cashier should check that the petty cash book has been balanced and that the amount of cash held agrees with the balance shown in the book. If there is any discrepancy, this should be referred to the accounts supervisor immediately.

2    The petty cashier should ensure that each week or month is started with the imprest amount of cash which has been agreed with the accounts supervisor.

3    The petty cash is to be kept securely in a locked cash box, and control kept of the keys.

4    Petty cash vouchers (in number order) are to be provided on request.

5    Petty cash is paid out against correctly completed petty cash vouchers after checking that:

– the voucher is signed by the person receiving the money

– the voucher is signed by the person authorising payment (the petty cashier or a manager)

– a receipt (or other supporting evidence) is attached to the petty cash voucher, and that receipt and petty cash voucher are for the same amount

– the amount being claimed is within the authorised limit of the petty cashier

6    The petty cash book is written up (to include calculation of VAT amounts when appropriate); it is important that the petty cash book is accurate.

7    Completed petty cash vouchers are stored safely – filed in numerical order. The vouchers will need to be kept for at least six years. They may

be needed by the auditors or in the event of other queries. Completed petty cash books will also need to be retained.

8     A surprise check of petty cash will be made by the accounts supervisor – at any one time the cash held plus amounts of petty cash vouchers should equal the imprest amount.

9     At the end of each week or month the petty cash book is to be balanced.

10    Details of the total of each expenses column are given to the person who looks after the double-entry accounts so that the amount of each expense can be entered into the double-entry system.

11    An amount of cash is drawn from the cashier equal to the amount of payments made (less any sundry receipts), in order to restore the imprest amount.

12    The petty cash book and cash in hand are to be presented to the accounts supervisor for checking.

13    Any discrepancies are to be dealt with promptly; these may include:

– petty cash claims that have not been authorised

– insufficient supporting evidence (eg missing receipt) attached to the petty cash voucher

– amounts being claimed which exceed the authorised limit of the petty cashier

– a receipt and petty cash voucher total differing – the matter should be queried with the person who made the purchase

– a difference between the totals of the expenses columns and the amount of the total payments column in the petty cash book – check the addition of the columns, the figures against the vouchers, the VAT calculations (does the VAT plus the expense column amount equal the total amount?)

– a difference between the cash in the petty cash box and the balance shown in the petty cash book – if this is not an arithmetic difference it may be a case of theft, and should be reported promptly to the accounts supervisor

– where discrepancies and queries cannot be resolved, they should be referred to the accounts supervisor

## CHECKING THE CASH

An important aspect of petty cash, which has been noted in the previous section, is that the petty cashier must ensure that the amount of cash held is what it should be. This process – known as reconciling the petty cash book with cash in hand – takes place on different occasions, as follows:

- at the beginning of the weekly or monthly period of the petty cash book, the petty cashier should check that the amount of cash held agrees with the balance shown in the book – this is usually the imprest amount

- at any one time during the week or month the amount of cash held plus the amounts of petty cash vouchers which have been paid out should be equal to the imprest amount – a surprise check may be made by the accounts supervisor

- at the end of the week or month, the amount paid out by the petty cashier will be reimbursed from cash book – this should restore the cash in hand to the imprest amount

Any difference in cash – whether  a shortfall or a surplus – at any stage during the week or month should be investigated promptly and, if it cannot be resolved, should be referred to the accounts supervisor.

**Case Study**

## CHECKING THE CASH

### situation

Jameson Limited keeps an amount of petty cash in a locked box in the office. The imprest amount is £100 which is restored at the beginning of each month.

The following payments were made in April and have been recorded in the petty cash book:

| | | |
|---|---|---|
| 6 April | Stationery | £12.50 |
| 10 April | Taxi fare | £10.00 |
| 14 April | Post office | £4.55 |
| 20 April | Window cleaning | £12.00 |
| 25 April | Donation to charity | £10.00 |

At 30 April the petty cash remaining in the locked box comprised:

1 x £10 note, 7 x £5 notes, 5 x £1 coins, 1 x 50p coin, 1 x 20p coin, 1 x 10p coin, 2 x 5p coins, 1 x 2p coin, 3 x 1p coins

## solution

- total payments for April are £49.05
- therefore cash remaining should be £100.00 – £49.05 = £50.95
- actual cash remaining is:

|  | as at 30 April | |
|---|---|---|
|  | number held | value £ |
| £10 notes | 1 | 10.00 |
| £5 notes | 7 | 35.00 |
| £1 coins | 5 | 5.00 |
| 50p coins | 1 | 0.50 |
| 20p coins | 1 | 0.20 |
| 10p coins | 1 | 0.10 |
| 5p coins | 2 | 0.10 |
| 2p coins | 1 | 0.02 |
| 1p coins | 3 | 0.03 |
| TOTAL |  | 50.95 |

- therefore, at 30 April, the petty cash book reconciles (agrees) with cash in hand

**Notes on the Case Study:**

- if there is a discrepancy, it should be investigated promptly and, if it cannot be resolved should be referred to the accounts supervisor

- from a practical point of view it is advisable to keep the cash in the form of lower denomination notes and a stock of coins – these will make it easier to pay out the amounts of petty cash claims (with less risk of error) than if larger denomination notes, such as £50 and £20, are used

## HOW PETTY CASH BOOK FITS INTO THE ACCOUNTING SYSTEM

Over the last few pages we have seen how low-value cash payments for small purchases and expenses are recorded firstly in the petty cash book and secondly in the general ledger (and sometimes also in purchases ledger). As the petty cash book is the first place in the accounting system to record these transactions, it is the book of prime entry for low-value cash payments.

In accounting systems the petty cash book is:

- either the book of prime entry for low-value cash payments <u>and</u> the double-entry account for petty cash (kept in general ledger)

- or the book of prime entry only, with a separate petty cash account (see page 239) kept in general ledger in order to complete double-entry bookkeeping

## as a book of prime entry and double-entry account

The diagram below shows the petty cash book performing two functions within the accounting system:

- as the **book of prime entry** for low-value cash payments
- as **part of the double-entry** system

This diagram shows the flow involving:

- financial documents – petty cash vouchers
- the petty cash book as a book of prime entry
- double-entry bookkeeping, involving petty cash and the other ledgers

---

### petty cash payments in the accounting system

**FINANCIAL DOCUMENTS**
petty cash vouchers for low-value purchases
and expenses payments

**BOOK OF PRIME ENTRY – PETTY CASH BOOK**
entries recording low-value purchases
and expenses payments

**DOUBLE-ENTRY BOOKKEEPING – PETTY CASH BOOK**

    **debit**   VAT account with total of VAT column
    *and*
    **debit**   appropriate expense account with total of each
            column

    **credit**  petty cash book payments column

**Note on the double-entry:**
If payments are made to trade payables through petty cash book (eg to J Jones in the Case Study on page 229), the debits will be to:
– purchases ledger control account in the general ledger
– trade payables' subsidiary account in the purchases ledger

### petty cash book solely as a book of prime entry

The alternative to the above is for the accounting system to treat petty cash book solely as a book of prime entry, in which case a separate double-entry account – **petty cash account** – is used in the general ledger.

The use of a petty cash account, using the petty cash book of Wyvern Traders (from the Case Study), is shown below.

## PETTY CASH ACCOUNT

As noted above, where an accounting system treats petty cash book solely as a book of prime entry, a **petty cash account** is used in general ledger to complete double-entry. From Wyvern Traders' petty cash book (on page 230) the totals of receipts and payments are entered in petty cash account (which has been given the account number GL0180) as follows:

**GENERAL LEDGER**

| Dr | | | Petty cash account (GL0180) | | | | Cr |
|---|---|---|---|---|---|---|---|
| 20-4 | | | £ | 20-4 | | | £ |
| 5 Apr | Balance b/d | | 100.00 | 9 Apr | Petty cash book PCB30 | | 62.00 |
| 9 Apr | Petty cash book | | | 9 Apr | Balance c/d | | 100.00 |
| | PCB30 | | 10.00 | | | | |
| 9 Apr | Bank CB55 | | 52.00 | | | | |
| | | | 162.00 | | | | 162.00 |
| 10 Apr | Balance b/d | | 100.00 | | | | |

**Notes:**

■ the debit 'balance b/d' on 5 April of £100.00 is the same as the opening balance in petty cash book – see page 230. This is the imprest amount for this petty cash book

■ the credit entry for 'petty cash book PCB30' on 9 April of £62.00 is the total of the expenses columns from petty cash book. These amounts are debited to their respective accounts in general ledger, as already seen on page 232

■ the debit entry for 'petty cash book PCB30' on 9 April for £10.00 is the receipt of cash from Jo Lee – payment for the purchase of postage stamps. This amount is credited to the relevant account – here postages account – in general ledger, as already seen on page 232

■ the debit entry for 'bank CB55' on 9 April for £52.00 is the reimbursement of petty cash in order to restore the imprest amount. The requisition form for this is shown on page 233

■ the 'balance c/d' on 9 April (and brought down on 10 April) for £100.00 is the new balance on petty cash book, ready for next week's transactions

■ in petty cash account, the cross reference to petty cash book enables a transaction to be followed through the accounting system – from book of prime entry to double-entry account – to ensure that it is complete

## Chapter Summary

■ The petty cash book records low-value cash payments for small purchases and expenses incurred by a business.

■ Petty cash receipts are recorded on the debit side; payments are recorded on the credit side.

■ Transactions recorded in the petty cash book include:
  – stationery items
  – small items of office supplies
  – casual wages
  – window cleaning
  – bus, rail and taxi fares incurred on behalf of the business
  – meals and drinks incurred on behalf of the business
  – postages
  – tips and donations

■ The petty cash book is controlled by the petty cashier.

■ Petty cash book is kept using either the imprest system or the non-imprest system.

■ The petty cashier writes up the petty cash book from petty cash vouchers, which are analysed to various expense columns.

■ At regular intervals – weekly or monthly – the data from the completed petty cash book is transferred to general ledger where the total of each expenses column is debited to the relevant account.

■ The petty cash book is the book of prime entry for low-value cash payments.

■   The petty cash book may combine the roles of:

–   the book of prime entry for low-value cash payments

–   the double-entry account for petty cash

■   When the petty cash book is used as the book of prime entry only, a petty cash account in general ledger completes double-entry bookkeeping.

**Key Terms**

| | |
|---|---|
| **petty cash book** | records low-value cash payments for small purchases and expenses; is the book of prime entry for low-value cash payments (and may also be the double-entry account for petty cash) |
| **petty cashier** | the person responsible for the petty cash book |
| **petty cash voucher** | financial document against which payments are made out of petty cash |
| **imprest system** | where the money held in the petty cash float is restored to the same amount for the beginning of each week or month |
| **non-imprest system** | where the petty cash supply is not topped up to the same value each time |
| **petty cash float** | amount of money held at any one time by the petty cashier |
| **expenses columns** | used in the petty cash book to record payments under various headings to suit the circumstances of the business |
| **petty cash account** | double-entry account in the general ledger used when the petty cash book is treated solely as the book of prime entry; it shows the total payments made by the petty cashier during the week or month, and records receipts from bank account, together with the opening and closing balances |

# Activities

**10.1** The petty cash book:

| | | |
|---|---|---|
| (a) | Is a financial document | |
| (b) | Is a part of double-entry bookkeeping only | |
| (c) | Is the book of prime entry for low-value cash payments | |
| (d) | Records and analyses expenses payments on the debit side | |

Which **one** of these options is correct?

**10.2** A petty cash voucher:

| | | |
|---|---|---|
| (a) | Is a financial document against which payments are made out of petty cash | |
| (b) | Is used to draw cash from bank to top-up the petty cash float | |
| (c) | Is passed to the bookkeeper for posting to the general ledger expenses accounts | |
| (d) | Is used to restore the imprest amount of the cash float | |

Which **one** of these options is correct?

**10.3** Most petty cash books operate using the imprest system. This means that:

| | | |
|---|---|---|
| (a) | The petty cashier draws money from the cashier as and when required | |
| (b) | The cashier has to authorise each petty cash payment | |
| (c) | A copy has to be kept of each petty cash voucher | |
| (d) | The petty cashier starts each week or month with a fixed amount of money | |

Which **one** of these options is correct?

**10.4** When the total of a petty cash book's column for VAT is transferred to the VAT account in the general ledger, will it be recorded as a debit or credit entry in general ledger?

| | |
|---|---|
| Debit | |
| Credit | |

**10.5** The petty cashier of the business where you work tops up the petty cash at the end of the month with £75 withdrawn from the bank. What will be the entries in the general ledger?

**General ledger**

| Account name | Amount £ | Debit | Credit |
|---|---|---|---|
| | | | |
| | | | |

**10.6** The business for which you work is registered for VAT. The following petty cash amounts include VAT at 20% and you are required to calculate the amount that will be shown in the VAT column and the appropriate expense column (remember that VAT amounts should be rounded down to the nearest penny):

**(a)** £9.60

**(b)** £4.80

**(c)** £2.40

**(d)** £2.46

**(e)** £5.60

**(f)** £3.48

**(g)** £8.76

**(h)** 96p

**(i)** 99p

**(j)** £9.43

**10.7**    The following petty cash book shows a number of transactions of Nelson and Company for March 20-9. The petty cash book is kept solely as a book of prime entry.

| | | | | | | | | | | |
|---|---|---|---|---|---|---|---|---|---|---|
| | | | | **Petty Cash Book** | | | | | | **PCB20** |
| **Date**<br>20-9 | **Details** | **Amount**<br>£ | **Date**<br>20-9 | **Details** | **Amount**<br>£ | **VAT**<br>£ | **Travel**<br>£ | **Postages**<br>£ | **Stationery**<br>£ | **Ledger**<br>£ |
| 1 Mar | Balance b/d | 100.00 | | | | | | | | |
| | | | 4 Mar | Taxi fare | 6.72 | 1.12 | 5.60 | | | |
| | | | 6 Mar | Post office | 6.80 | | | 6.80 | | |
| | | | 9 Mar | Pens | 4.80 | 0.80 | | | 4.00 | |
| | | | 11 Mar | Rail fare | 5.46 | | 5.46 | | | |
| 12 Mar | J Hart<br>(postages) | 8.50 | | | | | | | | |
| | | | 16 Mar | Envelopes | 2.88 | 0.48 | | | 2.40 | |
| | | | 18 Mar | P Andrews (PL) | 13.50 | | | | | 13.50 |
| | | | 19 Mar | Rail fare | 10.60 | | 10.60 | | | |
| | | | 20 Mar | Post office | 4.75 | | | 4.75 | | |
| | | | 23 Mar | Tape | 3.84 | 0.64 | | | 3.20 | |
| | | | 25 Mar | Post office | 5.10 | | | 5.10 | | |
| | | | 27 Mar | Taxi fare | 9.12 | 1.52 | 7.60 | | | |
| | | | | | 73.57 | 4.56 | 29.26 | 16.65 | 9.60 | 13.50 |
| 31 Mar | Bank | 65.07 | | | | | | | | |
| | | | 31 Mar | Balance c/d | 100.00 | | | | | |
| | | 173.57 | | | 173.57 | | | | | |
| 1 Apr | Balance b/d | 100.00 | | | | | | | | |

**(a)**    You are to transfer the data from the petty cash book into the general ledger accounts (including cash book) as at 31 March 20-9. Note that a petty cash account is required.

**(b)**    Show the entry that will be recorded in the purchases ledger as at 31 March 20-9.

**10.8** On returning from holiday, you are told to take charge of the petty cash book of Carr Trading. This is kept using the imprest system, the float being £150.00 at the beginning of each month. Expenses columns are used for VAT, travel, postages, stationery, meals, and miscellaneous.

There are a number of transactions for the month which have been authorised. All transactions, unless otherwise indicated, include VAT at 20%. Petty cash voucher numbers are not required.

20-3

| 1 Aug | Balance of cash £150.00 |
| 4 Aug | Taxi fare £9.60 |
| 6 Aug | Post office £5.50 (no VAT) |
| 9 Aug | Marker pens £3.84 |
| 11 Aug | Rail fare £10.50 (no VAT) |
| 12 Aug | Window cleaner £14.40 |
| 16 Aug | Large envelopes £4.80 |
| 18 Aug | Donation to charity £10.00 (no VAT) |
| 19 Aug | Rail fare £10.60 (no VAT) |
| 20 Aug | Post office £8.30 (no VAT) |
| 23 Aug | Roll of packing tape £2.40 |
| 25 Aug | Post office £1.50 (no VAT) |
| 27 Aug | Taxi fare £14.40 |

**You are to:**

• enter the transactions for the month in the petty cash book (PCB42)

• total the expenses columns

• restore the imprest amount of petty cash book to £150.00 by transfer from the cash book

• balance the petty cash book at 31 August 20-3 and bring down the balance on 1 September

**10.9** Towan Limited keeps an amount of petty cash in a locked box in the office. The imprest amount is £150 which is restored at the beginning of each month.

The following payments were made in June and have been recorded in the petty cash book:

| | | |
|---|---|---|
| 3 June | Post office | £5.85 |
| 7 June | Window cleaning | £12.50 |
| 10 June | Envelopes | £7.25 |
| 15 June | Meal allowance | £8.00 |
| 18 June | Donation to charity | £10.00 |
| 20 June | Pens | £9.47 |
| 24 June | Post office | £3.65 |

At 30 June the petty cash remaining in the locked box comprised:

3 x £10 notes, 8 x £5 notes, 15 x £1 coins, 11 x 50p coins, 6 x 20p coins, 11 x 10p coins, 5 x 5p coins, 6 x 2p coins, 11 x 1p coins

**You are to** complete the following:

**(a)**

| Total of petty cash payments for June | £ |
|---|---|
| Cash remaining should be | £ |

Actual cash remaining is:

| | as at 30 June | |
|---|---|---|
| | number held | value £ |
| £10 notes | | |
| £5 notes | | |
| £1 coins | | |
| 50p coins | | |
| 20p coins | | |
| 10p coins | | |
| 5p coins | | |
| 2p coins | | |
| 1p coins | | |
| TOTAL | | |

| Amount of discrepancy (if any) | £ |
|---|---|

**(b)**   State what action should be taken when a petty cash book cannot be reconciled with cash in hand.

# 11 The initial trial balance

## this chapter covers...

*In Chapter 3 we saw how it is necessary to balance the traditional form of account (the 'T' account) from time-to-time, according to the needs of the business.*

*In this chapter we list in two columns the balance of each account from the ledger, distinguishing between those accounts which have debit balances and those which have credit balances.*

*These two columns of debit and credit balances form the initial trial balance.*

*The two columns are totalled and if the two totals are the same, it proves that the accounting records are arithmetically correct.*

*If the two totals are not the same, it shows that there is an error, either in the addition of the columns or in the double-entry bookkeeping. This error should be traced and corrected.*

*This chapter shows how to prepare a trial balance manually. Many accounting systems use computer accounting, where the computer prints out a trial balance, in which case the totals should agree.*

*Later in the chapter we look at the differences between:*

■ *capital expenditure and revenue expenditure*

■ *capital income and revenue income*

*We see why it is important to classify this income and expenditure correctly in the double-entry system – if this is not done, the accounts may show a false financial position for the business.*

## BALANCING THE ACCOUNTS

Before an initial trial balance can be extracted, it is necessary to balance each account in the general ledger. The balance brought down needs to be calculated correctly and shown on the correct side of the account. It is the balance brought down figure that is used in the initial trial balance.

Before moving on to the initial trial balance, do make sure that you are able to balance accounts accurately – please refer back to Chapter 3 if you wish to review this process.

## PREPARING AN INITIAL TRIAL BALANCE

An initial trial balance is prepared – or extracted – from the accounting records in order to make an initial check of the arithmetical accuracy of the double-entry bookkeeping, ie that the debit entries equal the credit entries.

**A trial balance is a list of the balances of every account from general ledger (including cash book and petty cash book), distinguishing between those accounts which have debit balances and those which have credit balances.**

A trial balance is prepared at regular intervals – often at the end of each month – and the balances are set out in two totalled columns, a debit column and a credit column.

Read the notes set out below and refer at the same time to the example trial balance shown on the next page.

■ the debit and credit columns are totalled and the totals should agree. In this way the trial balance proves that the accounting records are arithmetically correct

■ the balance for each account listed in the trial balance is the amount brought down after the accounts have been balanced

■ the order of accounts within the trial balance could be set out

 – in alphabetical order, or

 – in random order, or

 – in the order of final accounts, that is income and expenditure items from the statement of profit or loss, followed by asset, liability and capital items from the statement of financial position

## Trial balance of Ace Suppliers as at 31 January 20-4

| Account name | Debit £ | Credit £ |
|---|---|---|
| Purchases | 7,500 | |
| Sales | | 16,000 |
| Sales returns | 250 | |
| Purchases returns | | 500 |
| Sales ledger control | 1,550 | |
| Purchases ledger control | | 900 |
| Rent | 1,000 | |
| Wages | 1,500 | |
| Heating and lighting | 1,250 | |
| Office equipment | 5,000 | |
| Machinery | 7,500 | |
| Inventory at 1 Jan 20-4 | 2,500 | |
| Petty cash | 200 | |
| Bank (cash at bank) | 4,850 | |
| Value Added Tax | | 1,200 |
| J Williams: loan | | 7,000 |
| Capital | | 10,000 |
| Drawings | 2,500 | |
| | 35,600 | 35,600 |

## a note about the asset of inventory

We have seen in earlier chapters how businesses use separate purchases and sales accounts to record when the goods in which they trade are bought and sold. The reason for using separate accounts for purchases and sales is because there is usually a difference between the buying price and the selling price – the latter is higher and gives the business its profit. At least once a year, however, a business values the inventory it has on the shelves of the shop, for example, or in the warehouse. As inventory is an asset of a business, the valuation is recorded as a debit to inventory account. This means that there will – for most businesses – be a debit balance on inventory account representing the value of inventory held at the beginning of the financial year. This balance will continue until such time as the inventory is formally valued again – often at the end of the financial year.

The debit balance for inventory is shown in the trial balance, as seen above.

# DEBIT AND CREDIT BALANCES – GUIDELINES

Certain accounts always have a debit balance, while others always have a credit balance. The lists set out below act as a guide, and will also help in your understanding of the initial trial balance.

## debit balances

**Debit balances** are assets and expenses, and include:

- purchases account
- sales returns account
- non-current asset accounts, eg premises, motor vehicles, machinery, office equipment, etc
- inventory account – the inventory valuation, usually at the beginning of the year
- expenses accounts, eg wages, telephone, rent, discount allowed
- drawings account
- sales ledger control account (which records the total balances of trade receivables)
- petty cash account
- cash account

## credit balances

**Credit balances** are liabilities, income and capital, and include:

- sales account
- purchases returns account
- income accounts, eg rent received, commission received, fees received, discount received
- capital account
- loan account
- purchases ledger control account (which records the total balances of trade payables)

**Notes:**

- **Bank account** can be either debit or credit – it will be:
  - debit when the business has money in the bank
  - credit when it is overdrawn
- **Value Added Tax account** can be either debit or credit – it will be:
  - debit when VAT is due to the business
  - credit when the business owes VAT to HM Revenue & Customs

## IF THE INITIAL TRIAL BALANCE DOESN'T BALANCE . . .

If the initial trial balance fails to balance, ie the two totals are different, there is an error (or errors):

- either in the addition of the trial balance
- and/or in the double-entry bookkeeping

### how to find an error

The procedure for finding the error(s) is as follows:

- check the addition of the trial balance
- check that the balance of each account has been correctly entered in the trial balance, and under the correct heading, ie debit or credit
- check that the balance of every account in general ledger has been included in the trial balance, together with the balance of cash book and petty cash book
- check that analysis columns from the cash book (for VAT), and from the petty cash book (for VAT and expenses) have been entered to the general ledger accounts
- check the calculation of the balance on each account
- calculate the amount that the trial balance is wrong, and then look in the accounts for a transaction for this amount: if one is found, check that the double-entry bookkeeping has been carried out correctly
- halve the amount by which the trial balance is wrong, and look for a transaction for this amount: if it is found, check the double-entry bookkeeping
- if the amount by which the trial balance is wrong is divisible by nine, then the error may be a reversal of figures, eg £65 entered as £56, or £45 entered as £54
- if the trial balance is wrong by a round amount, eg £10, £100, £1,000, the error is likely to be in the calculation of the account balances
- if the error(s) is still not found, it is necessary to check the bookkeeping transactions since the date of the last trial balance, by going back to the financial documents and books of prime entry

The accounts supervisor needs to be informed if the trial balance still does not balance; he or she will give guidance as to what is to be done.

The Case Study that follows shows how an initial trial balance is constructed from a list of account balances.

**Case
Study**

# INITIAL TRIAL BALANCE

## situation

You work as an accounts assistant for Severn Valley Stationery. The company sells office products and equipment to businesses in its area.

Today the accounts supervisor has asked you to work on preparing an initial trial balance as at 30 April 20-4. The supervisor has given you the following list of balances to be transferred to the trial balance.

You are to place the figures in the debit or credit column, as appropriate, and to total the debit and credit columns.

| Account name | Amount £ | Debit £ | Credit £ |
|---|---|---|---|
| Vehicles | 20,500 | | |
| Inventory | 11,945 | | |
| Bank (overdraft) | 8,297 | | |
| Petty cash | 110 | | |
| Sales ledger control | 28,368 | | |
| Purchases ledger control | 12,591 | | |
| VAT owing to HM Revenue & Customs | 2,084 | | |
| Capital | 23,237 | | |
| Loan from bank | 20,500 | | |
| Sales | 84,837 | | |
| Sales returns | 1,089 | | |
| Purchases | 51,054 | | |
| Purchases returns | 2,210 | | |
| Discount allowed | 105 | | |
| Discount received | 215 | | |
| Vehicle expenses | 3,175 | | |
| Wages | 22,864 | | |
| Rent and rates | 8,210 | | |
| Advertising | 2,174 | | |
| Heating and lighting | 968 | | |
| Travel costs | 1,476 | | |
| Telephone | 732 | | |
| Postages | 591 | | |
| Miscellaneous expenses | 610 | | |
| Totals | – | | |

### solution

You take each balance in turn and enter it in either the debit balance column or the credit balance column.

You use the following guidelines:

| DEBIT BALANCES (to go in the debit column) | CREDIT BALANCES (to go in the credit column) |
|---|---|
| • purchases | • sales |
| • sales returns | • purchases returns |
| • expenses (including discount allowed) | • income (including discount received) |
| •  inventory | • capital |
| • sales ledger control | • purchases ledger control |
| • VAT (when refund is due from HM Revenue & Customs) | • VAT (when owed to HM Revenue & Customs) |
| • bank (cash at bank) | • bank (overdraft) |
| • cash | • loan/bank loan |
| • petty cash | |
| • non-current assets | |
| • drawings | |

When you have entered the balances in the appropriate column, you then total the two columns of the trial balance – if the debit and credit totals are the same, this proves that the accounting records are arithmetically correct. If the trial balance doesn't balance, you follow the procedures for finding error(s) along the lines of those set out on page 252.

The initial trial balance of Severn Valley Stationery as at 30 April 20-4 then appears as shown on the next page.

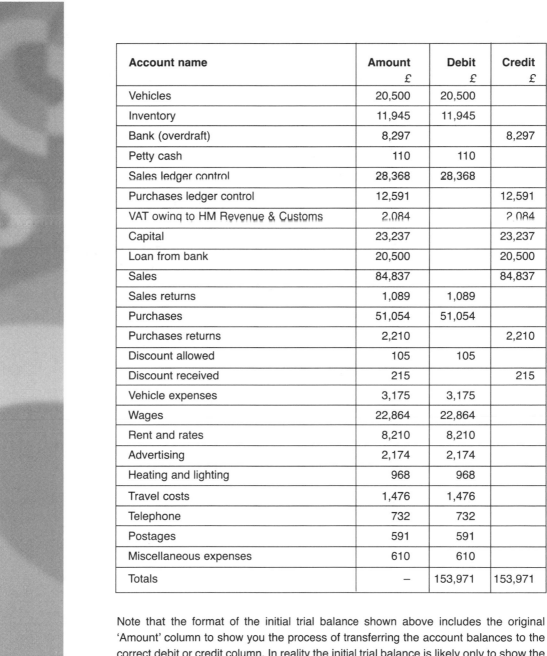

| Account name | Amount £ | Debit £ | Credit £ |
|---|---|---|---|
| Vehicles | 20,500 | 20,500 | |
| Inventory | 11,945 | 11,945 | |
| Bank (overdraft) | 8,297 | | 8,297 |
| Petty cash | 110 | 110 | |
| Sales ledger control | 28,368 | 28,368 | |
| Purchases ledger control | 12,591 | | 12,591 |
| VAT owing to HM Revenue & Customs | 2,084 | | 2,084 |
| Capital | 23,237 | | 23,237 |
| Loan from bank | 20,500 | | 20,500 |
| Sales | 84,837 | | 84,837 |
| Sales returns | 1,089 | 1,089 | |
| Purchases | 51,054 | 51,054 | |
| Purchases returns | 2,210 | | 2,210 |
| Discount allowed | 105 | 105 | |
| Discount received | 215 | | 215 |
| Vehicle expenses | 3,175 | 3,175 | |
| Wages | 22,864 | 22,864 | |
| Rent and rates | 8,210 | 8,210 | |
| Advertising | 2,174 | 2,174 | |
| Heating and lighting | 968 | 968 | |
| Travel costs | 1,476 | 1,476 | |
| Telephone | 732 | 732 | |
| Postages | 591 | 591 | |
| Miscellaneous expenses | 610 | 610 | |
| Totals | – | 153,971 | 153,971 |

Note that the format of the initial trial balance shown above includes the original 'Amount' column to show you the process of transferring the account balances to the correct debit or credit column. In reality the initial trial balance is likely only to show the debit and credit money columns. It will also be headed up with the name of the business and the date of the trial balance.

The trial balance of Severn Valley Stationery is shown in its final form on the next page.

## Severn Valley Stationery
## Trial Balance as at 30 April 20-4

| Account name | Debit £ | Credit £ |
|---|---|---|
| Vehicles | 20,500 | |
| Inventory | 11,945 | |
| Bank (overdraft) | | 8,207 |
| Petty cash | 110 | |
| Sales ledger control | 28,368 | |
| Purchases ledger control | | 12,591 |
| VAT owing to HM Revenue & Customs | | 2,084 |
| Capital | | 23,237 |
| Loan from bank | | 20,500 |
| Sales | | 84,837 |
| Sales returns | 1,089 | |
| Purchases | 51,054 | |
| Purchases returns | | 2,210 |
| Discount allowed | 105 | |
| Discount received | | 215 |
| Vehicle expenses | 3,175 | |
| Wages | 22,864 | |
| Rent and rates | 8,210 | |
| Advertising | 2,174 | |
| Heating and lighting | 968 | |
| Travel costs | 1,476 | |
| Telephone | 732 | |
| Postages | 591 | |
| Miscellaneous expenses | 610 | |
| Totals | 153,971 | 153,971 |

## CAPITAL AND REVENUE EXPENDITURE AND INCOME

In the double-entry bookkeeping system, it is important to distinguish between:

■ **capital expenditure** and **revenue expenditure**

■ **capital income** and **revenue income**

The reason for making the distinction between these two types of classification is to ensure that the accounting system shows the true financial position for the business.

### capital expenditure

**Capital expenditure is expenditure incurred on the purchase, alteration or improvement of non-current assets.** Non-current assets are items purchased by a business for use on a long-term basis.

Included in capital expenditure are such costs as:

■ delivery of non-current assets

■ installation of non-current assets

■ improvement (but not repair) of non-current assets

■ legal costs of buying property

An example of capital expenditure is the purchase of a car for use in the business.

Note that we use the word 'capitalised' to mean that an item has been treated as capital expenditure.

### revenue expenditure

**Revenue expenditure is expenditure incurred on purchases made by the business and on running expenses.**

Included in revenue expenditure are the costs of:

■ purchases made by the business

■ maintenance and repair of non-current assets owned by the business

■ administration of the business

■ selling and distributing the goods or products in which the business trades

An example of revenue expenditure is the cost of petrol or diesel for the car used in the business.

## capital expenditure and revenue expenditure – the differences

In the accounting system, it is important to classify correctly capital expenditure and revenue expenditure. An error in the double-entry accounting may show a false financial position for the business. For example, if the cost of the car was shown as an expense instead of as a non-current asset, the business will show a large motoring expense during the year but will not record that it owns the car as a non-current asset: in other words, the accounts will show an incorrect picture of the business.

Study the following examples: they show the differences between capital expenditure and revenue expenditure.

■ **£30,000 cost of building an extension to the factory, which includes £1,000 for repairs to the existing factory**

– capital expenditure £29,000

– revenue expenditure £1,000 (because it is for repairs to an existing non-current asset)

■ **a plot of land has been bought for £20,000, the legal costs are £750**

– capital expenditure £20,750 (the legal costs are included in the capital expenditure, because they are the cost of acquiring the non-current asset, ie the legal costs are 'capitalised')

■ **the business' own employees are used to install a new air conditioning system: wages £1,000, materials £1,500**

– capital expenditure £2,500 (an addition to the property); note that, in cases such as this, the amounts for revenue expenditure, ie wages and materials purchases, will need to be reduced to allow for the transfer to capital expenditure

■ **own employees used to repair and redecorate the premises: wages £500, materials £750**

– revenue expenditure £1,250 (repairs and redecoration are running expenses)

■ **purchase of a new machine £10,000, payment for installation and setting up £250**

– capital expenditure, £10,250 (costs of installation of a non-current asset are capitalised)

Only by recording capital expenditure and revenue expenditure correctly in the double-entry accounting system can the business know the correct expenses amount and the correct amount of non-current assets it owns.

### capital income

**Capital income is income received from non-regular ('one-off') transactions.**

Included in capital income are receipts from:

■ sales of non-current assets

■ loans raised from banks and other lenders

■ capital, or increases in capital, paid in by the owner of the business

### revenue income

**Revenue income is income received from sales made by the business and other regular amounts of income.**

Included in revenue income are the receipts from:

■ sales made by the business

■ rent from business premises rented out

■ commission for work done by the business on behalf of other businesses

■ cash discount for prompt settlement of amounts due to suppliers

### recording capital income and revenue income

As with capital and revenue expenditure it is important to record capital income and revenue income correctly in the double-entry accounting system so as not to show a false financial position. For example, if the money received from the sale of a non-current asset was shown as income from sales it would increase the sales figure and, at the same time, there would be no record against the non-current asset of the amount it was sold for.

| **Chapter Summary** | |
|---|---|
| | ■ An initial trial balance is prepared by taking the balances brought down of each account in the ledger and setting them out in debit and credit columns. |
| | ■ Debit balances include accounts for purchases, sales returns, non-current assets, inventory, expenses, sales ledger control, petty cash, and cash. |
| | ■ Credit balances include accounts for sales, purchases returns, income, capital, loan and purchases ledger control. |
| | ■ The balances of bank account and VAT account can be either debit or credit – depending on the circumstances. |
| | ■ In the initial trial balance the totals of the columns for debit and credit balances should be the same. |

- The initial trial balance checks the arithmetical accuracy of the double-entry bookkeeping, ie that the debit entries equal the credit entries.

- If the initial trial balance fails to balance, there is an error (or errors):
  - *either* in the addition of the trial balance
  - *and/or* in the double-entry bookkeeping

- Any error (or errors) must be traced and corrected.

- Expenditure is classified between capital expenditure and revenue expenditure.

- Income is classified between capital income and revenue income.

- In the double-entry system, it is important to classify capital and revenue expenditure and income correctly so as not to show a false position.

| **Key Terms** | | |
|---|---|---|
| **initial trial balance** | list of the balances of every account from general ledger (including cash book and petty cash book), distinguishing between those accounts which have debit balances and those which have credit balances | |
| **debit balances** | include assets, expenses, drawings, purchases, sales returns, petty cash, cash | |
| **credit balances** | include liabilities, income, capital, sales, purchases returns, bank overdraft | |
| **capital expenditure** | expenditure incurred on the purchase, alteration or improvement of non-current assets | |
| **revenue expenditure** | expenditure incurred on purchases made by the business and on running expenses | |
| **capital income** | income received from non-regular transactions | |
| **revenue income** | income received from sales made by the business and other regular amounts of income | |

# Activities

**11.1** Which **one** of the following accounts always has a debit balance?

| | | |
|---|---|---|
| (a) | Capital account | |
| (b) | Purchases account | |
| (c) | Sales account | |
| (d) | Purchases returns account | |

**11.2** Which **one** of the following accounts always has a credit balance?

| | | |
|---|---|---|
| (a) | Sales returns account | |
| (b) | Premises account | |
| (c) | Capital account | |
| (d) | Wages account | |

**11.3** Prepare the initial trial balance of Jane Greenwell as at 31 March 20-9, from the following list of balances:

| | £ |
|---|---|
| Bank (overdraft) | 1,250 |
| Purchases | 850 |
| Petty cash | 48 |
| Sales | 1,940 |
| Purchases returns | 144 |
| Trade payables | 1,442 |
| Equipment | 2,704 |
| Van | 3,200 |
| Inventory at 1 April 20-8 | 1,210 |
| Sales returns | 90 |
| Trade receivables | 1,174 |
| Wages | 1,500 |
| Capital | 6,000 |

**11.4** You work as an accounts assistant for Pershore Products. The accounts supervisor has asked you to work on preparing an initial trial balance as at 30 June 20-2. The supervisor has given you the following list of balances to be transferred to the trial balance.

You are to place the figures in the debit or credit column, as appropriate, and total the debit and credit columns.

| Account name | Amount £ | Debit £ | Credit £ |
|---|---|---|---|
| Office equipment | 12,246 | | |
| Bank (cash at bank) | 3,091 | | |
| Petty cash | 84 | | |
| Inventory | 11,310 | | |
| Capital | 22,823 | | |
| Drawings | 2,550 | | |
| VAT owing to HM Revenue & Customs | 3,105 | | |
| Loan from bank | 8,290 | | |
| Purchases ledger control | 17,386 | | |
| Sales ledger control | 30,274 | | |
| Sales | 82,410 | | |
| Purchases | 39,496 | | |
| Purchases returns | 2,216 | | |
| Sales returns | 3,471 | | |
| Discounts received | 298 | | |
| Discounts allowed | 517 | | |
| Wages | 20,212 | | |
| Advertising | 4,390 | | |
| Insurance | 1,045 | | |
| Heating and lighting | 1,237 | | |
| Rent and rates | 4,076 | | |
| Travel costs | 854 | | |
| Postages | 721 | | |
| Telephone | 954 | | |
| Totals | – | | |

**11.5** You work as an accounts assistant for Arley Limited. The accounts supervisor has asked you to work on preparing an initial trial balance as at 31 December 20-6. The supervisor has given you the following list of balances to be transferred to the trial balance.

You are to place the figures in the debit or credit column, as appropriate, and total the debit and credit columns.

| Account name | Amount £ | Debit £ | Credit £ |
|---|---|---|---|
| Sales | 101,269 | | |
| Sales returns | 3,476 | | |
| Purchases | 54,822 | | |
| Purchases returns | 4,107 | | |
| Sales ledger control | 25,624 | | |
| Purchases ledger control | 18,792 | | |
| Discounts received | 399 | | |
| Discounts allowed | 210 | | |
| Rent and rates | 3,985 | | |
| Advertising | 4,867 | | |
| Insurance | 1,733 | | |
| Wages | 31,246 | | |
| Heating and lighting | 3,085 | | |
| Postages | 1,211 | | |
| Telephone | 985 | | |
| Travel costs | 2,311 | | |
| Miscellaneous expenses | 107 | | |
| Capital | 22,489 | | |
| Vehicles | 22,400 | | |
| Inventory | 12,454 | | |
| Petty cash | 85 | | |
| Bank (overdraft) | 6,291 | | |
| VAT owing to HM Revenue & Customs | 3,054 | | |
| Loan from bank | 12,200 | | |
| Totals | – | | |

**11.6** Classify the following as either *capital expenditure* or *revenue expenditure* by putting a tick in the relevant column of the table below.

|  |  | Capital Expenditure | Revenue Expenditure |
|---|---|---|---|
| (a) | Purchase cost of vehicles |  |  |
| (b) | Rent paid on premises |  |  |
| (c) | Payments for purchases |  |  |
| (d) | Legal fees paid relating to the purchase of property |  |  |
| (e) | Cost of redecoration of the office |  |  |
| (f) | Cost of installation of air-conditioning in the office |  |  |
| (g) | Wages cost of own employees used to build extension to the stockroom |  |  |
| (h) | Cost of installation and setting up of a new machine |  |  |

**11.7** Classify the following as either *capital income* or *revenue income* by putting a tick in the relevant column of the table below.

|  |  | Capital Income | Revenue Income |
|---|---|---|---|
| (a) | Rent received |  |  |
| (b) | Commission received |  |  |
| (c) | Receipt from sale of old office equipment |  |  |
| (d) | Bank loan received |  |  |
| (e) | Receipts from sales |  |  |
| (f) | Discounts received |  |  |
| (g) | Receipt from increase in owner's capital |  |  |
| (h) | Receipt from sale of property |  |  |

# Answers to chapter activities

## CHAPTER 1: THE ACCOUNTING SYSTEM

**1.1**    (b)    A sale requiring immediate payment

**1.2**    True

**1.3**    (c)    Cash book, petty cash book, sales day book

**1.4**    (a)    Ledger accounts

**1.5**    (b)    A customer who owes money to a business

**1.6**    (c)    One debit and one credit

**1.7**    (b)    Trade payables

**1.8**    (a)    An amount owed by that business

**1.9**    **(a)**    £10,500

      **(b)**    £6,720

      **(c)**    £3,000

      **(d)**    £155,000

      **(e)**    Sales ledger and purchases ledger control accounts


## CHAPTER 2:  FINANCIAL DOCUMENTS FOR SALES

**2.1**    **(a)**    purchase order
      **(b)**    delivery note
      **(c)**    invoice
      **(d)**    statement of account
      **(e)**    credit note

**2.2**    **(a)**    prompt payment discount
      **(b)**    trade discount
      **(c)**    bulk discount

**2.3**    £159.50 − £47.85 discount = £111.65 plus VAT of £22.33 (rounded down) = **£133.98**

**2.4**

|  | Total £ | Discount £ | Net total £ | VAT £ | Invoice total £ |
|---|---|---|---|---|---|
| **(a)** | 160.00 | 32.00 | 128.00 | 25.60 | 153.60 |
| **(b)** | 400.00 | 80.00 | 320.00 | 64.00 | 384.00 |
| **(c)** | 40.00 | none | 40.00 | 8.00 | 48.00 |
| **(d)** | 8,000.00 | 1,600.00 | 6,400.00 | 1,280.00 | 7,680.00 |

**2.5** **(a)**

|   | Total £ | Discount £ | Net total £ | VAT £ | Invoice total £ |
|---|---|---|---|---|---|
| 1 | 100.00 | 20.00 | 80.00 | 16.00 | 96.00 |
| 2 | 1,650.00 | 330.00 | 1,320.00 | 264.00 | 1,584.00 |
| 3 | 2,500.00 | 500.00 | 2,000.00 | 400.00 | 2,400.00 |
| 4 | 10,900.00 | 2,180.00 | 8,720.00 | 1,744.00 | 10,464.00 |

**(b)**

|   | Total £ | PPD £ | Net total £ |
|---|---|---|---|
| 1 | 96.00 | 4.80 | 91.20 |
| 2 | 1,584.00 | 79.20 | 1,504.80 |
| 3 | 2,400.00 | 120.00 | 2,280.00 |
| 4 | 10,464.00 | 523.20 | 9,940.80 |

**(c)** Credit note

**2.6** **(a)** Numeric coding – invoice & credit note: invoice 10982, credit note 2378

**(b)** Alphabetic coding – invoice & credit note: product code ASPS

**(c)** Alpha-numeric coding – account No HS234, postcode MR7 4EF

**2.7** **(a)** Incorrect discount rate applied (10%), wrong addition for total. Goods total should be £76.00, VAT £15.20 and final total £91.20.

**(b)** Total before discount should be £250.00. Corrected figures: goods total £225.00 (after deduction of 10% discount), VAT £45.00, final total £270.00.

**2.8** Statement should be dated 31 July 20-3 and addressed to Mr Simpson.
The entries are:

| 20-3 |   | Debit £ | Credit £ | Balance £ |
|---|---|---|---|---|
| 1 July | Balance b/f | 58.75 |   | 58.75 |
| 4 July | Cheque received |   | 58.75 | 00.00 |
| 8 July | Invoice 10982 | 348.00 |   | 348.00 |
| 14 July | Credit note 2378 |   | 34.80 | 313.20 |
|   |   |   | **TOTAL** | 313.20 |

## CHAPTER 3: DOUBLE-ENTRY AND THE ACCOUNTING EQUATION

3.1 (c) Books of prime entry

3.2 (b) Sales ledger

3.3 (a) Money in is a debit, money out is a credit

3.4

|  | Debit | Credit |
|---|---|---|
| Payment of wages |  | ✔ |
| Cash received from sales | ✔ |  |
| Payment of an invoice by a credit customer | ✔ |  |
| Payment of an insurance premium |  | ✔ |
| Loan received from a finance company | ✔ |  |
| Loan repayment made |  | ✔ |
| Bank charges |  | ✔ |

3.5

|  | Debit | Credit |
|---|---|---|
| Payment of wages | Wages | Bank |
| Payment of insurance | Insurance | Bank |
| Money received from sales | Bank | Sales |
| Purchases made | Purchases | Bank |
| Loan received from the bank | Bank | Loan |
| Loan repayment | Loan | Bank |
| Telephone bill paid | Telephone | Bank |
| Rates bill paid | Rates | Bank |
| Rent received from office let out | Bank | Rent received |

**3.6**

| Account | 20-3 | DR or CR | Details | Amount |
|---|---|---|---|---|
| Sales | 1 May | Cr | Bank | 975.00 |
| | 11 May | Cr | Bank | 456.70 |
| Telephone | 6 May | Dr | Bank | 265.00 |
| Insurance | 12 May | Dr | Bank | 678.00 |
| Bank Loan | 14 May | Cr | Bank | 5,000.00 |
| Purchases | 15 May | Dr | Bank | 2,760.90 |

**3.7**   **Debit balances**: Purchases, Expenses, Customer Accounts, Assets

**Credit balances**: Capital, Liabilities, Supplier Accounts, Sales, Income

**3.8**

| | Debit | Credit |
|---|---|---|
| Asset bought by the business | ✔ | |
| Liability (eg bank loan taken out) | | ✔ |
| Capital introduced by the owner | | ✔ |
| Sales made by the business | | ✔ |
| Purchases made by the business | ✔ | |
| Expenses of the business | ✔ | |
| Customer who owes the business money | ✔ | |
| Supplier who is owed money by the business | | ✔ |

**3.9**   (b)   Assets – Liabilities = Capital

**3.10**

| Assets £ | Liabilities £ | Capital £ |
|---|---|---|
| 120,000 | 45,000 | 75,000 |
| 156,000 | 61,000 | 95,000 |
| 265,500 | 86,500 | 179,000 |
| 88,000 | 38,000 | 50,000 |
| 127,500 | 37,500 | 90,000 |
| 345,700 | 136,700 | 209,000 |

**3.11**

| Transaction | Debit | Credit |
|---|---|---|
| Increase in capital account | | ✔ |
| Increase in liability account | | ✔ |
| Decrease in asset account | | ✔ |
| Decrease in liability account | ✔ | |
| Increase in asset account | ✔ | |

**3.12**

| Dobit | | | Bank Account | | Credit |
|---|---|---|---|---|---|
| Date | Details | £ | Date | Details | £ |
| 20-4 | | | 20-4 | | |
| 3 Feb | Capital | 10,000 | 10 Feb | Purchases | 750 |
| 4 Feb | Bank Loan | 25,000 | 14 Feb | Rates | 450 |
| 6 Feb | Sales | 1,340 | 15 Feb | Purchases | 2,760 |
| 18 Feb | Sales | 860 | 21 Feb | Advertising | 138 |
| 25 Feb | Sales | 2,640 | 28 Feb | Wages | 3,560 |

| Account | 20-3 | DR or CR | Details | Amount £ |
|---|---|---|---|---|
| Capital | 3 Feb | Cr | Bank | 10,000 |
| Bank loan | 4 Feb | Cr | Bank | 25,000 |
| Sales | 6 Feb | Cr | Bank | 1,340 |
| | 18 Feb | Cr | Bank | 860 |
| | 25 Feb | Cr | Bank | 2,640 |
| Purchases | 10 Feb | Dr | Bank | 750 |
| | 15 Feb | Dr | Bank | 2,760 |
| Rates | 14 Feb | Dr | Bank | 450 |
| Advertising | 21 Feb | Dr | Bank | 138 |
| Wages | 28 Feb | Dr | Bank | 3,560 |

**3.13** **(a)**

| Dr | Solo Supplies Account (Purchases Ledger) | | | | Cr |
|---|---|---|---|---|---|
| 20-3 | Details | £ | 20-3 | Details | £ |
| 31 Mar | Balance c/d | 506.75 | 23 Mar | Purchases | 248.00 |
| | | | 25 Mar | Purchases | 78.75 |
| | | | 30 Mar | Purchases | 180.00 |
| | | 506.75 | | | 506.75 |
| | | | 1 Apr | Balance b/d | 506.75 |

**(b)**

| Dr | Atletico Supplies Account (Purchases Ledger) | | | | Cr |
|---|---|---|---|---|---|
| 20-3 | Details | £ | 20-3 | Details | £ |
| 23 Mar | Purchases returns | 80.00 | 24 Mar | Purchases | 120.00 |
| 26 Mar | Purchases returns | 70.00 | 27 Mar | Purchases | 360.00 |
| 31 Mar | Balance c/d | 500.00 | 30 Mar | Purchases | 170.00 |
| | | 650.00 | | | 650.00 |
| | | | 1 Apr | Balance b/d | 500.00 |

**(c)**

| Dr | Trajan Sports Account (Sales Ledger) | | | | Cr |
|---|---|---|---|---|---|
| 20-3 | Details | £ | 20-3 | Details | £ |
| 23 Mar | Sales | 450.00 | 24 Mar | Sales returns | 80.00 |
| 26 Mar | Sales | 70.00 | 30 Mar | Sales returns | 70.00 |
| 27 Mar | Sales | 180.00 | 31 Mar | Balance c/d | 550.00 |
| | | 700.00 | | | 700.00 |
| 1 Apr | Balance b/d | 550.00 | | | |

**(d)**

| Dr | Office Expenses Account (General Ledger) | | | | | Cr |
|---|---|---|---|---|---|---|
| 20-3 | Details | £ | 20-3 | Details | | £ |
| 4 Mar | Bank | 75.20 | | | | |
| 6 Mar | Bank | 191.00 | | | | |
| 8 Mar | Bank | 34.65 | | | | |
| 15 Mar | Bank | 63.46 | 31 Mar | Balance c/d | | 364.31 |
| | | 364.31 | | | | 364.31 |
| 1 Apr | Balance b/d | 364.31 | | | | |

## CHAPTER 4: ACCOUNTING FOR SALES, RETURNS, AND DISCOUNTS

**4.1** (a) Sales day book

**4.2** (a) Sales invoice; sales day book; sales account; sales ledger control account; customer's account

**4.3** (c) Debit discounts allowed; debit VAT; credit sales ledger control

**4.4** **(a)**
- The financial documents for credit sales transactions are sales invoices that have been checked and authorised.
- The details and amounts of the invoices are entered into sales day book. In the money columns of sales day book is recorded:
  - total column, the final total of each invoice
  - VAT column, the VAT amount shown on each invoice
  - net column, the net ('goods or services total') amount of each invoice
- After sales day book has been written up for the week or month, it is totalled and the information from it is transferred into the double-entry system.
- The bookkeeping entries are:
  - the total of the total column is debited to sales ledger control account in general ledger
  - the total of the VAT column is credited to VAT account in general ledger
  - the total of the net column is credited to sales account in general ledger
  - the amounts from the total column for each separate transaction are debited to the subsidiary accounts of the customers in sales ledger

**(b)**
- The financial documents for sales returns transactions are credit notes issued that have been checked and authorised.
- The details and amounts of the credit notes are entered into sales returns day book. In the money columns of the sales returns day book is recorded:
  - total column, the final total of each credit note
  - VAT column, the VAT amount shown on each credit note
  - net column, the net ('goods or services total') amount of each credit note
- After sales returns day book has been written up for the week or month, it is totalled and the information from it is transferred into the double-entry system.
- The bookkeeping entries are:
  - the total of the total column is credited to sales ledger control account in general ledger
  - the total of the VAT column is debited to VAT account in general ledger
  - the total of the net column is debited to sales returns account in general ledger
  - the amounts from the total column for each separate transaction are credited to the subsidiary accounts of the customers in sales ledger

**4.5 (a)**

| Sales Day Book | | | | | | SDB50 |
|---|---|---|---|---|---|---|
| Date | Details | Invoice number | Account code | Total £ | VAT £ | Net £ |
| 20-5 | | | | | | |
| 2 Apr | Malvern Stores | 4578 | SL110 | 66.00 | 11.00 | 55.00 |
| 5 Apr | Pershore Retailers | 4579 | SL145 | 78.00 | 13.00 | 65.00 |
| 7 Apr | E Grainger | 4580 | SL055 | 33.60 | 5.60 | 28.00 |
| 9 Apr | P Wilson | 4581 | SL172 | 69.60 | 11.60 | 58.00 |
| 12 Apr | M Kershaw | 4582 | SL090 | 91.20 | 15.20 | 76.00 |
| 14 Apr | D Lloyd | 4583 | SL095 | 79.20 | 13.20 | 66.00 |
| 19 Apr | A Cox | 4584 | SL032 | 39.60 | 6.60 | 33.00 |
| 22 Apr | Dines Stores | 4585 | SL048 | 122.40 | 20.40 | 102.00 |
| 23 Apr | Malvern Stores | 4586 | SL110 | 56.40 | 9.40 | 47.00 |
| 26 Apr | P Wilson | 4587 | SL172 | 42.00 | 7.00 | 35.00 |
| 29 Apr | A Cox | 4588 | SL032 | 98.40 | 16.40 | 82.00 |
| 30 Apr | Totals for month | | | 776.40 | 129.40 | 647.00 |
| | | | | GL1200 | GL2200 | GL4100 |

**(b)**

## GENERAL LEDGER

| Dr | | | Sales ledger control account  (GL1200) | | | Cr |
|---|---|---|---|---|---|---|
| 20-5 | | £ p | 20-5 | | | £ p |
| 30 Apr Sales Day Book SDB50 | | 776.40 | | | | |

| Dr | | | Value added tax account  (GL2200) | | | Cr |
|---|---|---|---|---|---|---|
| 20-5 | | £ p | 20-5 | | | £ p |
| | | | 30 Apr Sales Day Book SDB50 | | | 129.40 |

| Dr | | | Sales account  (GL4100) | | | Cr |
|---|---|---|---|---|---|---|
| 20-5 | | £ p | 20-5 | | | £ p |
| | | | 30 Apr Sales Day Book SDB50 | | | 647.00 |

## SALES LEDGER

| Dr | | | | Malvern Stores  (SL110) | | Cr |
|---|---|---|---|---|---|---|
| 20-5 | | | £ p | 20-5 | | £ p |
| 2 Apr Sales | | SDB50 | 66.00 | | | |
| 23 Apr Sales | | SDB50 | 56.40 | | | |

| Dr | | | | Pershore Retailers  (SL145) | | Cr |
|---|---|---|---|---|---|---|
| 20-5 | | | £ p | 20-5 | | £ p |
| 5 Apr Sales | | SDB50 | 78.00 | | | |

| Dr | | | | E Grainger  (SL055) | | Cr |
|---|---|---|---|---|---|---|
| 20-5 | | | £ p | 20-5 | | £ p |
| 7 Apr Sales | | SDB50 | 33.60 | | | |

| Dr | | | | P Wilson  (SL172) | | Cr |
|---|---|---|---|---|---|---|
| 20-5 | | | £ p | 20-5 | | £ p |
| 9 Apr Sales | | SDB50 | 69.60 | | | |
| 26 Apr Sales | | SDB50 | 42.00 | | | |

| Dr | | | M Kershaw (SL090) | | | Cr |
|---|---|---|---|---|---|---|
| 20-5 | | | £ p | 20-5 | | £ p |
| 12 Apr | Sales | SDB50 | 91.20 | | | |

| Dr | | | D Lloyd (SL095) | | | Cr |
|---|---|---|---|---|---|---|
| 20-5 | | | £ p | 20-5 | | £ p |
| 14 Apr | Sales | SDB 50 | 79.20 | | | |

| Dr | | | A Cox (SL032) | | | Cr |
|---|---|---|---|---|---|---|
| 20-5 | | | £ p | 20-5 | | £ p |
| 19 Apr | Sales | SDB 50 | 39.60 | | | |
| 20 Apr | Sales | SDB 50 | 08.10 | | | |

| Dr | | | Dines Stores (SL048) | | | Cr |
|---|---|---|---|---|---|---|
| 20-5 | | | £ p | 20-5 | | £ p |
| 22 Apr | Sales | SDB 50 | 122.40 | | | |

**4.6** **(a)**

| Sales Returns Day Book | | | | | | SRDB18 |
|---|---|---|---|---|---|---|
| Date 20-5 | Details | Credit note number | Account code | Total £ | VAT £ | Net £ |
| 8 Apr | Pershore Retailers | 572 | SL145 | 24.00 | 4.00 | 20.00 |
| 12 Apr | E Grainger | 573 | SL055 | 33.60 | 5.60 | 28.00 |
| 16 Apr | D Lloyd | 574 | SL095 | 39.60 | 6.60 | 33.00 |
| 28 Apr | Malvern Stores | 575 | SL110 | 24.00 | 4.00 | 20.00 |
| 30 Apr | A Cox | 576 | SL032 | 48.00 | 8.00 | 40.00 |
| 30 Apr | Totals for month | | | 169.20 | 28.20 | 141.00 |
| | | | | GL1200 | GL2200 | GL4110 |

**(b)**

**GENERAL LEDGER**

Dr            **Sales ledger control account (GL1200)**            Cr

| 20-5 | | | £ p | 20-5 | | | £ p |
|---|---|---|---|---|---|---|---|
| 30 Apr | Sales Day Book | SDB50 | 776.40 | 30 Apr | Sales Returns Day Book | SRDB18 | 169.20 |

Dr            **Value added tax account (GL2200)**            Cr

| 20-5 | | | £ p | 20-5 | | | £ p |
|---|---|---|---|---|---|---|---|
| 00 Apr | Sales Returns Day Book | SRDB18 | 28.20 | 30 Apr | Sales Day Book | SDB50 | 120.40 |

Dr            **Sales returns account (GL4110)**            Cr

| 20-5 | | | £ p | 20-5 | | | £ p |
|---|---|---|---|---|---|---|---|
| 30 Apr | Sales Returns Day Book | SRDB18 | 141.00 | | | | |

**Note:** sales account not shown – see answer to Activity 4.4

**SALES LEDGER**

Dr            **Pershore Retailers (SL145)**            Cr

| 20-5 | | | £ p | 20-5 | | | £ p |
|---|---|---|---|---|---|---|---|
| 5 Apr | Sales | SDB50 | 78.00 | 8 Apr | Sales Returns | SRDB18 | 24.00 |

Dr            **E Grainger (SL055)**            Cr

| 20-5 | | | £ p | 20-5 | | | £ p |
|---|---|---|---|---|---|---|---|
| 7 Apr | Sales | SDB50 | 33.60 | 12 Apr | Sales Returns | SRDB18 | 33.60 |

Dr            **D Lloyd (SL095)**            Cr

| 20-5 | | | £ p | 20-5 | | | £ p |
|---|---|---|---|---|---|---|---|
| 14 Apr | Sales | SDB50 | 79.20 | 16 Apr | Sales Returns | SRDB18 | 39.60 |

Dr            **Malvern Stores (SL110)**            Cr

| 20-5 | | | £ p | 20-5 | | | £ p |
|---|---|---|---|---|---|---|---|
| 2 Apr | Sales | SDB50 | 66.00 | 28 Apr | Sales Returns | SRDB18 | 24.00 |
| 23 Apr | Sales | SDB50 | 56.40 | | | | |

Dr            **A Cox (SL032)**            Cr

| 20-5 | | | £ p | 20-5 | | | £ p |
|---|---|---|---|---|---|---|---|
| 19 Apr | Sales | SDB50 | 39.60 | 30 Apr | Sales Returns | SRDB18 | 48.00 |
| 29 Apr | Sales | SDB50 | 98.40 | | | | |

**4.7**   **(a)**   **General ledger**

| Account name | Amount £ | Debit | Credit |
|---|---|---|---|
| Sales | 10,600 | | ✔ |
| Value Added Tax | 2,120 | | ✔ |
| Sales ledger control | 12,720 | ✔ | |

**Sales ledger**

| Account name | Amount £ | Debit | Credit |
|---|---|---|---|
| Bowne Ltd | 960 | ✔ | |
| Jamieson & Co | 4,944 | ✔ | |
| Pottertons | 3,888 | ✔ | |
| Wells plc | 2,928 | ✔ | |

**(b)**   **General ledger**

| Account name | Amount £ | Debit | Credit |
|---|---|---|---|
| Sales returns | 1,520 | ✔ | |
| Value Added Tax | 304 | ✔ | |
| Sales ledger control | 1,824 | | ✔ |

**Sales ledger**

| Account name | Amount £ | Debit | Credit |
|---|---|---|---|
| Lloyd & Co | 576 | | ✔ |
| Wyvern Stores | 1,248 | | ✔ |

**(c)**   **General ledger**

| Account name | Amount £ | Debit | Credit |
|---|---|---|---|
| Discounts allowed | 50 | ✔ | |
| Value Added Tax | 10 | ✔ | |
| Sales ledger control | 60 | | ✔ |

**Sales ledger**

| Account name | Amount £ | Debit | Credit |
|---|---|---|---|
| Sanchos Ltd | 24 | | ✔ |
| Belton Stores | 36 | | ✔ |

**4.8**

| Customer | Sales ledger account code |
|---|---|
| Dymock Trading Co | DYM003 |
| Hedgehog Fashions | HED001 |
| Jones & Co | JON002 |

**Note:** Dymock Trading Co is numbered '003' because an '002' account number has been allocated already for 'D'; similarly for Jones & Co where '001' has been allocated already for 'J'.

**4.9** **(a)** and **(b)**

**Sales day book**

| Date 20-9 | Details | Invoice number | Total £ | VAT £ | Net £ | Sales type 1 £ | Sales type 2 £ |
|---|---|---|---|---|---|---|---|
| 30 June | Yanez & Co | 1621 | 1,440 | 240 | 1,200 | | 1,200 |
| 30 June | Napier Stores | 1622 | 1,920 | 320 | 1,600 | 1,600 | |
| 30 June | Beale Ltd | 1623 | 768 | 128 | 640 | | 640 |
| | **Totals** | | 4,128 | 688 | 3,440 | 1,600 | 1,840 |

## CHAPTER 5: PROCESS PAYMENTS FROM CUSTOMERS

**5.1** (d) Invoice, sales ledger account, customer statement

**5.2** (b) The prompt payment discount percentage is shown

**5.3** **(a)** The remittance advice does not take account of the credit note issued on 10 November and so includes an overpayment of £49.00. Cool Socks should advise the customer, Trends, of this discrepancy and suggest that an adjustment could be made when the next month's payment is due, the credit remaining on the account for the time being.

**(b)** The remittance advice does not include payment of an invoice for £625.85 issued on 17 November and so the discrepancy is an underpayment. As the amount is large, Cool Socks should contact Vogue Limited and ask for payment. If the invoice is disputed, the problem should be looked into and resolved as soon as possible.

**(c)** RTC Fashions have underpaid their account because they have deducted 5% prompt payment discount when it was not offered (it is not included in the terms on the Chico Importers invoice). Additionally they have adjusted and underpaid the VAT by £5.60. Chico Importers should either ask RTC Fashions for payment of the shortfall of £33.60 immediately or advise them of the problem and suggest that an adjustment could be made when the next month's payment is due, the debit remaining on RTC Fashions' account for the time being. The decision depends on the relationship that exists between the supplier and customer.

## CHAPTER 6: PROCESS DOCUMENTS FROM SUPPLIERS

**6.1** **(a)** Purchase order

**(b)** Delivery note

**(c)** Goods received note

**(d)** Invoice

**(e)** Credit note

**6.2** A delivery note is sent by the seller with the goods, a goods received note is an internal document used by the purchaser to record and action any discrepancies found when the goods arrive.

**6.3** (a) The delivery note and the invoice

**6.4** Credit note

**6.5** The errors are:

(a) the goods were delivered to the wrong address

(b) an incorrect customer discount has been applied (10% instead of 15%)

(c) the wrong goods were sent (product code 4574 instead of 4573)

The total should have been £95 less 15% discount = £80.75 plus VAT of £16.15 = £96.90

The email should point out these errors and state that the disks are being returned for credit.

**6.6** **(a)** Errors on credit note:

– Wrong reference – should be 17643

– Product code incorrect – should be 919BK

– Should be gel pens, not rollerball pens

– credit should be for 2 boxes, not 3

As the goods received are correct, the email should point out the errors on the credit note and ask for a revised document to be issued.

**(b)**

| supplier a/c reference | general ledger a/c number |
|---|---|
| HE001 | 5010 |

**CHAPTER 7: ACCOUNTING FOR PURCHASES, RETURNS AND DISCOUNTS**

**7.1**  (c)  Purchases returns day book

**7.2**  (d)  Credit note issued; purchases returns day book; purchases returns account; purchases ledger control account; supplier's account

**7.3**  (b)  Debit purchases ledger control; credit discounts received; credit VAT

**7.4**  **(a)**  •  The financial documents for credit purchases transactions are purchases invoices, received from suppliers, that have been checked and authorised.

   •  The details and amounts of the invoices are entered into the purchases day book. In the money columns of purchases day book is recorded:

      –  total column, the final total of each invoice

      –  VAT column, the VAT amount shown on each invoice

      –  net column, the net ('goods or services total') amount of each invoice

   •  After purchases day book has been written up for the week or month, it is totalled and the information from it is transferred into the double-entry system.

   •  The bookkeeping entries are:

      –  the total of the total column is credited to purchases ledger control account in general ledger

      –  the total of the VAT column is debited to VAT account in general ledger

      –  the total of the net column is debited to purchases account in general ledger

      –  the amounts from the total column for each separate transaction are credited to the subsidiary accounts of the suppliers in purchases ledger

**(b)** • The financial documents for purchases returns transactions are credit notes, received from suppliers, that have been checked and authorised.

• The details and amounts of the credit notes are entered into purchases returns day book. In the money columns of the purchases returns day book is recorded:

– total column, the final total of each credit note

– VAT column, the VAT amount shown on each credit note

– net column, the net ('goods or services total') amount of each credit note

• After purchases returns day book has been written up for the week or month, it is totalled and the information from it is transferred into the double-entry system.

• The bookkeeping entries are:

– the total of the total column is debited to purchases ledger control account in general ledger

– the total of the VAT column is credited to VAT account in general ledger

– the total of the net column is credited to purchases returns account in general ledger

– the amounts from the total column for each separate transaction are debited to the subsidiary accounts of the suppliers in purchases ledger

**7.5** **(a)**

| Purchases Day Book | | | | | | PDB36 |
|---|---|---|---|---|---|---|
| **Date**<br>**20-5** | **Details** | **Invoice**<br>**number** | **Account**<br>**code** | **Total**<br>£ | **VAT**<br>£ | **Net**<br>£ |
| 2 Apr | Severn Supplies | 6789 | PL721 | 300.00 | 50.00 | 250.00 |
| 5 Apr | I Johnstone | A241 | PL604 | 252.00 | 42.00 | 210.00 |
| 9 Apr | L Murphy | 2456 | PL659 | 222.00 | 37.00 | 185.00 |
| 15 Apr | Mercia Manufacturing | X457 | PL627 | 216.00 | 36.00 | 180.00 |
| 19 Apr | AMC Enterprises | AMC 456 | PL520 | 414.00 | 69.00 | 345.00 |
| 26 Apr | S Green | 2846 | PL574 | 474.00 | 79.00 | 395.00 |
| 30 Apr | Totals for month | | | 1,878.00 | 313.00 | 1,565.00 |
| | | | | GL2350 | GL2200 | GL5100 |

**(b)**

## GENERAL LEDGER

| Dr | Value added tax account (GL2200) | | | | | Cr |
|---|---|---|---|---|---|---|
| 20-5 | | | £ p | 20-5 | | £ p |
| 30 Apr | Purchases Day Book | PDB36 | 313.00 | | | |

| Dr | Purchases ledger control account (GL2350) | | | | | Cr |
|---|---|---|---|---|---|---|
| 20-5 | | | £ p | 20-5 | | £ p |
| | | | | 30 Apr | Purchases Day Book PDB36 | 1,878.00 |

| Dr | Purchases account (GL5100) | | | | | Cr |
|---|---|---|---|---|---|---|
| 20-5 | | | £ p | 20-5 | | £ p |
| 30 Apr | Purchases Day Book | PDB36 | 1,565.00 | | | |

## PURCHASES LEDGER

| Dr | Severn Supplies (PL721) | | | | | Cr |
|---|---|---|---|---|---|---|
| 20-5 | | | £ p | 20-5 | | £ p |
| | | | | 2 Apr | Purchases PDB36 | 300.00 |

| Dr | I Johnstone (PL604) | | | | | Cr |
|---|---|---|---|---|---|---|
| 20-5 | | | £ p | 20-5 | | £ p |
| | | | | 5 Apr | Purchases PDB36 | 252.00 |

| Dr | L Murphy (PL659) | | | | | Cr |
|---|---|---|---|---|---|---|
| 20-5 | | | £ p | 20-5 | | £ p |
| | | | | 9 Apr | Purchases PDB36 | 222.00 |

| Dr | Mercia Manufacturing (PL627) | | | | | Cr |
|---|---|---|---|---|---|---|
| 20-5 | | | £ p | 20-5 | | £ p |
| | | | | 15 Apr | Purchases PDB36 | 216.00 |

| Dr | AMC Enterprises (PL520) | | | | | Cr |
|---|---|---|---|---|---|---|
| 20-5 | | | £ p | 20-5 | | £ p |
| | | | | 19 Apr | Purchases PDB36 | 414.00 |

| Dr | S Green (PL574) | | | | | Cr |
|---|---|---|---|---|---|---|
| 20-5 | | | £ p | 20-5 | | £ p |
| | | | | 26 Apr | Purchases PDB36 | 474.00 |

**7.6**  **(a)**

| Purchases Returns Day Book | | | | | | PRDB11 |
|---|---|---|---|---|---|---|
| Date | Details | Credit note number | Account code | Total £ | VAT £ | Net £ |
| 20-5 | | | | | | |
| 7 Apr | Severn Supplies | 225 | PL 721 | 60.00 | 10.00 | 50.00 |
| 14 Apr | L Murphy | X456 | PL 659 | 96.00 | 16.00 | 80.00 |
| 21 Apr | AMC Enterprises | 3921 | PL 520 | 150.00 | 25.00 | 125.00 |
| 29 Apr | S Green | SG247 | PL 574 | 81.60 | 13.60 | 68.00 |
| 30 Apr | Totals for month | | | 387.60 | 64.60 | 323.00 |
| | | | | GL2350 | GL2200 | GL5110 |

**(b)**                          **GENERAL LEDGER**

| Dr | | Value added tax account  (GL2200) | | | | Cr |
|---|---|---|---|---|---|---|
| 20-5 | | | £ p | 20-5 | | £ p |
| 30 Apr | Purchases Day Book | PDB36 | 313.00 | 30 Apr | Purchases Returns Day Book  PRDB11 | 64.60 |

| Dr | | Purchases ledger control account  (GL2350) | | | | Cr |
|---|---|---|---|---|---|---|
| 20-5 | | | £ p | 20-5 | | £ p |
| 30 Apr | Purchases Returns Day Book  PRDB11 | | 387.60 | 30 Apr | Purchases Day Book  PDB36 | 1,878.00 |

| Dr | | Purchases returns account  (GL5110) | | | | Cr |
|---|---|---|---|---|---|---|
| 20-5 | | | £ p | 20-5 | | £ p |
| | | | | 30 Apr | Purchases Returns Day Book  PRDB11 | 323.00 |

**Note:** purchases account not shown – see answer to Activity 7.5

**PURCHASES LEDGER**

| Dr | Severn Supplies (PL721) | | | | Cr |
|---|---|---|---|---|---|
| 20-5 | | £ p | 20-5 | | £ p |
| 7 Apr | Purchases Returns | | 2 Apr | Purchases PDB36 | 300.00 |
| | PRDB11 | 60.00 | | | |

| Dr | L Murphy (PL659) | | | | Cr |
|---|---|---|---|---|---|
| 20-5 | | £ p | 20-5 | | £ p |
| 14 Apr | Purchases Returns | | 9 Apr | Purchases PDB36 | 222.00 |
| | PRDB11 | 96.00 | | | |

| Dr | AMC Enterprises (PL520) | | | | Cr |
|---|---|---|---|---|---|
| 20-5 | | £ p | 20-5 | | £ p |
| 21 Apr | Purchases Returns | | 19 Apr | Purchases PDB36 | 414.00 |
| | PRDB11 | 150.00 | | | |

| Dr | S Green (PL574) | | | | Cr |
|---|---|---|---|---|---|
| 20-5 | | £ p | 20-5 | | £ p |
| 29 Apr | Purchases Returns | | 26 Apr | Purchases PDB36 | 474.00 |
| | PRDB11 | 81.60 | | | |

**7.7 (a)  General ledger**

| Account name | Amount £ | Debit | Credit |
|---|---|---|---|
| Purchases | 8,040 | ✔ | |
| Value Added Tax | 1,608 | ✔ | |
| Purchases ledger control | 9,648 | | ✔ |

**Purchases ledger**

| Account name | Amount £ | Debit | Credit |
|---|---|---|---|
| Seng Ltd | 1,152 | | ✔ |
| Peall & Co | 2,832 | | ✔ |
| Knightons | 4,176 | | ✔ |
| Galeazzi plc | 1,488 | | ✔ |

**(b)**    **General ledger**

| Account name | Amount £ | Debit | Credit |
|---|---|---|---|
| Purchases returns | 1,440 | | ✔ |
| Value Added Tax | 288 | | ✔ |
| Purchases ledger control | 1,728 | ✔ | |

**Purchases ledger**

| Account name | Amount £ | Debit | Credit |
|---|---|---|---|
| Martin & Co | 1,056 | ✔ | |
| Wentworth Stores | 672 | ✔ | |

**(c)**    **General ledger**

| Account name | Amount £ | Debit | Credit |
|---|---|---|---|
| Discounts received | 60 | | ✔ |
| Value Added Tax | 12 | | ✔ |
| Purchases ledger control | 72 | ✔ | |

**Purchases ledger**

| Account name | Amount £ | Debit | Credit |
|---|---|---|---|
| Kumar Ltd | 12 | ✔ | |
| Prior & Co | 60 | ✔ | |

**7.8**

| Supplier | Purchases ledger account code |
|---|---|
| Bridon Ltd | BRI003 |
| Foster & Co | FOS001 |
| Hirst & Co | HIR002 |

**Note:** Bridon Ltd is numbered '003' because an '002' account number has been allocated already for 'B'; similarly for Hirst & Co where '001' has been allocated already for 'H'.

**7.9**    **(a)** and **(b)**

**Purchases day book**

| Date 20-4 | Details | Invoice number | Total £ | VAT £ | Net £ | Purchases type 1 £ | Purchases type 2 £ |
|---|---|---|---|---|---|---|---|
| 30 June | Canoy Ltd | C350 | 1,608 | 268 | 1,340 | 1,340 | |
| 30 June | McVeigh & Co | 5148 | 2,340 | 390 | 1,950 | | 1,950 |
| 30 June | Robinsons | R/862 | 2,952 | 492 | 2,460 | 2,460 | |
| | **Totals** | | 6,900 | 1,150 | 5,750 | 3,800 | 1,950 |

## CHAPTER 8: PREPARE PAYMENTS TO SUPPLIERS

**8.1**   (c)    The supplier statement and the supplier's purchases ledger account in the books of the buyer

**8.2**   (a)    Supplier invoice

**8.3**   (b)    Deduct £250 from the amount owing to the supplier as shown on the statement

**8.4**   (c)    To accompany a cheque when paying a supplier

**8.5**    Invoice £150 on 8 March ref 76333 has been entered twice on the statement of account but only once in the purchases ledger. It is likely to be a duplication and should be queried with Luxon Traders. The likely outcome is a payment of £100 (invoice for £150 less credit note for £50).

**8.6**    Credit note £72.90 on 22 April appears in the purchases ledger but not on the supplier statement. Having checked that the credit note has been correctly posted to the purchases ledger account, you should query it with A Krauss Trading, as they  may have posted it to the wrong account, or not posted it at all. The likely outcome is a payment of £269.85 (invoices for £233.25 and £109.50 less credit note for £72.90).

**8.7**

| BACS REMITTANCE ADVICE | | | FROM: Hetherington Limited Unit 23 Wessex Estate Langborne Road Seatown SE8 5VZ |
|---|---|---|---|
| TO  Aldersgate Supplies<br>10 Aldersgate Street, London<br>EC1A 7GH | | | date: 3 October 20-5 |

| date | your reference | our reference | payment amount £ |
|---|---|---|---|
| 08 09 20-5 | Invoice 10945 | PO85262 | 120.75 |
| 14 09 20-5 | Invoice  10963 | PO85271 | 380.25 |
| 20 09 20-5 | Credit note 109 | PO85248 | (46.00) |
| | | TOTAL | 455.00 |

THIS AMOUNT HAS BEEN PAID BY BACS CREDIT TRANSFER DIRECTLY INTO YOUR BANK ACCOUNT AT HRBC BANK ACCOUNT NO 79001875 SORT CODE 41 22 01

**8.8**

**REMITTANCE ADVICE**

FROM:
Hetherington Limited
Unit 23 Wessex Estate
Langborne Road
Seatown SE8 5VZ

TO  Sutherland & Co
67 Great March Street
Eastwick, EA3 9JN

date: 5 June 20-5

| date | your reference | our reference | payment amount £ |
|------|----------------|---------------|------------------|
| 23 May 20-5 | Invoice 7856 | 472984 | 345.90 |
| 29 May 20-5 | Credit note 4562 | 472076 | (87.50) |
| | | CHEQUE TOTAL | 258.40 |

---

**Southern Bank PLC**
Mereford Branch
16 Broad Street, Mereford MR1 7TR

date  *5 June 20-5*

97-76-54

Pay  *Sutherland & Co* ———————————————— only

*Two hundred and fifty eight pounds 40p* ———————

Account payee only

£ **258.40**

HETHERINGTON LTD

123456    97 76 54    68384939

Director

**CHAPTER 9: CASH BOOK**

**9.1** (d) The book of prime entry for bank receipts and payments

**9.2**

# GENERAL LEDGER

| Dr | | **Capital account** | | Cr |
|---|---|---|---|---|
| 20-7 | | £ | 20-7 | £ |
| | | | 30 Apr Cash CB70 | 2,000 |
| | | | 30 Apr Bank CB70 | 8,000 |

| Dr | | **Bank loan account** | | Cr |
|---|---|---|---|---|
| 20-7 | | £ | 20-7 | £ |
| | | | 30 Apr Bank CB70 | 5,000 |

| Dr | | **Rent account** | | Cr |
|---|---|---|---|---|
| 20-7 | | £ | 20-7 | £ |
| 30 Apr Bank | CB70 | 1,000 | | |

| Dr | | **Wages account** | | Cr |
|---|---|---|---|---|
| 20-7 | | £ | 20-7 | £ |
| 30 Apr Cash | CB70 | 800 | | |

| Dr | | **Drawings account** | | Cr |
|---|---|---|---|---|
| 20-7 | | £ | 20-7 | £ |
| 30 Apr Bank | CB70 | 500 | | |

| Dr | | **Vehicles account** | | Cr |
|---|---|---|---|---|
| 20-7 | | £ | 20-7 | £ |
| 30 Apr Bank | CB70 | 10,000 | | |

**9.3** **(a)** True

**(b)** False – the balance b/d of £918 on 1 May shows that, according to the cash book, there is a bank overdraft.

**(c)**                                       **GENERAL LEDGER**

Dr                                        **Sales account**                                        Cr

| 20-5 | | | £ | 20-5 | | | £ |
|------|---|---|---|------|---|---|---|
| | | | | 30 Apr | Cash | CB32 | 40 |

Dr                                  **Commission received account**                                  Cr

| 20-5 | | | £ | 20-5 | | | £ |
|------|---|---|---|------|---|---|---|
| | | | | 30 Apr | Bank | CB32 | 48 |

Dr                                **Sales ledger control account**                                Cr

| 20-5 | | | £ | 20-5 | | | £ |
|------|---|---|---|------|---|---|---|
| | | | | 30 Apr | Bank | CB32 | 2,400 |

Dr                                     **Bank loan account**                                     Cr

| 20-5 | | | £ | 20-5 | | | £ |
|------|---|---|---|------|---|---|---|
| | | | | 30 Apr | Bank | CB32 | 2,000 |

Dr                              **Purchases ledger control account**                              Cr

| 20-5 | | | £ | 20-5 | | | £ |
|------|---|---|---|------|---|---|---|
| 30 Apr | Bank | CB32 | 3,200 | | | | |

Dr                                     **Purchases account**                                     Cr

| 20-5 | | | £ | 20-5 | | | £ |
|------|---|---|---|------|---|---|---|
| 30 Apr | Bank | CB32 | 96 | | | | |

Dr                                 **Office equipment account**                                 Cr

| 20-5 | | | £ | 20-5 | | | £ |
|------|---|---|---|------|---|---|---|
| 30 Apr | Bank | CB32 | 2,600 | | | | |

Dr                                       **Wages account**                                       Cr

| 20-5 | | | £ | 20-5 | | | £ |
|------|---|---|---|------|---|---|---|
| 30 Apr | Bank | CB32 | 1,550 | | | | |

Dr                                  **General expenses account**                                  Cr

| 20-5 | | | £ | 20-5 | | | £ |
|------|---|---|---|------|---|---|---|
| 30 Apr | Cash | CB32 | 80 | | | | |

**(d)**

### SALES LEDGER

| Dr | Lindum Limited | | | Cr |
|---|---|---|---|---|
| 20-5 | £ | 20-5 | | £ |
| | | 30 Apr Bank | CB32 | 2,400 |

### PURCHASES LEDGER

| Dr | | Mereford Mills | | Cr |
|---|---|---|---|---|
| 20-5 | £ | 20-5 | | £ |
| 30 Apr Bank | CB32 3,200 | | | |

**9.4** (c) Bank transfer from a trade receivable for £1,350

**9.5** (a) Cheque to a trade payable for £870

**9.6** (a), (b) and (d) are true; (c) is false

**9.7** **(a)** and **(b)**

| Dr (Receipts) | | | | | | | | |
|---|---|---|---|---|---|---|---|---|
| Date | Details | Account code | Cash | Bank | VAT | Cash sales | Trade receivables | Other income |
| 20-7 | | | £ | £ | £ | £ | £ | £ |
| 12 May | Balances b/d | | 205 | 825 | | | | |
| 12 May | Sales | GL | | 600 | 100 | 500 | | |
| 13 May | Sales | GL | 180 | | 30 | 150 | | |
| 13 May | T Jarvis | SL | | 155 | | | 155 | |
| 14 May | Sales | GL | | 720 | 120 | 600 | | |
| 15 May | Cash | C | | 250 | | | | |
| 15 May | Sales | GL | 288 | | 48 | 240 | | |
| 16 May | Wyvern Council | SL | | 560 | | | 560 | |
| | | | 673 | 3,110 | 298 | 1,490 | 715 | – |
| 17 May | Balances b/d | | 387 | 1,816 | | | | |

**Cr (Payments)**

| Date | Details | Account code | Cash £ | Bank £ | VAT £ | Cash purchases £ | Trade payables £ | Other expenses £ |
|------|---------|--------------|--------|--------|-------|------------------|------------------|------------------|
| 20-7 | | | | | | | | |
| 12 May | Rent | GL | | 255 | | | | 255 |
| 13 May | Terry Carpets | PL | | 363 | | | 363 | |
| 14 May | Trade Supplies | PL | | 145 | | | 145 | |
| 14 May | Purchases | GL | 36 | | 6 | 30 | | |
| 15 May | Bank | C | 260 | | | | | |
| 15 May | Longlife Carpets | PL | | 291 | | | 291 | |
| 16 May | Purchases | GL | | 240 | 40 | 200 | | |
| 16 May | Balances c/d | | 387 | 1,816 | | | | |
| | | | 673 | 3,110 | 46 | 230 | 799 | 255 |

**(c)**

**SALES LEDGER**

| Dr | T Jarvis | | Cr |
|----|----------|---|----|
| 20-7 | £ | 20-7 | £ |
| | | 13 May   Bank | 155 |

| Dr | Wyvern Council | | Cr |
|----|----------------|---|----|
| 20-7 | £ | 20-7 | £ |
| | | 16 May   Bank | 560 |

**PURCHASES LEDGER**

| Dr | Terry Carpets | | Cr |
|----|---------------|---|----|
| 20-7 | £ | 20-7 | £ |
| 13 May   Bank | 363 | | |

| Dr | Trade Supplies | | Cr |
|----|----------------|---|----|
| 20-7 | £ | 20-7 | £ |
| 14 May   Bank | 145 | | |

| Dr | Longlife Carpets | | Cr |
|----|------------------|---|----|
| 20-7 | £ | 20-7 | £ |
| 15 May   Bank | 291 | | |

**9.8**  **(a)**  **Cash book – credit side**

| Details | Cash £ | Bank £ | VAT £ | Trade payables £ | Cash purchases £ | Vehicle expenses £ |
|---|---|---|---|---|---|---|
| Balance b/f | | | | | | |
| Knowles & Co | 30 | | 5 | | 25 | |
| S Goulding | 96 | | 16 | | 80 | |
| Liyan Ltd | | 920 | | 920 | | |
| Nelson Street Garage | | 132 | 22 | | | 110 |
| Sandhu & Co | | 645 | | 645 | | |
| **Totals** | 126 | 1,697 | 43 | 1,565 | 105 | 110 |

**(b)**  **Cash book – debit side**

| Details | Cash £ | Bank £ | Trade receivables £ | Other income £ |
|---|---|---|---|---|
| Balance b/f | 254 | 1,598 | | |
| Watkin Ltd | | 429 | 429 | |
| P Pandya | | 1,522 | 1,522 | |
| Matt Martin | 235 | | | 235 |
| **Totals** | 489 | 3,549 | 1,951 | 235 |

**(c)**  £363

**(d)**  £1,852

**(e)**  Debit

**CHAPTER 10: PETTY CASH BOOK**

**10.1** (c)   Is the book of prime entry for low-value cash payments

**10.2** (a)   Is a financial document against which payments are made out of petty cash

**10.3** (d)   The petty cashier starts each week or month with a fixed amount of money

**10.4** Debit

**10.5** **General ledger**

| Account name | Amount £ | Debit | Credit |
|---|---|---|---|
| Petty cash book/Petty cash account | 75.00 | ✔ | |
| Bank | 75.00 | | ✔ |

**10.6**

| | Expense (excluding VAT) | VAT | Total |
|---|---|---|---|
| | £ | £ | £ |
| **(a)** | 8.00 | 1.60 | 9.60 |
| **(b)** | 4.00 | 0.80 | 4.80 |
| **(c)** | 2.00 | 0.40 | 2.40 |
| **(d)** | 2.05 | 0.41 | 2.46 |
| **(e)** | 4.67 | 0.93 | 5.60 |
| **(f)** | 2.90 | 0.58 | 3.48 |
| **(g)** | 7.30 | 1.46 | 8.76 |
| **(h)** | 0.80 | 0.16 | 0.96 |
| **(i)** | 0.83 | 0.16 | 0.99 |
| **(j)** | 7.86 | 1.57 | 9.43 |

**10.7 (a)** | | | **GENERAL LEDGER**

| Dr | | | Value added tax account | | | Cr |
|---|---|---|---|---|---|---|
| 20-9 | | | £ | 20-9 | | £ |
| 31 Mar | Petty cash book | PCB20 | 4.56 | | | |

| Dr | | | Travel account | | | Cr |
|---|---|---|---|---|---|---|
| 20-9 | | | £ | 20-9 | | £ |
| 31 Mar | Petty cash book | PCB20 | 29.26 | | | |

| Dr | | | Postages account | | | Cr |
|---|---|---|---|---|---|---|
| 20-9 | | | £ | 20-9 | | £ |
| 31 Mar | Petty cash book | PCB20 | 16.65 | 12 Mar | Petty cash book | PCB20 | 8.50 |

| Dr | | | Stationery account | | | Cr |
|---|---|---|---|---|---|---|
| 20-9 | | | £ | 20-9 | | £ |
| 31 Mar | Petty cash book | PCB20 | 9.60 | | | |

| Dr | | | Purchases ledger control account | | | Cr |
|---|---|---|---|---|---|---|
| 20-9 | | | £ | 20-9 | | £ |
| 31 Mar | Petty cash book | PCB20 | 13.50 | | | |

| Dr | | | Petty cash account | | | Cr |
|---|---|---|---|---|---|---|
| 20-9 | | | £ | 20-9 | | £ |
| 1 Mar | Balance b/d | | 100.00 | 31 Mar | Petty cash book | PCB20 73.57 |
| 31 Mar | Petty cash book | PCB20 | 8.50 | 31 Mar | Balance c/d | 100.00 |
| 31 Mar | Bank | CB | 65.07 | | | |
| | | | 173.57 | | | 173.57 |
| 1 Apr | Balance b/d | | 100.00 | | | |

| Dr | | | Cash book | | | Cr |
|---|---|---|---|---|---|---|
| 20-9 | | | Bank | 20-9 | | Bank |
| | | | | 31 Mar | Petty cash | PCB20 65.07 |

**(b)** | | | **PURCHASES LEDGER**

| Dr | | | P Andrews | | | Cr |
|---|---|---|---|---|---|---|
| 20-9 | | | £ | 20-9 | | £ |
| 18 Mar | Petty cash book | PCB20 | 13.50 | | | |

**10.8**

| Petty Cash Book | | | | | | | | | | PCB42 |
|---|---|---|---|---|---|---|---|---|---|---|
| Date 20-3 | Details | Amount | Date 20-3 | Details £ | Amount £ | VAT £ | Travel £ | Postages £ | Stationery £ | Misc £ |
| 1 Aug | Balance b/d | 150.00 | | | | | | | | |
| | | | 4 Aug | Taxi fare | 9.60 | 1.60 | 8.00 | | | |
| | | | 6 Aug | Post office | 5.50 | | | 5.50 | | |
| | | | 9 Aug | Marker pens | 3.84 | 0.64 | | | 3.20 | |
| | | | 11 Aug | Rail fare | 10.50 | | 10.50 | | | |
| | | | 12 Aug | Window cleaner | 14.40 | 2.40 | | | | 12.00 |
| | | | 16 Aug | Envelopes | 4.80 | 0.80 | | | 4.00 | |
| | | | 18 Aug | Donation | 10.00 | | | | | 10.00 |
| | | | 19 Aug | Rail fare | 10.60 | | 10.60 | | | |
| | | | 20 Aug | Post office | 8.30 | | | 8.30 | | |
| | | | 23 Aug | Printing tape | 2.40 | 0.40 | | | 2.00 | |
| | | | 25 Aug | Post office | 1.50 | | | 1.50 | | |
| | | | 27 Aug | Taxi fare | 14.40 | 2.40 | 12.00 | | | |
| | | | | | 95.84 | 8.24 | 41.10 | 15.30 | 9.20 | 22.00 |
| 31 Aug | Bank | 95.84 | | | | | | | | |
| | | | 31 Aug | Balance c/d | 150.00 | | | | | |
| | | 245.84 | | | 245.84 | | | | | |
| 1 Sep | Balance b/d | 150.00 | | | | | | | | |

**10.9**   **(a)**

| Total of petty cash payments for June: | | £56.72 |
|---|---|---|
| Cash remaining should be: | | £93.28 |
| Actual cash remaining is: | | |
| | *as at 30 June* | |
| | number held | value £ |
| £10 notes | 3 | 30.00 |
| £5 notes | 8 | 40.00 |
| £1 coins | 15 | 15.00 |
| 50p coins | 11 | 5.50 |
| 20p coins | 6 | 1.20 |
| 10p coins | 11 | 1.10 |
| 5p coins | 5 | 0.25 |
| 2p coins | 6 | 0.12 |
| 1p coins | 11 | 0.11 |
| TOTAL | | 93.28 |
| Amount of discrepancy (if any) | | £   nil |

**(b)**   If there is a discrepancy – whether a shortfall or a surplus – it should be investigated promptly and, if it cannot be resolved, should be referred to the accounts supervisor.

**CHAPTER 11: THE INITIAL TRIAL BALANCE**

**11.1**  (b)  Purchases account

**11.2**  (c)  Capital account

**11.3**  **Trial balance of Jane Greenwell as at 31 March 20-9**

| Name of account | Dr £ | Cr £ |
|---|---|---|
| Bank (overdraft) | | 1,250 |
| Purchases | 850 | |
| Petty cash | 48 | |
| Sales | | 1,940 |
| Purchases returns | | 144 |
| Trade payables | | 1,442 |
| Equipment | 2,704 | |
| Van | 3,200 | |
| Inventory at 1 April 20-8 | 1,210 | |
| Sales returns | 90 | |
| Trade receivables | 1,174 | |
| Wages | 1,500 | |
| Capital | | 6,000 |
| | 10,776 | 10,776 |

**11.4**

| Account name | Amount £ | Debit £ | Credit £ |
|---|---|---|---|
| Office equipment | 12,246 | 12,246 | |
| Bank (cash at bank) | 3,091 | 3,091 | |
| Petty cash | 84 | 84 | |
| Inventory | 11,310 | 11,310 | |
| Capital | 22,823 | | 22,823 |
| Drawings | 2,550 | 2,550 | |
| VAT owing to HM Revenue & Customs | 3,105 | | 3,105 |
| Loan from bank | 8,290 | | 8,290 |
| Purchases ledger control | 17,386 | | 17,386 |
| Sales ledger control | 30,274 | 30,274 | |
| Sales | 82,410 | | 82,410 |
| Purchases | 39,496 | 39,496 | |
| Purchases returns | 2,216 | | 2,216 |
| Sales returns | 3,471 | 3,471 | |
| Discounts received | 298 | | 298 |
| Discounts allowed | 517 | 517 | |
| Wages | 20,212 | 20,212 | |
| Advertising | 4,390 | 4,390 | |
| Insurance | 1,045 | 1,045 | |
| Heating and lighting | 1,237 | 1,237 | |
| Rent and rates | 4,076 | 4,076 | |
| Travel costs | 854 | 854 | |
| Postages | 721 | 721 | |
| Telephone | 954 | 954 | |
| Totals | | 136,528 | 136,528 |

**11.5**

| Account name | Amount £ | Debit £ | Credit £ |
|---|---|---|---|
| Sales | 101,269 | | 101,269 |
| Sales returns | 3,476 | 3,476 | |
| Purchases | 54,822 | 54,822 | |
| Purchases returns | 4,107 | | 4,107 |
| Sales ledger control | 25,624 | 25,624 | |
| Purchases ledger control | 18,792 | | 18,792 |
| Discounts received | 399 | | 399 |
| Discounts allowed | 210 | 210 | |
| Rent and rates | 3,985 | 3,985 | |
| Advertising | 4,867 | 4,867 | |
| Insurance | 1,733 | 1,733 | |
| Wages | 31,246 | 31,246 | |
| Heating and lighting | 3,085 | 3,085 | |
| Postages | 1,211 | 1,211 | |
| Telephone | 985 | 985 | |
| Travel costs | 2,311 | 2,311 | |
| Miscellaneous expenses | 107 | 107 | |
| Capital | 22,489 | | 22,489 |
| Vehicles | 22,400 | 22,400 | |
| Inventory | 12,454 | 12,454 | |
| Petty cash | 85 | 85 | |
| Bank (overdraft) | 6,291 | | 6,291 |
| VAT owing to HM Revenue & Customs | 3,054 | | 3,054 |
| Loan from bank | 12,200 | | 12,200 |
| Totals | | 168,601 | 168,601 |

**11.6**

|  |  | Capital Expenditure | Revenue Expenditure |
|---|---|:---:|:---:|
| (a) | Purchase cost of vehicles | ✔ | |
| (b) | Rent paid on premises | | ✔ |
| (c) | Payments for purchases | | ✔ |
| (d) | Legal fees paid relating to the purchase of property | ✔ | |
| (e) | Cost of redecoration of the office | | ✔ |
| (f) | Cost of installation of air-conditioning in the office | ✔ | |
| (g) | Wages cost of own employees used to build extension to the stockroom | ✔ | |
| (h) | Cost of installation and setting up of a new machine | ✔ | |

**11.7**

|  |  | Capital Income | Revenue Income |
|---|---|:---:|:---:|
| (a) | Rent received | | ✔ |
| (b) | Commission received | | ✔ |
| (c) | Receipt from sale of old office equipment | ✔ | |
| (d) | Bank loan received | ✔ | |
| (e) | Receipts from sales | | ✔ |
| (f) | Discounts received | | ✔ |
| (g) | Receipt from increase in owner's capital | ✔ | |
| (h) | Receipt from sale of property | ✔ | |

# Index

for your notes